The
HANDBOOK of THE
PROJECT
MANAGEMENT

2nd Edition

A Practical Guide to
Effective Policies and Procedures

Trevor L Young

**KOGAN
PAGE**

London and Sterling, VA

First published in 1996
First paperback edition 1998
Second edition published in Great Britain and the United States in 2003 by Kogan
Page Limited
Reprinted 2004

120 Pentonville Road
London N1 9JN
UK
www.kogan-page.co.uk

22883 Quicksilver Drive
Sterling VA 20166–2012
USA

© Trevor L. Young, 1996, 2003

ISBN 0 7494 3965 3

British Library Cataloguing in Publication Data

A CIP record for this book is available from the British Library.

Library of Congress Cataloging-in-Publication Data
Young, Trevor L. (Trevor Leonard), 1940–
  Handbook of project management: a practical guide to effective
policies and procedures / Trevor L. Young. – 2nd ed.
  p. cm.
Includes bibliographical references and index.
  ISBN 0-7494-3965-3
1. Project management–Handbooks, manuals, etc. I. Title.
HD69.P75Y68 2003
658.4´04–dc21
                                               2003005106

Typeset by Saxon Graphics Ltd, Derby
Printed and bound in Great Britain by Biddles Ltd, King's Lynn, Norfolk

Contents

Preface to the second edition   *vii*

Part 1 The programme and project environment   **1**

1   **Introduction**   3
        What is special about programmes and projects?   4
        Who is this book for?   5

2   **Change: programmes and projects**   7
        Change and the programme and project manager   8
        What is a project?   9
        Projects and sub-projects   10
        What is a programme?   13
        An example programme   14
        Why programme management?   15
        What is programme management?   17
        What is project management?   18
        Why is programme management different from project
           management?   19
        What is different about programme and project management?   20
        How are programmes and projects derived?   22
        The dynamic life cycle   24
        The dynamic action cycle   25
        The programme and project process phase gates   27
        Is the phase gate a constraint?   29
        Is this control necessary?   30
        Summary   31

3 Organizing for programme management   **32**
Organizing for ownership   34
Establishing the programme steering team   35
Continuous improvement and problem solving: are they projects? 38
The programme register   38
Operating a programme register   40
The key responsibilities of the programme steering team   42
Meetings of the programme steering team   43
Managing the portfolio: selection of programmes and projects   46
The inputs to effective selection   48
The secondary screening   49
The result of effective selection   51
Summary   53

4 The key roles   **54**
The project steering team administrator   55
The sponsor   56
The programme manager   56
The project manager   57
The functional manager   57
Frequently used terms   58
The stakeholders   59
Managing stakeholders   61
Customer satisfaction   64
The programme and project manager as a leader   65
The dimensions of leadership   67
Programmes, projects and teamwork   70
Building your team   72
Summary   73

Part 2 The programme and project processes and techniques   **77**

5 Starting up: ideas and opportunities for projects   **79**
The fundamental data needs   80
What are the constraints?   81
What data do the programme steering team require?   82
Preparing the initial business case   83
Through Gate Zero to Gate One   84
Presenting the business case to the programme steering team   89
The kick-off meeting   90
Project documentation   94
The project brief and specification   98
Summary   100

6	**Defining the project**	**102**
	What is necessary to define a project?	103
	The stakeholder list	103
	The project brief	106
	The scope of work statement	108
	Risk management	110
	Risk assessment	113
	Quantifying identified risks	117
	Risk monitoring	123
	Getting your project definition approved	124
	Summary	127

7	**Planning your project**	**130**
	What is not going to be done?	130
	Who needs to be involved?	131
	Where does planning start?	131
	Identifying the key stages	133
	The project work breakdown structure	136
	Allocating responsibility	136
	What is an estimate?	139
	Estimating the durations	141
	Contingencies	144
	Time-limited scheduling and estimates	145
	Identifying the critical path of your project	146
	The Programme Evaluation and Review Technique	147
	Analysing the logic diagram	150
	Using the PERT analysis data	150
	Analysing your resource requirements	155
	Optimizing your schedule	157
	Reviewing your project risk log	161
	Reviewing your project budget	162
	Intermediate phase gates	162
	Seeking approval to launch your project	164
	Summary	165

8	**Launching your project**	**168**
	Establishing key stage work plans	168
	Deriving a milestone schedule	171
	Critical success factors	173
	Ensuring effective communication	175
	Project status reports	176
	Deriving a meetings schedule for your project	179
	Managing project changes	180

Holding a launch meeting   187
Summary   190

9   Executing the project work   192
    The project control system   193
    Monitoring progress   197
    Managing issues   201
    Reviewing project issues   208
    Tracking your project   209
    Taking corrective action   215
    Problem solving   216
    Progress meetings   220
    Progress reporting   223
    Projects and conflict   224
    Encouraging good time management   228
    Controlling the project costs   236
    The regular 'gotchas'   243
    Approaching the closure phase   246
    Summary   247

10 Closing your project   250
    Why have a closure phase?   251
    Establishing completion criteria   252
    The acceptance process   254
    The close-out meeting   255
    Evaluating your project   259
    Closing down the project   260
    Post-project evaluation   262
    Post-project appraisals   266
    What next?   267
    Summary   269

11 Using a computer   271
    What can software do?   272
    Using a software program   276
    What software does not do   278
    Selecting project software   279
    The programme management office   280

    Postscript   282

    Appendix 1: Glossary of terms   283
    Appendix 2: Further reading   289
    Index   291

Preface to the second edition

Welcome to this new edition. Project management continues to improve both in the tools and techniques available to you and in their application to achieve successful results. Several changes have been made in this edition, the most significant being the introduction of the concepts of programme management.

The book has been divided into two parts. Part 1 looks at the programme and project environment. This includes how programmes have evolved and relate to projects and introduces the process for managing an idea or opportunity as it progresses from initial selection on through the different phases of a programme or project. The concept of phase gates to allow senior management control over the programme and project activities is included. These techniques depend very much on organizing for programme and project management, ensuring that the strategically appropriate programmes and projects are selected to create a portfolio of active projects and programmes. Finally in Part 1, the roles and their responsibilities are discussed to enable effective management of the portfolio.

Part 2 has been extensively revised to ensure that the processes and techniques described fit the programme and project environment. The detailed processes for managing an opportunity through each phase gate to completion have been enhanced with new material. The risk management process has been modified to include quantitative risk assessment. The issue management process and the change management process have been extensively revised on the basis of practical experience. Additional cost control and earned value analysis techniques have been added. Finally, the project closure process has been enhanced.

This book is based on over 30 years' experience in the project environment, and in that time I have learnt much from others – and much the hard way of 'try it and see if it works'. I could not begin to list all those who have helped me on that journey, working together at different times to achieve a successful project outcome. Programme management has not been easily understood in many companies. I would like to acknowledge the huge amount of commitment and support from Ken Foster and thank him for the many hundreds of satisfying hours we have spent together persuading others of the value of the techniques in this book. I thank Ken also for his many suggestions and helpful comments on the material in Part 1. Finally, I thank Christine, my wife, for tolerance, patience and the support she gave to help me complete this project on time.

Part 1

The programme and project environment

Part 1 is focused on understanding the steps that an organization needs to take to create an effective environment for success in programme and project management. This includes understanding the terminology and the organizational structure changes advisable to take advantage of a programme-oriented environment in the business.

Part 1 also looks at the steps necessary to institute a formalized approach to programme and project selection and at understanding the essential roles and their responsibilities that are required for these processes to be effective.

1

Introduction

During the past decade the skills of project management have become increasingly recognized as highly desirable for managers at all levels in an organization. Most people today can benefit from the application of these skills to some parts of their daily operations. The rapid growth of global markets and the introduction of Total Quality Management, continuous improvements and, more recently, the drive to redesign business processes all require these skills to some degree. All are aimed at improving organizational effectiveness and performance in a highly competitive world marketplace. The world marketplace is continually changing and every organization, irrespective of the service or product it offers, must accept that internal change is a normal process to meet the demands of external change.

The successful and effective implementation of change employs specific skills that have traditionally been owned by a select group of technical professionals. This is no longer true, and the skills of managing change are essential for everyone in an organization at all levels. Change always requires a cultural shift for everyone:

- introducing new processes;
- finding new and better procedures and working practices;
- throwing off the old habits to create a more dynamic and flexible organization;
- being able to react effectively to market forces;
- searching for ways to maintain competitiveness;
- searching for ways to seek new horizons.

To carry out such change requires some special skills. Project management has long provided a structured and organized way to achieve success every time, but has been buried deep inside technical and engineering departments as part of their exclusive domain. Unfortunately, it is not surprising that project management has been regarded as too complicated and as a result is frequently misunderstood and very poorly practised in other parts of the business.

WHAT IS SPECIAL ABOUT PROGRAMMES AND PROJECTS?

If you ask anyone what is special about projects, expect to get a confused variation of responses. The Channel Tunnel, Concorde, North Sea oil rigs, motorways, inner-city development, landing on the moon, the Taj Mahal, the Pyramids and countless others are readily recognized as 'projects'. Certainly all can be termed 'special' – all have a clearly recognizable specific result at the point of completion and we can see the result thanks to the use of modern technology and communications. Each is unique and unlikely to be repeated again in quite the same way with identical results. These large undertakings involve a wide range of technical skills and, often, large numbers of people. At the other end of the spectrum many unique but much smaller undertakings occur in every type of organization; they use fewer people but still require many skills to produce a desired result. All these activities involve change since they are concerned to create something that does not yet exist. The sum of the activities directed towards a specific result is regarded as a *project*.

In recent years the term *programme* has entered the project environment and, not unexpectedly, caused considerable confusion. Originally it was perceived as a management tool, just a convenient way of grouping some projects together so that they all came under the responsibility of one senior manager. This apparently reduced the burden of reporting effort required but conveniently hid from view many of the issues and delays occurring. Others saw a programme as an ongoing specialized activity with no clear end-point, such as, for example, marketing campaigns and space exploration. Fortunately, a more rigorous understanding of programmes has now been accepted, with significant benefits. Programme and project management is now more widely accepted as an essential business discipline for all professions.

Such activities are frequently carried out outside the normal operations that keep the mainstream activity of the organization moving to satisfy its customers. Programme and project management is seen as a burden on people, one demanding valuable time and resources. It incurs a commitment of expenditure of today's profits to generate future enhanced performance and benefits.

WHO IS THIS BOOK FOR?

Anyone involved in programmes or projects, regardless of their status or role in an organization, will benefit from reading this book. But that is not its real purpose. The book is written with two specific aims:

- to give managers in the organization a better understanding of programme and project management and how to establish an effective environment to achieve results;
- to give you, the programme or project manager, a guide to help you improve performance using well tried and tested tools and techniques.

The skills of project management are not the only tools you will need to become more effective, yet many of these tools are valuable in your everyday work. It is clearly recognized that you do not spend all your time managing programmes or projects and it is more likely to be an occasional responsibility at some time in your career.

The book has been carefully designed to meet your needs if:

- you are looking to help your organization become better organized to select and manage a programme and project portfolio;
- you are looking to develop the skills of effective programme and project management to help you in your work as a member of a team;
- you are about to start work on a programme or project, having just been appointed to the role of programme or project manager;
- you have managed programmes or projects already but are seeking to improve your skills and welcome an opportunity to review your present knowledge, add some new tools and techniques to your personal skill set and improve your performance;
- you have an involvement in programmes and projects and need to coach others in the application of the appropriate tools and techniques in a proven process.

This is not an academic textbook offering you complex theories to learn. The tools and techniques of effective and successful programme and project management are practical and relatively simple to understand. This does not mean they are always easy to apply, because of the complexity of the work and the effects of scale. The emphasis is on business programmes and projects, which are often small and of short duration when compared to highly technical or construction projects.

The book is written as a pocket guide, so it is not a book to read once and place in the bottom draw of your desk, never to see the light of day again! It is a tool to be used frequently to help you, remind you and support what you do at each step along the road from start-up of an opportunity for a programme or project through to successful completion. Throughout you will find practical tips and checklists for each step to help you achieve the results expected.

Enjoy and be successful.

2

Change: programmes and projects

Change in today's world affects everyone. You face a changing environment both in your private life and in the business world in which you work. Some of these changes are beyond your control, such as the weather, which not only changes with the passing seasons, but seems to be changing in its behaviour with the passing years.

Not all change is so automatic and uncontrolled. You can choose to create change in your life by taking carefully framed decisions. You choose to change jobs, move house, or adopt a different lifestyle as an expression of your personal desires and as a means of satisfying your current needs.

However, frequently you face changes that you do not choose because the decision is taken by another. You do not like an increase in taxation but someone decides it is essential for the greater good of the economy. Such change is obligatory for all, and you have to face consequential changes and take decisions to further adapt your lifestyle to accommodate the reduction in income. Similarly, others at work take decisions about how you must work or what you do; you have no input to the change and you are expected to accept the new environment that results. Technological advances continue to affect you at an increasing pace, creating additional stress through the need to keep up to date. Much of this change is a subtle, cumulative process that erodes the comfortable habits you have created over time, disturbing the normality and stability of familiarity. One thing is a certainty: the pace of change will continue to increase in the future. Your response determines your effectiveness in managing the process rather than letting the change manage you!

The consequences of change range from trivial through to very significant, affecting your response. Success in managing change is directly related to your ability to:

- understand the current reality;
- carefully design the change process;
- manage the consequences.

These processes help you to accept any change as an opportunity and a challenge. When you choose a change, you are positive and constructive about the consequences even if things do not work out as you expected. But an imposed change often creates negative and critical responses, with open opposition and even attempts to sabotage the desired results. Such reactions can occur regardless of the value of the change. The result is an impact on how the change process is managed to achieve a successful outcome.

CHANGE AND THE PROGRAMME AND PROJECT MANAGER

If you are to be successful in your management of change then you need to have a set of proven tools and techniques at your disposal to support your efforts. You cannot afford to ignore the nature of change and the impact on people, their reactions, fears and concerns about the future. Programmes and projects are concerned with creating change in an organized and structured manner. For you, the *programme* or *project manager*, achieving success is a measure of your ability to become an effective change agent.

You are faced with dealing with the fears that act to restrain the change process. At the same time, you demonstrate your enthusiasm and excitement at the prospect of achieving advances in the way your organization operates in the current and future business environment. This demands a wide range of people skills besides those traditionally associated with managing projects. You need to be able to:

- select the right team members with appropriate skills;
- recognize and understand the different types of personalities you must manage;
- set clear objectives and align people's personal goals;
- create a real sense of responsibility and obligation in the project team;
- manage a team as an interactive unit;
- create a sense of commitment in the team members, some of whom may have little interest in the results expected;

- coach, guide and actively support the individual team members;
- explain decisions and keep everyone informed of progress;
- establish a sustaining environment for effective dialogue and feed-back in the team and with other teams and their management;
- managing upwards to influence senior management and other line managers;
- managing third parties: contractors, suppliers, consultants;
- understanding the real needs of the end users of the results;
- satisfy the internal customer;
- handle conflicts effectively;
- demonstrate a concern for continuous improvement, questioning traditions and always seeking a better way of doing things;
- take a holistic view – seeing the bigger picture, understanding where the change fits into corporate strategy, other project activity and expected future changes.

This list may seem formidable, placing unexpected demands on your current skills. Moreover, there are additional management skills you will need to learn and improve as you become a more effective agent of change.

WHAT IS A PROJECT?

In most organizations the process of maintaining normal operations to meet the corporate objectives is the primary responsibility of the functional management. This includes the activities associated with improving effectiveness on a day-to-day basis through continuous improvement, seeking always to be better at the way the essential work is carried out. As you recognize, this is the traditional way to get things done because it is dependent on the habits and working practices generated by experience.

Projects vary considerably in size and duration. The project provides the organization with an alternative way of achieving results where the work to be done is likely to cross functional boundaries. It involves people in different parts or divisions of an organization, even different sites in the same or different countries. This allows you to use the most appropriate skills, gathered into a co-ordinated work unit to achieve results that would be difficult to accomplish in one department. The idea is not new, since most large pieces of work such as construction activities have always required a diverse range of particular skills. These skills are not within the capability of one individual.

The rapid advance of modern technology has created an enormous group of specialists, each with experience and extensive knowledge needed for the work. Even the smallest project today may call for this experience and knowledge from technologists, engineers, scientists, finance specialists, marketers, salespeople and others. Your job as the project manager is to obtain the services of these specialists, from wherever they live in the organization, to achieve a successful outcome. The *project* is a powerful mechanism for achieving that success.

The project is therefore something special by its nature and by the fact that it is perceived as being an activity outside normal operations. It may be defined as:

> a collection of linked activities carried out in an organized manner with a clearly defined start point and finish point, to achieve some specific results that satisfy the needs of an organization as derived from the organization's current business plans.

A project is therefore a temporary endeavour to achieve some specific objectives in a defined time. Because it is a practical activity carried out beyond normal operations, you will need to use a different approach to the work involved to achieve the desired results. The most unusual element of the project work is the particular effort you must use to manage a team whose membership is subject to continual change. Changes in the team's membership will occur partly because the range of skills required at any particular time is liable to change, and partly because of the varying availability of individuals from different departments, each of which has continually changing priorities.

It is difficult enough to build an effective team in a hierarchical structure with dedicated full-time members. Add the transitory nature of the project team and the job has increased complexity. You have to give additional attention to the essential skills of communication, negotiation and influencing others to keep everyone's focus on the project objectives.

PROJECTS AND SUB-PROJECTS

In many project situations it is clearly easy for you to break the work activity down into separate pieces. Each piece is still a large collection of work tasks. When the breakdown of the project shows pieces of work that can be carried out by just one department, function or specific location, it is convenient to create a sub-project. The sub-project has a small team dedicated to the work, with a project leader to manage the team. The sub-project is likely to be completed before the whole project is completed and then the resources working on the sub-project are released for other work or another sub-project.

The characteristics of projects

A project:

- ▓ has a specific purpose that can be readily defined;

- ▓ is unique because it is most unlikely to be repeated in exactly the same way by the same group of people to give the same results;

- ▓ is focused on the customer and customer expectations;

- ▓ is not usually routine work but may include routine-type tasks;

- ▓ is made up of a collection of activities that are linked together because they all contribute to the desired result;

- ▓ has clearly defined and agreed time constraints – a date when the results are required;

- ▓ is frequently complex because the work involves people in different departments and even on different sites;

- ▓ has to be flexible to accommodate change as the work proceeds;

- ▓ involves many unknowns: within the work itself, the skills of the people doing the work and the external influences on the project;

- ▓ has cost constraints, which must be clearly defined and understood to ensure that the project remains viable at all times;

- ▓ provides a unique opportunity to learn new skills;

- ▓ forces you to work in a different way because the 'temporary' management role is directly associated with the life of the project;

- ▓ challenges traditional lines of authority with perceived threats to the status quo;

- ▓ involves risks at every step of the process, risks that must be managed to sustain the focus on the desired results;

- ▓ may comprise more than one sub-project.

Figure 2.1 Project characteristics

A sub-project may be defined as:

> a key work element of a project; typically, a collection of closely related key stages with a defined start and stop date, defined objectives and deliverables.

One sub-project may be tightly integrated with other sub-project activities within the project. A sub-project cannot be justified as a stand-alone effort and does not normally produce revenue on a stand-alone basis.

It is important that you ensure that each sub-project has clearly defined ownership, with a project leader and appropriate team dedicated to the work. Sub-projects provide the organization with an opportunity to train aspiring project managers and learn the essential management skills to become effective.

There is often a problem of defining what is a project and what is a sub-project. The characteristics of projects apply to sub-projects. For a consistent approach it is convenient to establish some simple rules to show the key elements of each (Table 2.1).

A person-year is defined as 'one person dedicating 100 per cent of his or her time to the project work'. For example, if you use the definitions given in Table 2.1, for a piece of work to be classified as a project, it requires a minimum of:

- two people giving 100 per cent of their time for 12 months, or
- four people giving 100 per cent of their time for six months, or
- eight people giving 25 per cent of their time for 12 months.

Similarly, for a piece of work to be classified as a sub-project, it requires a minimum of:

- two people giving 100 per cent of their time for six months, or
- four people giving 100 per cent of their time for three months, or
- four people giving 25 per cent of their time for 12 months.

These rules can be extended to include key stages and tasks where required.

Table 2.1 Distinction between projects and sub-projects

Project	Sub-project
Requires at least two or more person-years of effort and involving more than one person	Requires at least one person-year or more of effort and involving more than one person
Comprises sub-projects, key stages, tasks and sub-tasks	Comprises key stages, tasks and sub-tasks
Not directly related to another active project	Directly related to an active project
May be directly part of an active programme and related to one or more other projects	Not directly part of an active programme except as part of an active related project

WHAT IS A PROGRAMME?

All organizations today recognize that they operate in an environment of change and must quickly react to forces that affect performance and potential growth. This need for quick reaction often leads to many projects becoming initiated, including some that are 'wild horses' or 'loose cannons'. Some of these projects can readily assume a size and duration far exceeding initial expectations. Such projects soon show the signs of the strain imposed on them: ineffective management, unclear objectives and inadequate resources. Many organizations have fallen into the trap of making their projects too big, often by default as the objectives are widened or because 'add-ons' to the original scope lead to 'scope creep'. Management issues are increased and such projects often acquire a legendary status in the organization. Dividing such large projects into smaller, more manageable pieces makes success much more likely and implementation easier.

To minimize such problems many organizations have adopted the concept of *programmes*. A programme is defined as:

> a collection of interdependent projects managed in a co-ordinated manner that together will provide the desired business outcomes.

A programme is always derived from a specific business strategy or part of a business plan. It is often a phased activity with target objectives and end dates for the initial phases well defined and committed. Subsequent phases are defined during the execution of the initial or preceding phase, allowing new, related projects to be initiated as appropriate. The interdependence of all the projects is an integral property of the programme. If any one project fails to deliver on time, the whole programme is put at risk and considerable cost over-runs could occur. In some circumstances the whole programme may suffer so badly that it is cancelled, with significant consequences for the organization and the people engaged on the work.

This may seem like a great way to organize all your projects: just collect them into groups and call them programmes. This is the potential trap for the unwary. The essential test for a programme is the interdependent nature of the projects it links. If a particular project's link is tentative and it is known that the deliverables of that project are primarily aimed at another customer then it is questionable whether it is really part of the programme. If you include such doubtfully related projects in your programme, you increase the probability of additional risks created by slippage or delays beyond your control. You just need to ensure that your business case and scope include the shared deliverables from that project and the dates when the results are expected to be available to your team.

Do not collect projects together into a programme just for reporting or management convenience. However, if a project yields a deliverable that may subsequently have an additional use either internally or for a customer, then you can still include it in your programme.

> The projects in a programme must have the same primary customer in their objectives. Collecting projects with different customers into a programme because the deliverables are useful will increase the risks to the programme's success.

AN EXAMPLE PROGRAMME

The easiest way to explain a programme is with a typical example. Suppose that the senior management team has concluded that in the current business climate it is essential to reduce production costs in the organization. Production is carried out in three locations, two in Europe and one in the Far East. The two European plants use a similar functional structure: plant general managers have responsibility for raw material purchasing, production lines, packaging and final shipment. The Far East plant has the same functions but each function has its own separate department and senior managers on the local management team. If costs cannot be reduced effectively the alternative is to close part or all of one European production unit. The cost of closure and moving production lines is clearly significant and should be avoided if possible. You have been given the objective of reducing production costs across the group by £20 million in the next financial year. This has given you 10 months to complete the work and show a successful outcome.

Your initial investigation has concluded that:

- Each European plant will be given an overall target cost reduction after discussions and agreement with the plant general managers. This cost reduction will be divided locally by the plant general manager between the purchasing, production lines, packaging and shipping departments by agreement within the local management team. This will need an experienced project manager to be appointed in each of the two plants.
- The plant in the Far East will be given separate target cost reductions for each department after discussions and agreement with each senior manager. This will require project managers to be appointed in each of the departments.
- The total cost reduction for all three plants will aggregate £20 million in the next financial year and you believe savings of £8 million can be achieved in the second half of the current financial year.

You have created a 'cost reduction programme' with six projects. Each of the European projects will have at least four sub-projects, one in each of the four departments. It may be appropriate to initiate further sub-projects as the work proceeds. Similarly, the four projects in the Far East plant may require sub-projects. In this way the total activity is broken down into manageable chunks using a team of selected specialists with appropriate skills to carry out the work.

As a business manager you are not particularly concerned with the detail and performance of each individual project and any subsequent sub-projects. Of primary interest to you is the total benefit achieved: a cost reduction of £20 million. You must maintain a continuing watch on the expected benefits from each project as the activity proceeds. One project may perform better and show signs of yielding a greater benefit than expected. You can then allow another project that is not performing to amend the scope or delay delivery of the expected benefits.

Your role as the programme manager requires you to focus on the relationship and relative importance of the six projects, ensuring that all arising issues are resolved promptly. Since the senior management team initiated the whole programme, the organization is acutely aware of the global importance of the programme. You can take major issues to the senior management team for a prompt resolution and protect the objectives. A typical structure for the cost reduction programme is shown in Figure 2.2. This approach allows you to add additional projects and sub-projects as the programme proceeds.

WHY PROGRAMME MANAGEMENT?

Programme management provides the organization with an opportunity to break down the work into a group of related and interdependent projects. The 'programme approach' allows you to separate, easily manageable chunks of work as discrete projects without losing the essential relationship between the projects to yield the desired programme objectives.

Benefits from projects usually start when the project is completed. Benefits from a programme, however, will often start to accrue when the first project or even a sub-project is completed, as shown in Figure 2.3. The projects and their sub-projects all have different completion dates. As more projects and sub-projects are completed, the benefits grow until the last project is completed and starts to yield benefits. Then the programme should start to yield the total planned benefit.

You will need all the skills you have acquired as a project manager to manage a programme effectively. You can consider the programme to be a

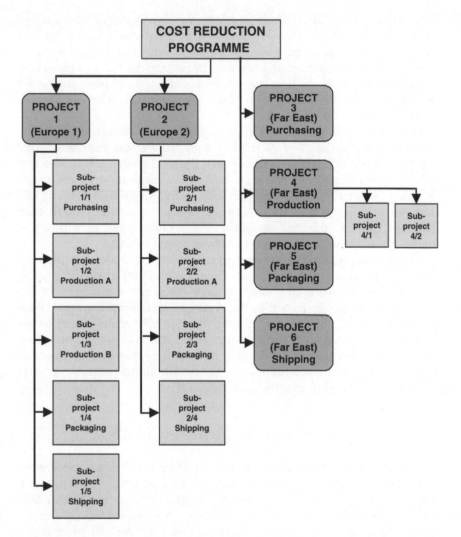

Figure 2.2 Example programme structure

'superproject' utilizing all the techniques you employ in carrying out a project.

All the methods discussed later in this book apply to the higher level of a programme. Every programme must have:

● senior management accountability;
● clearly defined objectives and benefits;
● a plan and schedule with defined start and end dates;

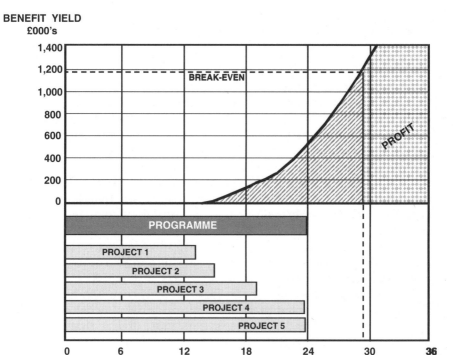

Figure 2.3 Programmes can yield benefits before completion

- a dynamic risk management process;
- an issue management process;
- a continuous performance review process.

In any programme all the projects must have well-defined objectives and benefits linked to the programme to realize the desired result.

WHAT IS PROGRAMME MANAGEMENT?

As we have seen, a programme is a collection of interdependent projects managed in a co-ordinated manner that together will provide the desired outcomes. Programme management is essentially the control system you use to achieve the desired results or outcomes. The phases and the dynamic life cycle comprise the dynamic process you are going to employ. So *programme management* may be defined as:

the utilization of project management and its inherent processes to manage effectively a collection of closely interdependent projects in a controlled and structured manner to achieve some clearly defined objectives identified as strategic needs.

The processes employed for programmes and projects are similar. Programme management is primarily concerned to satisfy strategic needs identified from business planning. Since it involves maintaining an overview of several interdependent projects, all active with differing time lines, programme management is closely linked to business management. Programmes generally use more resources simply because of their size and are often spread between several locations. The impact of progress or lack of it must be under constant review in terms of the business benefits expected, especially as benefits accumulate as projects complete and new ones start.

The programmes and projects that are approved as active at any time make up the *programme and project portfolio*. This portfolio is like an investment portfolio: some programmes and projects are low risk and a few are very high risk, and if all succeed, the business will benefit significantly. All are perceived as essential to success, but priorities do change as new opportunities arise, and the organization must ensure that adequate resources and funding are available. So, the definition of programme management can be extended further. It can now be defined as:

creating the environment where the portfolio of all active programmes and stand-alone projects is managed to yield defined benefits in pursuit of business strategic needs.

As with investments, we need to understand our portfolio – what is in it and why and how we will benefit. Programme management must create a suitable environment where well-informed business decisions can be made about the active programmes and projects, for effective business results. This is sometimes termed *portfolio management*.

WHAT IS PROJECT MANAGEMENT?

The management of your project is essentially the control system you use to achieve the right results or outcomes. As with a programme, the phases and the dynamic action cycle comprise the dynamic process you are going to employ, so project management may now be defined as:

a dynamic process that utilizes the appropriate resources in a controlled and structured manner to achieve some clearly defined objectives identified as strategic needs.

Project management is clearly carried out within an environment of set constraints, either from a programme or as a stand-alone project with a defined scope.

WHY IS PROGRAMME MANAGEMENT DIFFERENT FROM PROJECT MANAGEMENT?

Although it is easy to consider programme management and project management to be different disciplines, in practice they also have many similarities. Both require an essential understanding of project processes. A programme manager with no knowledge of how to lead a project team successfully is not likely to make a success of a programme. To lead a project team successfully a project manager must have a detailed understanding of all the processes employed in project management through the project phases.

Programme and project management have some common characteristics. Both:

- are objectives oriented – without objectives you have no outcomes;
- are change oriented – aimed at creating something the organization needs but does not have;
- are multi-disciplined – needing a wide range of skills to achieve success;
- benefit from opportunism – requiring short cuts to be taken and old norms to be bypassed;
- are performance oriented – requiring the setting of appropriate standards and quality of outputs;
- are control oriented – needing carefully designed controls to maintain the schedule;
- question tradition – demand that managers avoid getting trapped by the old ways of doing things.

The primary objective of programme management is to ensure that all the constituent projects together provide the benefit required, regardless of the performance of any individual project or sub-project. Other differences are listed in Table 2.2.

Too often the selection of team members for a project team is controlled less by the skill-set needed and more by 'who is available'. Always ensure you have some part in the selection process. You probably will not have a free hand to select who you want, but at least exert a strong influence. Many programmes and projects have run into difficulties because the wrong team members were selected at the outset. If programme and

Table 2.2 Differences between programme management and project management

Programme management	Project management
Is concerned with achieving benefits required by organization strategic objectives	Is a defined activity focused on delivering specific objectives as one piece of a programme or as a 'stand-alone' project
Is appropriate for managing and reviewing performance of a large number of constituent interdependent projects that may change with time	Is intended for an activity designed to achieve specific deliverables and benefits
Manages the impact and benefits of a group of closely aligned projects to ensure a smooth transition to a defined new environment	Aims to produce clearly defined benefits in a known environment
Manages risks and issues across the projects to minimize impact on the programme performance	Manages risks and issues within the project to minimize the impact on the project performance
Creates an environment that sets the constraints for all the projects in the programme	Creates an environment where constraints are set by the project scope

project management is accepted as an essential skill in your organization, you will find it possible to influence senior managers to support your efforts from the outset.

WHAT IS DIFFERENT ABOUT PROGRAMME AND PROJECT MANAGEMENT?

Compared with normal functional management, the principal difference is that you are operating in a temporary role. You are the manager of the team only for the life of the programme or stand-alone project and then you return to your other operational duties – or another programme with possibly a different team. This situation leads to some specific differences when compared to the 'fixed' functional hierarchical team that is part of the organizational structure.

In a fixed functional team, as the manager you:

- lead the team;
- have team members reporting direct to you alone;

- have a stable team membership in the medium to long term;
- create the conditions for good teamworking;
- set the team norms and behaviours with the team;
- decide responsibilities and coach team members in new skills;
- control the work of the team – input and output;
- build trust and respect in the team;
- encourage the personal growth and development of the team members;
- encourage sharing of information, opinions and feelings for the team's benefit;
- utilize the team's creative skills to improve team performance;
- appraise the team members' performance;
- set individual targets to improve performance;
- create a team identity.

The team you bring together for a programme or stand-alone project will almost certainly have come from different departments in the organization, maybe even different sites. Although you must attempt to do all the things just listed, you will have difficulty with some of them:

- Team members report to you only for their work on the programme or project and to their line manager for other work – unless they are fully dedicated to your new team.
- Your team membership is less likely to have stability, owing to changing priorities of the team members' line managers.
- With a changing team membership, conditions for good teamwork are more difficult to create.
- Often team members do not know each other, and setting team norms takes a considerable time.
- You are in a time-limited situation and can find little time for coaching; you need the skills immediately.
- Team members who do not know each other well are always hesitant to share information, opinions and feelings openly.
- You can appraise an individual only on his or her programme or project work; this individual may be working on more than one project at a time for different managers and still have line responsibilities. So who does the appraisal and how?
- Creating a team identity requires time and additional effort on your part to ensure that the team comes together regularly as a team to learn more about each other.

The organizational hierarchical structure is a matrix from which your team is drawn, and during the early stages of a programme or stand-alone project everyone is getting used to the situation of working with a different group of people. This can lead to more conflict than you would like, so pay particular attention to getting to know and understand the team members yourself through setting up regular one-to-one meetings with each.

Success in programme and project management is not going to be yours merely as a result of your using the right tools and techniques. It is only achieved through giving time to leading the team and overcoming these areas of potential difficulty, which will then reduce the risk of failure.

HOW ARE PROGRAMMES AND PROJECTS DERIVED?

As we have seen, the programme or project is a vehicle for carrying change to its intended conclusion, which is to give your organization something it does not currently have, but strongly desires. But where do the ideas for all this additional activity come from? You may feel the answer is obvious – the senior management, maybe. Yet anyone in the organization may come up with ideas. Creativity and idea generation are not the exclusive territory of the management. It is the people who do the day-to-day operational work who often have the best ideas for improving organizational performance, both in current operations and in terms of creating new products. To identify how programmes and projects are derived, it is appropriate to examine their sources in the organization.

Business planning

Every organization today engages in business planning in some manner. It is common to have a three- or five-year *corporate plan* and a shorter one-year *strategic plan*. The corporate plan will set the future direction of the organization and establish broad targets. The strategic plan is a more detailed documentation of how the organization will meet the corporate plan through the next financial year.

Incremental growth

Greater effort will be directed towards achieving the operational targets for the year. Everyone whose job contributes to achieving the growth of current operations set out in the strategy seeks to improve performance. Continuous improvement is not to be undertaken via an initiative or campaign; it should be part of everyday work and a way of life for everyone. Everyone should seek always to find better ways to do the job so as to make the organization more effective and more efficient.

Sometimes good ideas that come from continuous improvement activity in one part of the organization may have benefits for other functions. A considerable effort with a cross-functional team may then be needed to make a significant change effectively. The organization can gain considerably from treating this type of continuous improvement as a stand-alone project, because of the size and complexity of the work involved.

Step change growth

Most programme and project activity in an organization starts by someone recognizing the importance of addressing specific needs or opportunities now to yield increased defined benefits in the future. The purpose is to give the organization something that does not yet exist but is clearly defined as essential or highly desirable to support the process of achieving the strategic plan for the year. Some programmes may be of longer life and directed towards the corporate objectives within the three- or five-year plan.

It may be considered necessary to start a programme comprising several projects that are connected by a common overall objective, as in our earlier example of a cost reduction programme. All have one important characteristic: they involve a step change or quantum leap from current business process or operations. They are directly derived from the organization's vision for the future and form a significant contribution towards achieving that vision.

How does this affect you as the programme or project manager? You have an interest in success, and a key element of success is the team, ie the people doing the work. It is not enough to just hand out the work you decide is necessary. The people in the team must participate in all aspects of the work from the start-up and definition through to completion. You can get the team motivated, enthusiastic about the work and focused on the objectives if you can explain the context of the programme or project within the organization's strategy. Then everyone understands why the programme or project exists, its importance and its relative priority compared with other work.

Occasionally you may be faced with a mandatory project – a change controlled by an external requirement such as new UK legislation, EU directives or health and safety requirements. Such projects often do not arouse enthusiasm but are still important for the organization and are always part of strategy. After all, failure to comply may lead to legal and commercial difficulties or financial penalties.

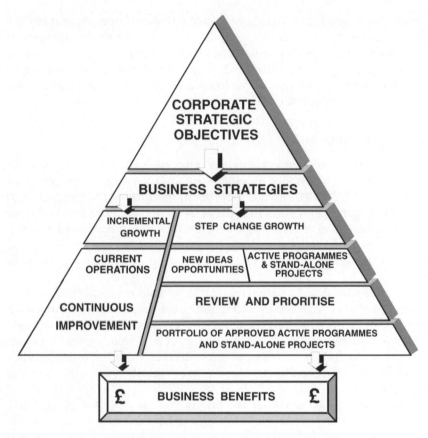

Figure 2.4 How programmes and projects are related to strategy

THE DYNAMIC LIFE CYCLE

Because the programme or project has such specific characteristics, all limited by time, it naturally goes through a life cycle, just as a product does. The difference here is that the life cycle is dynamic and subject to reiteration at any time during the project.

The front end of any programme or project is marked by the initial decision to proceed. This start-up is often very 'woolly' and ill defined, and will be discussed in more detail in Chapter 5.

All programmes and projects given an initial approval to start go through a similar life cycle, comprising four fundamental phases:

- **Opportunity identified**. An opportunity is identified for a new product, new system or process, new manufacturing facilities or business process. If it is considered a valid opportunity within the current strategy then it passes into Phase Zero.

- **Phase Zero: Selection**. An opportunity is examined in some detail and subjected to rigorous selection tests and criteria by the business group or department making the proposal. A decision must be made to proceed and commit resources to the work and pass into Phase One.
- **Phase One: Definition**. Phase One is the start of the real work once needs have been clearly identified and the project can be defined with the agreement of those people with an interest in the outcomes. Once all definition work is complete and approved then Phase Two can be entered.
- **Phase Two: Planning**. Phase Two is the processes of planning to derive a realistic schedule taking into account all the constraints that can be identified at this stage. When all those with an interest in the outcomes have approved the plans, the actual work can start, which is Phase Three.
- **Phase Three: Execution**. Phase Three involves launching the actual work, ensuring everyone understands the plan; the controls you impose on the process; and making sure the plan is always up to date with any changes that occur. When all work is successfully complete and no outstanding major issues are unresolved then entry to Phase Four is approved.
- **Phase Four: Closure**. Formal closure is agreed with the customer. All work is complete and the acceptance and handover signed off. Any follow-on activities are identified and assigned and the evaluation process is completed.

THE DYNAMIC ACTION CYCLE

In practice these phases are only a convenient way to help you to separate the programme or project work into blocks with a defined sequence. The reality is that no programme or project follows such a neat and simple process flow without a significant amount of reiteration. At any stage of the work you may have to:

- revise the definition and scope;
- replan part of the work;
- revise the schedule;
- solve problems;
- carry out recovery planning – to recover lost time;
- carry out contingency planning – in case a high-risk part of the work goes wrong.

The *action cycle* gives the basic steps that a programme or project (or any part of a project) must go through, with the phases identified earlier. Figure 2.5 shows the cycle in a graphic form.

Completion of any phase in the process requires a decision-making process to be invoked. The work done must be subjected to a rigorous review to determine the validity of allowing the programme or project to continue. This decision can commit the organization to using resources that do not exist, because of other commitments. Many questions must be asked by the management before this decision is made. Too often, rogue programmes or projects are allowed to continue unchecked and either subsequently fail owing to there being insufficient resources or seriously affect other important programmes by stealing their resources. Clearly, the

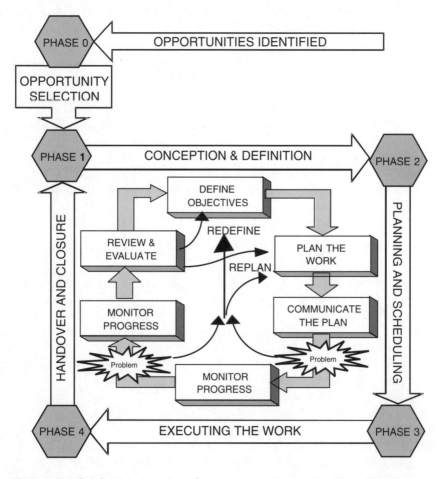

Figure 2.5 The dynamic action cycle

technical feasibility of continuing must be reviewed at the same time. In the past, many development projects (eg for a new product) have become 'runaway trains' consuming huge amounts of resources and still subsequently failing, with large debt write-offs. The risk of such situations occurring can be minimized by using a regular review and decision process.

At each of the steps in Figure 2.5 it may become necessary to recycle the process and redo some of the work. Such reiteration throughout the process maintains the dynamics. It provides a check that you are doing the right things to keep the work on track to the schedule and achieve the desired outcomes agreed with your customer.

THE PROGRAMME AND PROJECT PROCESS PHASE GATES

For any programme or project to achieve success it is essential to relate the progress through the dynamic action cycle to the organization's strategic needs. As the programme or project manager you will always demonstrate that your programme or project has clear objectives and that the work is on target. However, the senior management of the organization need to be kept informed and must remain convinced that the costs justify continuing with the work.

To achieve this open approach two essential elements are required:

- *Phase gates* (Figure 2.6) to provide entry to each phase of the dynamic action cycle. Each phase gate is opened to allow the work of the programme or project to proceed to the next phase.
- *The programme steering team* (PST). This team of senior managers of the organization meets at regular intervals to review the status of all active programmes and projects. The PST also approves opportunities to be investigated and sets the priorities. We will look in more detail at the PST and how it operates in Chapter 3.

The decision to open a phase gate for any programme or project is made only after a review by the PST. The decision is driven by a review of the programme or project that covers the following elements:

- current progress and identification of slippages;
- current risks and issues;
- the budget;
- priority ranking compared with other active programmes and projects;

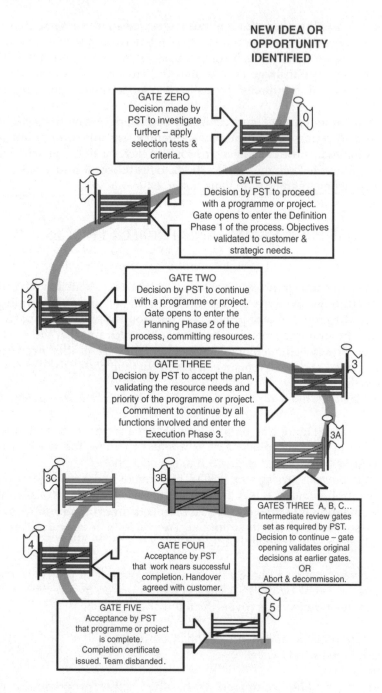

Figure 2.6 The programme and project process phase gates

- assessment that appropriate resources are available for the next phase;
- confirmation that the programme or project is still needed – alignment with strategic needs;
- a GO/NO GO decision either to continue or to cancel the programme or project.

The review outcome is dependent on information you present to the PST. Occasionally it may even be necessary for you to make specific recommendations concerning revisions to the objectives, scope or current plans, or even to cancel the work. This ensures that decisions are confronted at the appropriate time in the dynamic action cycle.

IS THE PHASE GATE A CONSTRAINT?

You may consider that the concept of phase gates is imposing more bureaucracy on you as the programme or project manager. The only apparent constraint is preventing some work in the next phase from starting early because resources are available and you keep the work rolling along.

The real purpose of the phase gate is to focus the mind of everyone with an interest in your programme or project, encouraging them to take a deep breath and ask 'where are we now?' After a detailed review the PST is primarily concerned to seek answers to three questions:

- *Is the programme or project still viable?* The PST must be satisfied that the planned benefits meet their original expectations and the costs have not exceeded the planned budget.
- *Is the priority the same relative to other programmes or projects?* The PST decides the relative priority of all active programmes and projects, taking into account the costs, benefits and resource availability.
- *Is funding still available?* The PST must decide to continue funding the work when reviewing all other commitments. In some circumstances the work may be slowed to make money available for other activities.

After a successful review, and if the answers to the above questions are satisfactory, the next phase gate is opened and a 'GO' decision recorded. However, the PST may instead decide on one of three primary options:

- Terminate – cancel the programme or project and initiate decommissioning procedures immediately to minimize collateral damage.
- Suspend work – stop all work temporarily for a specified period. This may be due to a change of priority, the need to move resources to another programme or a demand for a review of strategic needs.

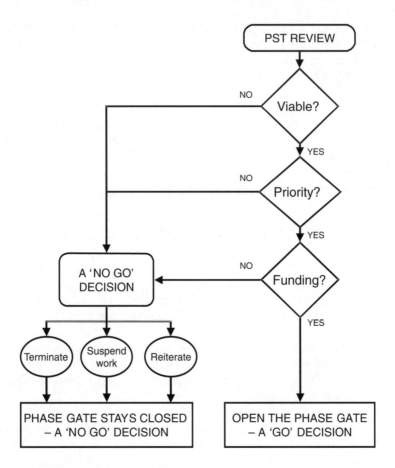

Figure 2.7 The phase gate decisions

- Reiterate – go back and repeat past work or additional work in the current phase, with revisions to the definition, scope or plans.

Any of these options will lead to a 'NO GO' decision. If the decision is 'Reiterate', then you will be expected to action the reasons for the decision and then present your programme or project again for review at a future meeting of the PST.

IS THIS CONTROL NECESSARY?

This amount of control may seem excessive when first considered. However, many organizations have now realized the importance of ensuring that expenditure is incurred on realistic business needs, and this approach provides a valuable process. This does not mean creativity is killed but it does direct all innovation into areas that benefit the business. It ensures that wild ideas are reviewed in the context of business strategy even if this is subsequently revised and involves the senior management team together in making such decisions.

Programme management is an *enabling process* that focuses on accountability for initiating and conducting programmes and projects to grow the business.

SUMMARY

- Programmes and projects are an essential part of a change process.
- Programme management:
  - enables informed decisions;
  - ensures focus on the business's strategic needs;
  - helps maintain control of business growth.
- Programmes and projects are a means to:
  - implement business strategies;
  - achieve step changes;
  - continuously improve business performance;
  - involve people across the organization;
  - break down functional barriers.
- Programmes and projects:
  - depend on people and effective teamwork;
  - are unique activities;
  - are concerned to create something that does not yet exist;
  - have specific and desired outcomes with clear benefits;
  - are subject to risk.
- All programmes and projects follow a dynamic life cycle:
  - selection;
  - definition;
  - planning;
  - execution;
  - closure.
- Programme and project management is different from other management roles because:
  - it is a temporary role only for the period of the life cycle;
  - the team membership is flexible and changes as project needs vary;
  - it is a time- and resource-limited activity.

3

Organizing for programme management

Chapter 2 introduced the concept of programmes as a way to manage the activities of an organization that are outside 'normal operations'. This approach has proved well suited to managing change, and particularly to developing new products or operating systems, or following specific new business activities. Many organizations suffer from having too many projects, or even programmes that were initiated only with regard to the content of the work, with the deliverables being seen as a benefit.

How are programmes and projects organized and managed in your organization? Do you find yourself in a situation where many of the projects use resources that are stretched beyond the limit of effectiveness? People are forced to hop from one project to another according to who shouts loudest, demanding results and progress. Inevitably confusion occurs and people start to question why they are doing the work. Many of these projects have been doomed to failure almost from the day they started. In this typical situation projects are spawned within functional departments in isolation from the corporate business strategy. You may already have functional responsibilities and the project work is an additional burden on your limited time. Success gives your manager the kudos for starting the project and you are left to get on with your day-to-day functional activities. When the project fails the outcome is quickly forgotten and never mentioned again.

No organization can successfully survive for long with such a situation prevailing. You will frequently come across the complaint that 'We have too many projects', and this is a signal that something is seriously at fault with the organizational culture. The operations of the business are usually managed and controlled with a traditional rigid structure of senior managers (or directors) responsible for specific parts of the business. Each senior manager manages an element of this structure, with middle-level and junior managers responsible for departments and sections, all staffed by the people who carry out the day-to-day work.

In this type of environment strategic planning is conducted at the senior manager level and may involve other managers. A decision to start a programme or project that will use resources of the business, possibly at the expense of other activities, is normally made by the senior management team. A programme or project manager is then appointed and a team allocated. The first problem occurs at this point. Who decides who is to join the team? Drawing the resources from different departments across the organization in a matrix (Figure 3.1) solves the problem, provided you can reach an agreement with all the individual managers concerned.

The core team are people assigned full time to the work. Unfortunately, securing the release of some of the people required for the core team and particularly the extended team could lead to difficulties, particularly as they probably are assigned only part time to the work of the programme or project. As a functional manager you would naturally take the position that your departmental work is more important!

Typical difficulties with this approach include:

- conflicts between functional work and project commitments;
- uncertain lines of accountability;
- unclear responsibilities – who is responsible for what?
- poor programme/project control – most will be late or delayed;

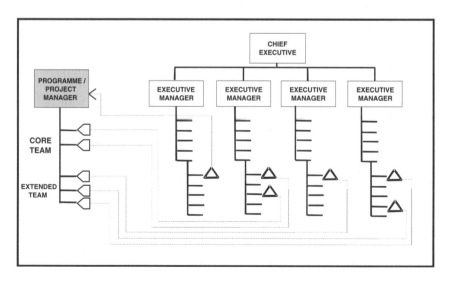

Figure 3.1 Programmes and projects in a matrix structure

- unclear view of resource utilization leading to individual overload;
- unclear responsibility for individual performance appraisal;
- no prioritization of programme/project activity from an organization overview position;
- 'programmes' and 'projects' being initiated at random at all levels and often hidden from view.

It is not surprising that problems such as these create a valid belief that programmes and projects need 100 per cent dedicated teams for success.

ORGANIZING FOR OWNERSHIP

To overcome these problems created by the confusion of having many programmes and projects supposedly 'active' requires a clearly defined organizational structure that is overlaid on the functional hierarchy. To ensure that all the potentially 'active' programmes and projects in the organization are adequately resourced would usually require a significant increase in staff numbers!

As we saw earlier, all the organization's activity is directed towards supporting the overall purpose of meeting corporate strategic objectives, either within normal operations or in an attempt to achieve the step changes desired by the organization (see Figure 2.3). This can be achieved successfully only through *a clear statement of ownership at each level in the organization, with clearly defined roles and responsibilities.*

It is essential that programmes and projects are not initiated as management whims at any level but are allowed only when it is demonstrated that they will make a clear contribution to corporate strategy. To ensure that this is the case, senior managers must be involved in the process and have defined responsibilities for the 'sponsorship' of all programme and project activity.

The individual *sponsors* come from this senior management team, where authority should be clearly defined. In Chapter 2 the concept of the *programme steering team* (PST) was introduced. The PST (Figure 3.2) is normally drawn from some or all of the senior management team. These senior managers each assume the role of sponsor for specific programmes and projects from the initial idea through to completion. The sponsor is the primary driver of the activity because this person has 'ownership' of the final benefits expected for the organization. When the PST approves a programme or project this person is clearly accountable to the senior management team to ensure that success is achieved. The sponsor must demonstrate that he or she 'owns' the programme or project and ensure that everything possible is done to ensure that a successful outcome is achieved. The high visibility of the sponsors and the PST giving total support does make sure that everyone in the organization focuses on the active programmes and projects, ie those designated as important to the successful attainment of the strategic objectives.

The PST must operate using the same methodology for programmes and projects as the teams carrying out the work. This creates a common understanding of the processes involved and obliges everyone involved to work with the dynamic action cycle and phase gates discussed in Chapter 2. With an effective PST a clear decision process exists on all aspects of programme and project work and you have a clear understanding to whom you are reporting. It also creates a clear sense of direction for all such activity in the organization, which prioritizes programmes and projects for the limited available resources.

ESTABLISHING THE PROGRAMME STEERING TEAM

Do your programmes and projects span cross-functional boundaries in the organization? It would be unusual if some do not, and this means your

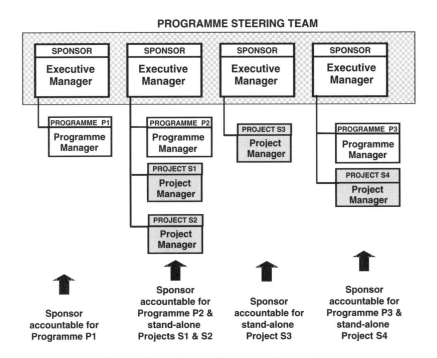

Figure 3.2 The programme steering team of sponsors

organization needs to have a PST. This will ensure that only the right projects that fit the business strategy are initiated, and the PST reinforces the priority of these activities across all functions.

However, do not confuse the PST described here with another approach you may come across in other project methodologies. In some circumstances a programme or project board or review board is established for a specific programme or project, meeting once a month to review progress. This board is usually chaired by the sponsor and includes selected individuals chosen for their knowledge, past experience or specialized skills to advise the sponsor on the conduct of the work. Such a board is totally internally focused on the programme or project and does not consider any other unrelated programme activities going on in the organization. Attempts have been made to establish programme or project boards for every programme and project initiated in the organization. This has created a situation where a small group of experts and managers spend a huge amount of time sitting in meetings, running from one board meeting to the next. The process serves only to add a layer of bureaucracy between the sponsor and the programme manager, and experience has shown that this leads to a much slower decision-making process. Such programme boards have often been found to be ineffective and add little value to the programme or project.

The PST is different because the membership is strictly confined to a group of *sponsors*, all having a keen interest in the matters discussed in their meetings. The PST must meet at regular intervals, usually monthly, to review the status of all active programmes and projects, initiate new projects and decide the prioritization of project activity in the organization. However, it is important to stress that this review is not a detailed investigation of all the elements of the work. The review is carefully designed to focus on specific elements of each active programme and project, as will be discussed further in a later section.

In very large organizations it is beneficial to have a PST at different levels (Figure 3.3). The *executive PST* is concerned to focus on programmes and projects that:

- Have a sponsor drawn from the executive PST.
- Cross division boundaries for support, technology and resources.
- Are considered major activities to achieve strategic objectives of the whole business.
- Are elevated from a *division programme steering team*. Although a programme or project may be totally confined within a division and its own departments, in certain circumstances the executive PST can choose to elevate the programme or project because of its strategic significance. A new sponsor from within the executive PST is then assigned.

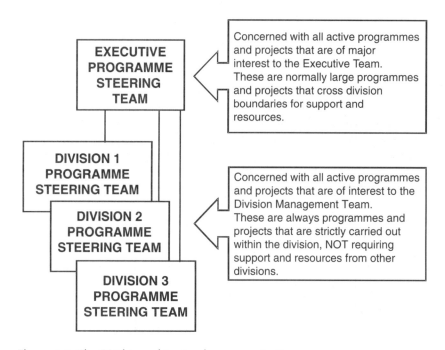

Figure 3.3 The PST hierarchies in a large organization

Each PST creates and maintains a *programme register* that lists:

- all ideas and opportunities currently under or awaiting investigation;
- all active programmes and projects;
- all recent programmes and projects that have been suspended, cancelled or completed.

If there is only one programme register in the organization then this is the active *programme and project portfolio* referred to in Chapter 2. However, if there is both an executive programme register and several division programme registers then the programme and project portfolio comprises all the programme registers in the organization.

The programme register is the key document for all PST meetings as it lists all 'step change growth' activities that are active. In Chapter 2 some guidance was given on the minimum requirements for a programme and project. It is most important for your organization to define clearly what is and what is not a project. Failure to make this definition available could lead to programme registers becoming littered with many activities that are no more than key stages of projects, or even just tasks.

CONTINUOUS IMPROVEMENT AND PROBLEM SOLVING: ARE THEY PROJECTS?

Continuous improvement activities are frequently labelled 'projects'. However, if we take the view that continuous improvement is really nothing more than a responsibility of the job then it cannot be a project – by definition it is continuous and has no end! Similarly, problem-solving activities are often given the project label. The activity is strictly focused on immediacy to solve a problem quickly and at minimum cost to maintain or restore production. If a longer-term solution is discovered that requires new equipment or systems to be designed and installed then it is only this that should become a project. As defined earlier, the proposed activity will have defined start and end dates. From experience it is well worth considering making these definitions very clear at the outset to avoid 'register clutter'. If you do not restrict what is entered on the programme register to true programmes and projects then it can take many months to investigate and clean up the list.

THE PROGRAMME REGISTER

The programme register is used to list: 1) all approved programmes and projects regardless of current status; 2) ideas and opportunities approved for further investigation. An example register template is shown in Figure 3.4.

The listing of ideas and opportunities is optional, but recommended in order to track progress, particularly as the investigation is using valuable resources. When such ideas or opportunities are subsequently approved as a programme or project then the unique identifier number remains on the list. The PST can decide to change the status at any time to 'Suspended' (S) or 'Cancelled' (T), when work will cease. It is suggested that the register be maintained on a database to allow subsequent reference. Programmes and projects that are completed or cancelled stay on the list for a fixed period – say three or six months. Suspended programmes and projects stay on the list until either reactivated or cancelled.

The example register lists some key information for each entry:

- description of the programme or project – the title;
- the name of the sponsor;
- the name of the programme/project manager;
- the date when the proposal or business case is submitted to the PST for approval;
- the date when the project brief (see Chapter 6) is approved by the PST;
- the date when the baseline plan is approved by the PST;

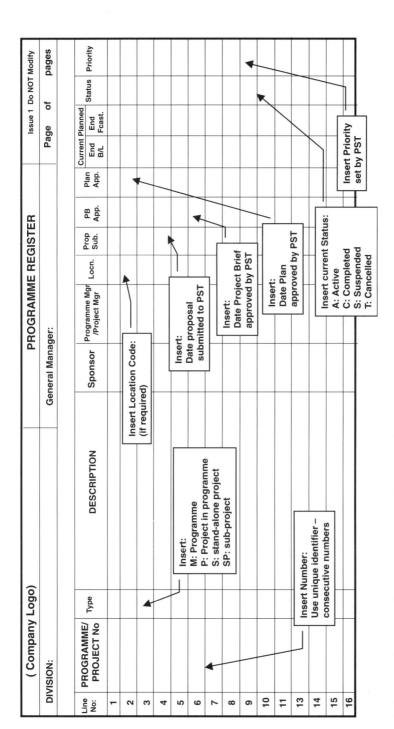

Figure 3.4 An example programme register template

- current end dates – baseline plan and current forecast;
- the current status – active, completed, suspended or cancelled.

Other data can be added as required, such as 'location code' for the location by site or otherwise of the programme manager or project manager.

The programme register is intended as a working document, so the data recorded must be regularly renewed to reflect the current situation for each sponsor and the PST.

OPERATING A PROGRAMME REGISTER

You need to ensure everyone understands some basic process rules to operate the programme register effectively. The executive register lists only the active programmes and projects approved by the executive PST. If required, ideas and opportunities can also be listed, provided:

- the initial proposal or business case has been submitted to the PST and approved for further investigation;
- the idea or proposal is directly linked to a business strategic objective;
- it is expected that the subsequent programme or project, if approved, will cross division boundaries in a significant way.

If division PSTs are established then the situation is different. The executive managers do not themselves normally manage any programmes or projects directly, as they are more likely to take on the role of sponsors for major activities. Then the division registers become very important. Each of the active programmes and projects is owned by one of the divisions, usually because this is where the initial idea was proposed, the resources are located and the work instigated. Some of the work may involve people in one or more other divisions, and these other divisions should list each of their activities on their own register as *either* a project linked to a programme in another division *or* a sub-project linked to a project in another division – this may be a stand-alone project or a project within a programme.

The division owning the programme must show all the projects and sub-projects on register using the location code to record where the work is being conducted. The key to ensuring accurate linkage of all these activities is the programme or project number, which is unique for all the divisions involved. An example is shown in Figure 3.5.

Other projects and sub-projects may be added as the programme proceeds. These are listed on the Division 1 register and on the registers of other divisions, as appropriate.

Why record the same information on different registers? Experience has shown several sound reasons for this procedure:

- Each register is owned by a different management team.
- Visibility of a strategic programme across the organization maintains focus on important activities.
- Each management team is responsible for the effective utilization of its resources.

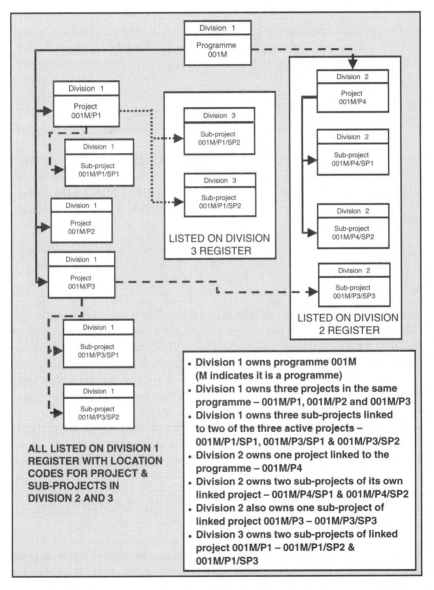

Figure 3.5 Example programme across three divisions

- Each management team must ensure that it does everything necessary to ensure that projects and sub-projects of programmes owned in other divisions are given the appropriate priority.

In the example shown in Figure 3.5 the members of the executive PST may decide that Programme 001M is a major strategic programme and elevate it to their register. If this happens:

- Programme 001M is listed on the executive PST programme register along with the projects and sub-projects to identify the locations.
- One of the executive PST members is assigned as sponsor for the whole programme.
- The programme remains listed on the Division 1 register along with the projects and sub-projects owned by Division 1.
- The projects and sub-projects owned in Divisions 2 and 3 are still listed on their respective registers.
- If required, the programme number and all its projects and sub-projects can be given a prefix (eg E001M) to indicate to everyone that this is now a major strategic programme for the business, with an executive sponsor. If it is a stand-alone project then the number changes from 002S to E002S.

> Elevating a programme to the executive register essentially labels it as a programme of key strategic importance that 'MUST NOT FAIL'.

Clearly, this process and maintenance of accurate registers is best managed and controlled using an electronic database on an organization intranet. The advantage of using this approach is that all ideas, opportunities, programmes and projects in the organization are assigned a unique identifier number in sequence as they are recorded, irrespective of which register owns the activity. If ideas and opportunities are listed on any register, each is recorded with the next available number, but no prefix or suffix is used until the decision to proceed is made by the appropriate PST. When this decision is taken, the appropriate suffix for a programme or stand-alone project can be added.

THE KEY RESPONSIBILITIES OF THE PROGRAMME STEERING TEAM

We shall take a closer look at the role and responsibilities of the sponsor in Chapter 4. For a PST to be effective, all the members must clearly understand their responsibilities when they meet together. They need to:

- ensure that all opportunities for programmes and projects are reviewed using agreed tests and criteria to enable the 'GO/NO GO' decision;
- maintain a focus on customer and business needs;
- ensure that all programmes and projects approved are strictly focused on business needs and aligned to strategic objectives;
- ensure that environmental influences (internal and external) are taken into account;
- ensure that adequate resources are available for all approved active programmes and projects;
- ensure that adequate funding is available to support the list of active programmes and projects;
- provide strategic direction and active support to programme and project managers;
- assign a priority ranking to all active programmes and projects;
- make decisions concerning resource conflicts;
- monitor process procedures to ensure these are followed and maintained;
- ensure that risk assessment is regularly reviewed and risks are managed;
- ensure that all escalated issues are promptly resolved, with assigned action plans;
- make 'GO/NO GO' decisions at the programme and project process phase gates.

The executive PST is the ultimate decision forum for all major problems, issues and cross-functional decisions to remove the obstacles to success. It should meet at regular intervals, preferably on a monthly cycle. Dates of meetings should preferably be fixed in the meetings diary for the year ahead. Division PSTs, if they are formed, should always ensure that they meet a few days before the executive PST to ensure that programme registers are updated with the latest information. In addition, this ensures that the divisions have all their programme and project progress and status reports updated in case the executive PST asks for a review.

MEETINGS OF THE PROGRAMME STEERING TEAM

It is inadvisable for the PST meeting to be an agenda item on another meeting. Even though the same group of managers need to be present, there are several risks to effectiveness:

- insufficient time for effective decision taking;
- confusion with earlier business of the meeting;

- lack of effective preparation for the PST;
- lack of time for proper review of the key active programmes and projects.

If some of the managers in the earlier part of the meeting are not required for the PST item then the meeting must break up for a short period anyway to allow people to leave. Extensive experience has shown that the PST meeting at any level in the organization is best set up as a completely separate meeting to allow adequate preparation time and ensure that everyone present is fully focused on the purpose of the meeting.

These meetings do tend to accumulate rather more paper than is desirable – unless conducted almost entirely using Web-based tools. As this is not always possible, the PST does need to have a permanent *PST administrator* who co-ordinates the meetings and collects together the essential papers for the meeting. A PST member should not fill this role. The administrator has many responsibilities, but before a PST meeting this person must ensure the following:

- The venue is organized.
- The PST members are reminded to attend, with no deputizing allowed.
- PST members (programme and project sponsors) are reminded they must report to the meeting on the status of their programmes and projects.
- The PST members are issued with documentation to read before the meeting:
  - the latest version of the programme register;
  - copies of status reports for all active programmes and projects (for details see Chapter 8);
  - summaries of proposals for new programmes or projects;
  - an action list with the current status of all actions, updated from the immediately preceding meeting;
  - a list of outstanding decisions (unresolved issues, opportunities, etc).

The administrator should also prepare the meeting agenda and issue this before the meeting. It is suggested that a standard framework for the agenda be used; for example:

1. welcome and opening remarks by the chairperson;
2. action list review of outstanding items (completed actions are history unless there are consequences, and need no further discussion);
3. review of the programme register – with the focus on changes since the last issue, guided by the PST administrator;

4. issues outstanding and new issues escalated to the PST for decisions;
5. review of one or more selected programmes or projects – a detailed review of the status and progress (optional);
6. opportunities for new programmes and projects;
7. action list – new actions added, with details, owner and target completion date;
8. closure of meeting.

The aim of the PST is to focus on the progress and status of all approved activities. This can normally be achieved from a review of the data in the programme register and the separate status reports. The emphasis should be on exceptions, not long reports of the good news about anything that should have happened anyway. The data in the reports are used by the sponsor to justify the request for a 'GO/NO GO' decision for a programme or project waiting at a phase gate for approval to proceed.

In certain circumstances the sponsor of a programme or the PST together may consider it appropriate to present a more detailed review of that programme under item 5 on the agenda. You cannot review everything on the register in one meeting but it is a good idea to select up to three key programmes on the register list for such reviews. This decision to hold a detailed review at any phase gate can also be driven by major process issues, resource problems, technology issues, lessons learnt, changes to benefits forecast or market changes.

However, it is important to understand this is not a project meeting, so the presentation of such a review needs to be structured around the current status. It is easy to put together a glitzy 30-slide show about the programme and what it will achieve. Keep this for the prospective customers; your sponsor and the PST know all about your programme. Keep the review focused on key elements:

- current and forecast customer base;
- changes to market forecasts;
- current (and previous) forecast completion dates;
- reasons for changes to forecasts;
- exceptions to plans;
- changes to customer and other key stakeholder expectations;
- issues outstanding;
- current risk level – current high risks and mitigation plans;
- current and forecast costs and return on investment, with reasons for any changes.

It is good practice for the programme or project manager to present to the PST, but if you are put in this position, do make sure you fully brief your sponsor before the meeting. If you present your sponsor with some surprises in the meeting you can expect some of your own after the meeting!

After the meeting the administrator is responsible for issuing the action list to the members of the PST and everyone assigned actions. The decisions list is issued to the members only, as each sponsor is responsible for passing down the decisions taken that affect his or her programmes and projects. The sponsors should ensure they inform their programme and project managers as quickly as possible. It is probable that the executive sponsors will be division managers, so it is relatively easy for them to pass on information from the executive PST meeting.

MANAGING THE PORTFOLIO: SELECTION OF PROGRAMMES AND PROJECTS

How can you ensure that the right programmes and projects are selected to help the business grow and make it more effective and profitable? There is no easy answer to this age-old question. Programmes and projects are by definition a proving ground for risk to demonstrate its effects on your efforts! As mentioned earlier, you may have been the unhappy victim of being pushed to work on a project that no one seemed to want except your manager. Managers have started many such activities on the basis of a whim or illogical self-belief. To be fair, some have got away with it too, as they proved to be right – sometimes. Unfortunately, most organizations can tell you the legendary tales of programmes and projects that failed and really should never have even started. It is not unknown for the same project to exist under different titles with the same objectives in separate departments! Competitive commitment is good, but such duplication within the organization is a huge waste of resources and operating costs.

It is a strange phenomenon that this month's 'good ideas' tend to look much more attractive than last month's. Consequently, the tendency is to dump last month's partially completed programmes and projects in favour of new ones. In a poorly controlled programme environment there is a high risk that the owners of the old ones will not let go and carry on regardless. As a result, all the programmes and projects suffer from a lack of available resources and all are threatened with failure as nothing is actually completed. Ultimately someone is brave enough to take the decision to cancel a large number of programmes and projects, leaving in his or her wake an unhappy band of dissatisfied customers and demotivated employees.

You can see how this situation has developed in Figure 3.6. This shows a typical organization with the apparent utilization of the available resources for a 12-month period. A significant portion of the resource pool is committed to normal operations and day-to-day problem solving.

You should always allow a small portion of the available resources for resolving major issues, engaging in disaster recovery activities (for a project in serious trouble) and conducting the initial investigation of new ideas and opportunities – the 'white space' (Figure 3.6). It is just good planning, and as these activities will happen anyway, they cannot be treated as just an additional burden on someone's time.

The resource left is available for programmes and projects. As each new programme or project is approved, resource commitments are made, usually in isolation of other activities. Before long, each new programme or project added to the list is committing resources that do not exist. This creates a rolling wave above the 'maximum available resource' line. This bow wave gets higher and higher with time as a major disaster looms.

The consequence of this situation is that the 'forecast' completion dates become impossible, and the reality is that the only date the portfolio can be completed is a vague 'expected' completion date that has no foundation in carefully prepared schedules. The longer this situation is allowed to

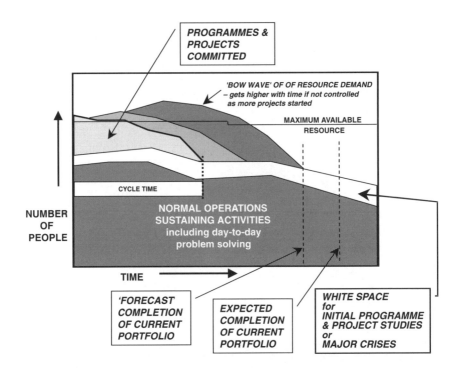

Figure 3.6 The case for portfolio management

continue, the worse matters become, with increasing dissatisfaction on the part of the recipients of the expected benefits.

THE INPUTS TO EFFECTIVE SELECTION

The selection of the programmes and projects aligned with current strategic needs can be carried out effectively only by means of a selection model that uses both qualitative and quantitative data to support a decision. Several such models have been published. Every organization must agree what data are required for the PST to make a decision. Whatever approach is used, a good understanding of the business processes is essential.

A typical list of data requirements is given in Checklist 1. This is a basic list you should consider when preparing the initial proposal or business case for submission to the PST. It is advisable to seek an interested potential sponsor before this submission is made, as this will inevitably help your case with the PST.

You may be required to apply specific tests to ensure the proposal meets stated strategic objectives. Sometimes a fantastic opportunity appears that does not align with current strategic objectives but you consider it is worth investigating. Now you must also consider how this opportunity will satisfy strategic needs of the business and prepare your case to convince the PST that it is valid to revise the current stated strategic objectives.

CHECKLIST 1: INPUTS TO THE PROGRAMME AND PROJECT SELECTION PROCESS

- The potential profit growth:
  - return on investment;
  - return on net assets;
  - break-even and payback period;
  - cost of risks;
  - net present value and/or internal rate of return;
  - benefit/cost ratio;
  - sensitivity analysis.
- Change to market share:
  - maintain current market position;
  - consolidate market position;
  - open up new markets.

- Changes to risk level:
  - technical risks;
  - scheduling risks;
  - organizational disruption;
  - impact on current customer base;
  - risk of not doing the programme or project;
  - why do it now?
- Maximize the utilization of current manufacturing capacity.
- Need for new manufacturing capacity.
- Maximize the utilization of existing resources (ie people).
- Need for additional people and/or skills.
- Possible improvement of the organization's public image and reputation.
- Possible improvements to the organization's internal culture:
  - elimination or improvement of existing business processes;
  - changes to job satisfaction;
  - reduction of administration burden.

Your objective is to prepare a business case and proposal that will satisfy the PST in the primary screening process. This screening is intended to allow the PST to make a decision at its first exposure to the opportunity you are providing. The PST has four options:

- Approve for further investigation – the idea has passed through Gate Zero. It's a good idea, so the PST approves the assembly of a small skilled team to investigate the idea in more detail.
- Assign to a 'WAIT LIST' for resubmission at a later date. The PST considers the idea to have merit but feels that it is not appropriate to proceed further at this time. The proposal is held for consideration again later.
- Reject for resubmission. The PST requires more specific information to enable it to come to a decision and requests a resubmission at a specified date.
- Reject the idea outright and dump it.

THE SECONDARY SCREENING

All those ideas and opportunities approved by the PST at the primary screening stage will then be subjected to a more detailed investigation with a nominated team. At this stage the focus is on expanding the initial proposal to understand the scope of work involved, how long it is likely to take to complete and what the resource needs are expected to be – people, skills and financial cost. It is important at this stage for the team to identify what the likely customers need and might expect from the outcomes of the programme or project. This exercise is no mean effort and could take some time to complete; you will also need to carry out some basic planning to enable a budget for the work to be estimated.

Although you may use many of the process techniques described later in this book, your final report to the PST is not necessarily binding on the final programme or project team appointed if PST approval is given. Remember that the programme or project manager appointed must still seek PST approval at all the later phase gates, so changes to the proposal originally approved at Phase Gate One are possible.

When the detailed investigation is completed, you can submit this to the PST for the secondary screening. Of course, not every idea can possibly be approved at this stage, if only because of cost or resource availability.

At the secondary screening the PST decision again has four possible options:

- Approve to proceed – the idea has passed through Phase Gate One. A programme or project manager is appointed and instructed to form a core team to proceed immediately with the approved budget.
- Assign the proposal to a 'WAIT LIST' for resubmission at a later date. The PST considers that the idea is one it wants to proceed with but has concerns about resources or funding and decides to delay the start date.
- Reject for resubmission. The PST requires more specific information to enable it to come to a decision, and requests a resubmission at a specified date.
- Reject the idea outright and dump it.

The core team appointed for the investigation of an idea or opportunity should ideally stay with the programme or project through the complete life cycle. In some organizations this is not always possible and a new team is assembled for the work.

The final business case approved by the PST at the secondary screening is effectively the charter for the programme or project and really should be updated as the PST approves all changes. This need for updating is often ignored because of time pressures, but configuration management is important. The PST may subsequently revisit the business case in the future so it is valuable to keep the document up to date, recording all revisions made up to completion date.

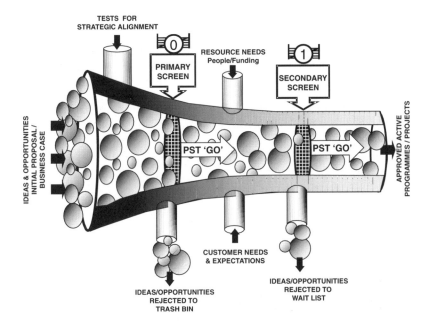

Figure 3.7 Programme and project selection – the pipeline

THE RESULT OF EFFECTIVE SELECTION

In Figure 3.6 we saw how uncontrolled initiation of programmes and projects creates a bow wave of resource needs that really do not exist. Adopting a more rigorous selection process will lead to a situation where this is avoided. The target is to eliminate the bow wave completely. It has been said that giving people 'stretched goals' overcomes the problem anyway because people will by nature work smarter and achieve the impossible! This is unrealistic and is more likely to lead to demotivation because of the imposed burdens, and the quality of the work done is likely to be questionable.

Effective selection leads to a number of benefits:

- The right programmes and projects are started at the right time.
- Timely customer and business needs are met.
- The timeline of committed programmes and projects is reduced.
- The previous forecast of completion of the portfolio is reduced.
- Additional programmes and projects can be started earlier.
- Additional programmes and projects can be completed earlier.
- The business revenue is maximized.

These benefits of effective selection are shown in Figure 3.8. The 'white space' is unaffected by this approach and must be retained for the reasons stated earlier. If a new opportunity proposed demands new skills and additional people, it is rapidly obvious that some questions need to be answered to find the resources:

- Can people be transferred from a low-priority programme or project?
- Can any programme or project on the portfolio list be delayed or suspended?
- Can resources available for the 'white space' be released?
- Is it necessary to recruit from outside the organization?

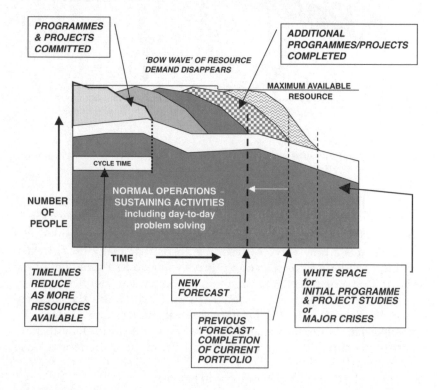

Figure 3.8 The target situation

Clearly, it would take longer to recruit new people than transfer them from another activity, and the PST is faced with a prioritization decision if it is considered essential to work on the new opportunity.

The technique is dependent on having accurate information about what people are doing and what is planned for their activities in the months ahead. Good management demands that some form of resource utilization mapping is carried out on a continuous basis. This is quite normal in most organizations for the short term. In a programme and project environment this planning process must extend to several months or longer to give the PST accurate data on resource commitments. This does not necessarily mean that timesheets are essential, but some form of time planning is needed across the whole organization. There is little point in estimating how long a group of tasks will take to complete if the estimate is not turned into a target commitment for the person doing the tasks. Software systems for the mapping of resources throughout the organization are now available and provide fairly accurate up-to-date information about all the commitments made on all active programmes and projects. Such systems integrate well with project management software, so that instant data on resources available can be obtained. These data are essential for the effective operation of the PST, both in approving new ideas and opportunities and in agreeing reassignments to resolve major issues and crises.

By using all these techniques the organization becomes more effective, focuses on programmes and projects that are completed on time and obtains the benefits of becoming more profitable, with delighted customers.

SUMMARY

- Each programme or project in the organization must be owned by a sponsor.
- All opportunities, programmes and projects are listed on a programme register.
- A programme steering team (PST) comprising sponsors approves all programmes and projects.
- In large organizations a hierarchy of PSTs can be established.
- A PST has clearly defined responsibilities and authority.
- Every PST:
  - creates and maintains a programme register;
  - has a PST administrator;
  - makes decisions to investigate or reject opportunities;
  - makes decisions to continue or cancel any programme or project at any time;
  - makes decisions to resolve major issues;
  - resolves cross-functional problems and obstacles to success.
- Programme and project selection must be a controlled process with specific tests for alignment with strategic objectives.
- The PST is the ultimate decision forum in the organization on all aspects of programme and project management.

4

The key roles

An effective programme and project environment demands that all the key roles are clearly defined and the responsibilities of each role are understood. The PST's primary responsibilities were discussed in Chapter 3. The other main players are:

- the PST administrator;
- the programme or project sponsor;
- the programme manager;
- the project manager;
- the functional managers;
- the stakeholders.

All are related in the project environment for the organization to create a climate for success.

The programme managers are accountable to their respective sponsor for their programme. The project managers of the projects in a programme are accountable to their programme manager for their respective projects. Programme managers are by default the sponsor for the projects in their programme. The project managers of stand-alone projects are accountable for their project to the sponsor.

The programme managers and project managers are obliged to co-ordinate their activities closely with the functional managers in the operations group. These functions or departments contain the resources that will be allocated either full- or part-time to project activities. Regular communication is essential to negotiate the release of human resources to become team members, and none of the active projects can proceed without the active support of the functional managers (Figure 4.1). Throughout the life of the project the functional managers play a key role in solving personnel or performance issues.

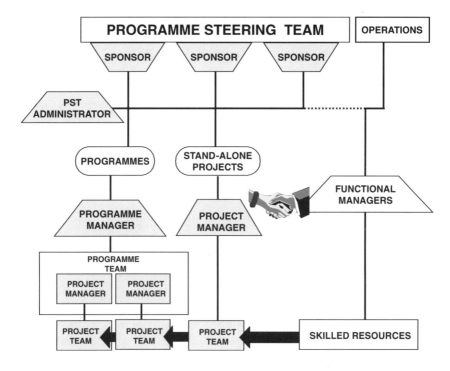

Figure 4.1 Role relationships

THE PROJECT STEERING TEAM ADMINISTRATOR

The PST appoints the PST administrator. This may be a full- or part-time position, depending on the size of the portfolio. Typical responsibilities for this role include the following:

- providing administrative support to the PST;
- tracking compliance with project process methodology;
- providing support and facilitation where appropriate;
- encouraging the spread of best practice;
- maintaining the programme register;
- encouraging communication;
- ensuring that all opportunities initiated adhere to the agreed process;
- ensuring that PST meetings are regular and effective;
- ensuring that PST decisions are communicated;
- contributing to the drive for excellence.

This role is key to the success of the PST and demands a person with significant practical experience of programme management and the processes and procedures employed to achieve success.

THE SPONSOR

The sponsor for any programme or project is accountable (to the PST) for the performance of his or her projects and must demonstrate concern for success to everyone involved. The sponsor's responsibilities include the following:

- being a member of the PST;
- ensuring that project objectives are always aligned to strategic needs;
- selecting the programme or project manager;
- approving the programme or project definition prior to PST approval;
- sustaining the programme or project direction;
- ensuring that priorities are maintained for all the sponsor's programmes or projects;
- having oversight of the process and procedures, budget and control;
- reacting promptly to issues escalated to him or her for decisions;
- maintaining support and commitment;
- approving programme and project plans, changes and status reports.

THE PROGRAMME MANAGER

The programme manager is accountable to the sponsor for the work from the initial kick-off through to closure. His or her responsibilities include the following:

- selecting the core team with the sponsor;
- maintaining a close working relationship with the sponsor;
- selecting the project managers of projects in the programme;
- identifying and managing the stakeholders;
- defining the programme and securing stakeholder approval;
- planning the programme and securing stakeholder approval;
- identifying and managing the risks;
- allocating and securing resource commitments;
- monitoring and tracking the progress of the programme and projects in the programme;
- supporting and guiding the project managers of projects in the programme;

- approving the definition and planning of projects in the programme;
- solving the problems that interfere with progress;
- controlling costs;
- leading the programme team;
- informing stakeholders of progress;
- delivering the programme deliverables and benefits on time;
- managing the performance of everyone involved.

THE PROJECT MANAGER

The project manager is accountable to the sponsor (for stand-alone projects) or the programme manager (for a project in a programme) for the project work from the initial kick-off through to closure. His or her responsibilities include the following:

- selecting the core team, together with the sponsor;
- maintaining a close working relationship with the sponsor;
- identifying and managing the project stakeholders;
- defining the project and securing stakeholder approval;
- planning the project and securing stakeholder approval;
- identifying and managing the risks;
- allocating and securing resource commitments;
- monitoring and tracking the project's progress;
- solving the problems that interfere with progress;
- controlling costs;
- leading the project team;
- informing stakeholders of progress;
- delivering the project deliverables and benefits on time;
- managing the performance of everyone involved with the project.

THE FUNCTIONAL MANAGER

The functional managers are key stakeholders and must have a clear understanding of the project's context, priority and strategic importance. Their responsibilities include the following:

- providing appropriate resources for projects;
- monitoring resource needs for all active projects;
- agreeing resource assignments;
- maintaining resource commitments;
- responding to technical problems;

- giving support and guidance to:
  - planning;
  - estimating;
  - project control;
- planning resource utilization;
- maintaining awareness of the status of supported projects;
- supervising the performance of resources;
- demonstrating concern for the on-time completion of projects.

A new term has appeared here: *stakeholders*. Stakeholders are the people who have a specific and clearly definable interest in your project – a stake, in gambling terms! They are an important group of people, as we shall see a little later in this chapter.

Of course, only the primary responsibilities are set out on the above lists, which can be expanded considerably for a particular organization. All of these roles are important to success in project work. You can see how a co-ordinated project community can develop in the organization and you are part of that structure now as a programme or project manager. It is appropriate to define some other terms you will use frequently in managing a programme or project.

FREQUENTLY USED TERMS

Responsibility

Responsibility is *the obligation to ensure that the project tasks or a piece of work is carried out efficiently, to the relevant quality standards and on time.* Your role demands that you create a climate in your team where responsibility is clearly defined and accepted. Without acceptance there is no commitment and the work is not done well or willingly.

> Responsibility is discrete to an individual and cannot be shared. A shared or split responsibility is no responsibility and generates a blame culture!

Authority

Authority is *the right to take and implement management decisions.* You can make decisions: it is just a process of generating options for a solution to a problem. You need authority to decide which to use and then implement the selected option. This authority is normally confined to taking decisions about people, equipment, materials and money. All these areas, directly or indirectly, involve spending or saving money and you must have a clear understanding about your limits. It is not common practice to define these limits in writing.

It is a good idea to get a clear statement of authority from your project sponsor, specific to the project work only. Make sure other managers are informed of the authority given to you for the project. This can support your efforts and improve co-operation once the real project work starts. You are expected to take technical decisions based on your knowledge and experience – or based on that in the team.

> Authority clearly defined and delegated at the outset speeds decisions and improves the probability of success. It is an essential part of empowerment.

Accountability

Accountability is *the management control over authority*. When you are given authority you are held to account for its effective use – and abuse! No authority means no accountability. If you fail to achieve a task on time, you have not fulfilled your obligations and therefore not carried out your responsibility effectively. Responsibility is often confused with account-ability, which is used as a threatening word to emphasize the priority or importance of some work.

> Accountability is the partner of authority – you are only accountable for the use of management authority that is given by delegation.

Confusion tends to occur about accountability for technical decisions. If you use your technical knowledge and skills when taking a decision, then you are accountable for that part that is purely technical. If it involves spending money and this is outside your authority then you must refer to your sponsor to take the decision.

THE STAKEHOLDERS

It is relatively easy to identify the stakeholders external to your organization. Anyone inside the organization who potentially at some time has an interest in your project is a stakeholder. You need to identify these people because they are certain to attempt to exert influence about how you manage the project. The team members come from different functions and their line managers have agreed to lose their resources for some of the working weeks ahead. The line managers are often *key stakeholders* – they can have a significant impact on your project if their priorities change and you lose a promised resource. Other key stakeholders include:

- your customer;
- your sponsor;
- the customer's user group;
- the finance department.

Many other people or departments across the organization will consider that they have a stake: production, quality, accounts, test, sales, marketing, personnel. If they do have a stake, you must consult them to determine their interest and how it may influence your project. This influence could take the form of a veto. All stakeholders have a hidden agenda about what they expect from your project and you need to expose these expectations before you define the project. This is not always easy where there is a political dimension to stakeholder needs and expectations; one need could be to hinder or stop the project!

Stakeholders are not only inside the organization; many external people are expecting to gain work from your project: suppliers, contractors, consultants and possibly government departments or agencies. All have their reasons for becoming involved in the project. You have no authority over any of your stakeholders and it is a formidable challenge to manage them effectively and gain their help and support.

CHECKLIST 2: IDENTIFYING AND MANAGING STAKEHOLDERS

Identify all potential stakeholders:

- Recognize which are the *key stakeholders*.
- Divide the list into internal and external stakeholders.
- What needs to be known about each of them?
- Where and how can information be gathered?
- Gather information about each:
  - What exactly is their interest?
  - Why are they interested?
  - What are they expecting to gain?
  - How will the project affect them?
  - Can they contribute valuable experience or knowledge?
  - What are their strengths and weaknesses?
  - Are there hidden agendas?

- What authority does this stakeholder have?
- Does this stakeholder have legal rights?
- Is this stakeholder in favour of the project?
- Will the project interfere with their operations?
- Could they seriously hinder or block the project's progress?
- Is there any history of behaviour from previous projects?
- Who is entitled to see the information gathered?

Prepare a list of stakeholders, then:

- Assign responsibility for the management of key stakeholders to yourself.
- Assign responsibility for the management of other stakeholders to team members.
- Review and update the list at regular intervals.
- Distribute the list to all stakeholders to show you recognize their interest.
- Meet with them regularly to understand changes to their needs.
- Keep them informed of progress.
- Involve them in your decisions when appropriate.
- Make use of their skills and experience in the project.

Identifying stakeholders is not just part of the project start-up. Many do not appear until later, so you must review your list of stakeholders at regular intervals. The relative importance of each changes with time and the stages of the project. If you fail to recognize or co-operate with any stakeholder, you take a serious risk. That stakeholder could force views or changes to your plans at a time that is least convenient to you and hinders progress. You are the project manager and must set the ground rules from the outset. Poor stakeholder control can lead to chaos and demotivation of your team!

MANAGING STAKEHOLDERS

There is still reluctance in many organizations to give project managers adequate authority and there are many occasions when decisions must be deferred to a higher level. Your sponsor has this authority and you should endeavour to have a close working relationship with this individual. Have sufficient authority clearly delegated to you to get the day-to-day work of the project done on time.

An effective sponsor can provide you with significant support through:

- responding rapidly to issues requiring high-level decisions;
- sustaining the priority of the project;
- sustaining the project direction to avoid 'scope creep';
- ensuring the work stays focused on strategic needs;
- building a working relationship with the customer;
- influencing other stakeholders.

Agree to meet with your sponsor at least weekly for a short update session on progress. The managing of issues is always preferably handled informally when possible.

Your next most important stakeholder is the customer, and a close working relationship is essential. Ensure you are working with the right person. You need to be sure you are working with someone who has final authority on behalf of the customer. Customers have a habit of changing their needs as the work proceeds because so many people in the customer's organization have an interest in your project. If communication is not effective, you may not be clearly informed of their revised expectations. You may even have multiple customers, which compounds your difficulties in attempting to satisfy all their expectations. Try to avoid having a committee to work with, as this will slow down decision making. Appointing a *customer representative* solves this problem if you can persuade the customer to use this approach and give the appointed individual authority to take decisions. Determining who is your true customer can present real challenges to you in practice.

Ask your sponsor to inform all your internal stakeholders about the strategic importance and priority of your project. This makes your job easier when you approach them later for active support of your efforts. Many of the stakeholders have valuable knowledge and experience. If appropriate, use this experience for your project and seek their input when you feel it can help the team. You can even bring a stakeholder into the 'extended team' for a time if he or she can make a specific contribution.

You need stakeholder support and commitment always, so part of your tactics is to feed that support using diplomacy and tact. You are the project manager, so they must understand your responsibilities and accept that you are in charge of the daily work of the team. You welcome positive suggestions and ideas and do not want covert criticism or interference that demotivates the team, destroys team spirit and promotes conflict.

The *stakeholder list* (see Chapter 6) is used in defining a project to list all known stakeholders for a project. This list is not intended to provide a convenient point of reference and then forgotten! It is the starting point for recording a more detailed database of information you have gathered about each stakeholder. These data can be used to derive a matrix (Figure 4.2) with which to categorize each stakeholder as one of four types:

- *decision maker* – one who provides resources or resolves issues;
- *direct influencer* – one who has a direct input to the project work or is impacted by the project activities or deliverables;
- *indirect influencer* – one with little or no direct input but may be needed to agree some actions to ensure the project's success;
- *observer* – one who is not apparently affected by the project but may choose to try to affect your activities.

In each of the four category columns, enter:

- a '+' sign for stakeholders who you consider are positive about the project;
- a '−' sign for stakeholders who you consider are negative about the project;
- an 'N' for stakeholders who you consider are neutral about the project.

With your team, decide what actions you can take now to turn negative and neutral stakeholders into positive and enthusiastic supporters. Assign actions to team members. Review how you intend to communicate with stakeholders and consider:

- what you need to tell them;
- how you will communicate with them;
- the frequency of this communication;
- how you will gather feedback.

STAKEHOLDER INFLUENCE MATRIX					PROJECT No:			
NAME	ROLE	CONTACT TEL. NO.	MANAGER	DECISION MAKER	DIRECT INFLUENCER	INDIRECT INFLUENCER	OBSERVER	OWNER
J. Turner	Customer	01793456278	G. Hadlow	✓ ✚				D.W .G
T. Woodrow	Ex-Sponsor	Int. 3586	B. Stewart	✓ ✚				D.W.G
L. Harmer	Tech Services Mgr	Int. 3871	T. Woodrow		✓ ✚			J.D.T
R. Driver	Sales Mgr	Int. 3844	H. Farmer			✓ N		G.W
G. Storm	Tech Dev Mgr	Int. 3868	F. Johnson				✓ ━	K.B.M.
D. Grant	Tech Mgr	Int. 3897	L. Harmer		✓ ━			J.D.T.
S. TRent	Prodn Director	Int. 3835	B. Stewart		✓ N			D.W.G.

Figure 4.2 Stakeholder influence matrix

Take care not to go into 'information overload', as busy people do not like long reports to read. They need short, objective and factual reports focused on their particular interest in the project. Keeping stakeholders involved throughout the project is a demanding task for you and needs tact and diplomacy to retain their support and make them feel important to the outcome.

A few words of caution

There are always plenty of people who are anxious to influence your project. Beware the people who claim stakeholder status just to get involved, when in reality they have no valid reason to influence the project. Seek your sponsor's support if necessary to ensure that the stakeholder list is restricted to people who have valid reasons to get involved and are keen to support you and your team to achieve success.

CUSTOMER SATISFACTION

It is essential for you to recognize that customer expectations directly relate to customer satisfaction. Unfortunately, there are degrees of satisfaction relating to the extent to which your customer perceives that you understand their expectations and, what is more important, meet them with the results achieved. Fall short of these expectations and you will have unhappy customers.

Your goal is to have a *delighted customer* by providing all the expected results to an acceptable quality and standard. Fall short on the quality or performance standards expected and you will only create a complaining customer.

In addition, the customer will expect you to deliver on time – that is, to an agreed schedule of delivery. This constitutes a promise by contract. Fail to deliver and you lose the respect of the customer and probably increase the project cost. This leaves you with a further issue of recovering the additional cost, and it is not too easy to convince a disgruntled customer that they should accept the overspend.

Customers also expect you and eventually your project team to serve them with professional competence. You must ensure that the right people with experience and appropriate skills are assigned to the project work, behave in a co-operative and friendly manner, and demonstrate a real concern to meet the customer's expectations. This means everyone working on the project must understand the customer's environment and the difficulties and constraints the customer faces. Do not add to the customer's problems; your job is to reduce them, so always avoid announcing surprises. The customer wants you to provide positive results, not a long list of excuses for poor performance and the problems of achieving results.

THE PROGRAMME AND PROJECT MANAGER AS A LEADER

To achieve success in your programme or project you need to use a collection of skills that demonstrate your ability to lead a team. You are working with and through others, using these skills to energize and direct a diverse group of people to give a high performance, willingly and enthusiastically throughout the life cycle. These people come from different parts of the organization, each of which has its culture through the leadership style of the departmental manager. You have to overcome these cultural variations to create a climate of co-operation and co-ordinate the efforts of the team members without direct line authority. Much has been written about leadership, the skills required and an appropriate style for different types of work. There is a diverse range of opinions about what makes an 'effective leader'. There are no common characteristics that you must have to be effective, and without which you are doomed to fail. At the core of leadership is your skill at influencing the behaviour of people to achieve your objectives.

QUALITIES OF AN EFFECTIVE PROJECT LEADER
A list of desirable qualities includes:

- flexibility and adaptability;
- ability to demonstrate significant initiative;
- assertiveness, confidence and verbal fluency;
- ambition, drive and commitment;
- effective communication and good listening skills;
- enthusiasm, imagination and creativity;
- being well organized and self-disciplined;
- being a generalist rather than a specialist – having technical awareness;
- being able to identify and facilitate problem solving;
- being able to make and take decisions promptly;
- ability to promote a motivating climate;
- ability to keep everyone focused on the project objectives;
- having been trained in project management tools and techniques;
- being experienced in project management processes and procedures;
- being respected by peers and management;
- being concerned to achieve success.

Figure 4.3 Qualities of the programme and project leader

One extreme of leadership style is to be an autocrat: you tell people what to do using a 'you will' approach. The other extreme is to be a democrat: information is shared; you consult widely and ask people to do the work using a 'will you' approach. The reality is that you adopt a style that is often subconsciously directed by:

- the situation and the prevailing environment;
- the type of work, its priority and urgency;
- the way the team reacts and behaves in the environment.

When a crisis hits, many people will tend to adopt a more autocratic style in the interest of getting a quick result. It is perceived that no time exists for consultation, ideas and suggestions are not encouraged, and consensus is avoided. The actions required are dictated in command and control mode. The democratic style is regarded as slower, encouraging people to give their ideas and opinions, always seeking a consensus so that the team is fully involved and well motivated to achieve results.

What is appropriate for the role of programme or project manager? There is no 'right' style – only a style that seems to work and that is appropriate with the people at the time. Your real skill as a leader is your ability to recognize what approach is appropriate at any particular time to get results. A programme or project is a very specialized situation because of the nature of the work, which is time and cost constrained, and the diverse range of skills and experience of people you do not know well.

To achieve the objectives you must use some particular skills to:

- ensure that the project tasks are completed on time to the quality desired;
- create co-ordination between the team members and develop teamwork;
- support the individual team members and develop their skills for the work.

These three elements of the leadership role are related and interdependent and you cannot ignore any one at the expense of the others. They are all directed in one fundamental direction: the objectives.

Keeping a balance between these three elements occupies much of your time as the leader. The actions you take at each stage of the work are focused on maintaining this balance, adopting a range of styles according to the prevailing situation. However, in any programme or project the people involved are not just yourself and the team. You have a *customer* – the person or group of people who expect to receive the outcomes, and a *sponsor* who is accountable to the PST for the results. There are also many others who have an interest in the journey you are going to take – the *stakeholders*.

THE DIMENSIONS OF LEADERSHIP

You can now see that the role of programme project manager is complex: managing a team and a diverse group of other people to achieve the objectives. Figure 4.4 shows the relationship between the key elements of leadership, the objectives and the stakeholders.

You spend much of your time *inner directed*, focusing on the tasks, developing and maintaining good teamwork and making sure you have the right skills in the team. You also spend time *outer directed* with your stakeholders to understand their needs and expectations, use their skills when appropriate and keep them informed of progress.

You must manage your stakeholders, not ignore them. They can influence your programme or project at any time with serious consequences to progress. They can change their minds at any time, cause delays and demand changes to your plans.

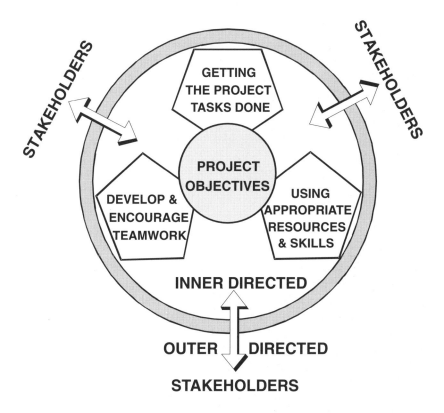

Figure 4.4 The programme and project manager's role relationships

In Chapter 2 we looked at the characteristics of a programme and project and the dynamic life cycle. Being aware of this dynamic cycle of actions throughout the programme or project is one of the three essential dimensions of leadership:

- identifying and managing the stakeholders throughout the project's life;
- managing the project's dynamic life cycle from definition through planning and execution to closure – all the tasks of the programme or project;
- managing the performance of yourself, the team and the stakeholders.

Success is directly related to balancing the time and effort you give to each of these dimensions from the start-up until you hand over the results to your Customer.

Managing the dynamic life cycle

Managing the dynamic life cycle involves you in controlling the tasks, the resources needed to complete the tasks on time and all the materials and equipment required. You must control the work to stay on track to a schedule derived from the plan, dealing with changes, managing risks and resolving issues that arise. Simultaneously you must demonstrate your concern for your team members and any other people engaged in carrying out the work. They are looking to you as the leader of the team to provide them with a congenial working environment and give support and guidance.

Chapters 5–10 take you through the life cycle processes and procedures and the actions you take as the programme or project manager to achieve a successful outcome.

Managing performance

As the programme or project manager, you must demonstrate throughout that you are concerned about the performance of everyone involved with the work. You are responsible for delivering the results expected by the *key stakeholders*, and evaluating your performance regularly will help you improve the way you do the job. Programme and project work requires effective teamwork. If the team is not well co-ordinated the work suffers and you then jump from crisis to crisis. However, effective co-ordination is made more difficult by the fact that the team members often come from different departments or even other sites. You must make an effort early to understand your team members and their working environment, what they hope to gain from the work and their personal objectives. The stakeholders should provide the drive, direction and climate for success. Ignore them and you court potential disaster!

CHECKLIST 3: MANAGING PERFORMANCE

Evaluate your own performance continuously. Pay particular attention to:

- helping and supporting your team members;
- coaching individual team members when opportunities arise;
- responding promptly to personal issues raised with you;
- demonstrating your continued enthusiasm;
- reviewing your decisions and being prepared to admit to mistakes if they happen;
- examining your management of time;
- evaluating your attention to detail in administering the work;
- seeking external help when appropriate;
- avoiding making promises you cannot or do not intend to fulfil.

Work closely with your team to:

- understand their personal objectives;
- keep all the team involved and well informed;
- establish clear responsibilities for the work;
- act promptly when conflict appears;
- encourage good communication within the team and with team members' line managers;
- recognize team effort and high performance;
- look after the team's interests at all times in the interests of success.

You must avoid continual fire-fighting, so ensure you:

- keep key stakeholders regularly informed of progress;
- get them committed to their promises of support;
- involve them in important decisions when replanning or when solving problems;
- monitor team members responsible for other stakeholders;
- encourage the team to maintain good communications with stakeholders.

PROGRAMMES, PROJECTS AND TEAMWORK

Because most programmes and projects involve more than one person, teamwork is crucial to achieve success. To get effective teamwork you start by taking a group of people from different backgrounds, with different experience, skills and personal needs, and build them into a cohesive working unit. If the team members are only giving part of their working day or week to your project activities, they have divided loyalties to different line managers and different working practices. The complexity increases if they are working in more than one programme or project team at the same time.

The first time you bring your core team together they are really a group of individuals. They may not have worked with each other before even if they know one another. They come from different functions and their normal operational environment conditions their behaviour at work. You are an unknown entity to them if they have not worked with you before. They expect you to break down the barriers and start to build the group into a team. This will test your communication skills to the limit as you get to know and understand your team – and they get to know and understand you. As the communication model in Figure 4.5 shows, you can change behaviour through effective communication.

Figure 4.5 The consequence of effective communication

This is a complex process but it is made a little easier by having a clear sense of direction. Everyone should know why he or she is in the team – apart from knowing that you selected them! They all have experience and skills you consider relevant to the project. Your objective is to harness their abilities, creativity and efforts to achieve a shared goal or outcome. If this potential is to benefit the organization, you must make sure you select the right team.

CHECKLIST 4: SELECTING TEAM MEMBERS

The criterion for selecting team members depends on the type of project. Ask:

- What is their relevant technical experience?
- Have they specialized knowledge essential to the project?
- Have they experience of similar projects?
- Have they worked in project teams before?
- Do they have relevant technical knowledge?
- What is their departmental authority?
- Have they other project commitments now?
- When do these commitments end?
- What is their capacity for project work (as a percentage of the working week)?
- What is their current non-project workload?
- Can this loading be reduced?
- What is their forecast future non-project workload?
- Can they be assigned for the whole project duration?
- Do they get on easily with other people?
- Do they like working alone?
- How do they feel about taking on a leadership role sometimes?
- Are they interested in joining your team?
- What do they expect to gain from joining your team?
- Do they have a track record of commitment to high performance?
- Are they well organized and good time managers?
- Do they take their current responsibilities seriously?
- Are they perceived as good team players?
- Is their line manager in agreement with the possible assignment?

Availability should not automatically guarantee selection.

Selecting team members solely on the basis of functional role is no guarantee the individual can contribute to your project team effectively. You must guard against the possibility that the setting up of a project team is seen as an opportunity by others to dump someone on you. This may be perceived as a training opportunity or as a chance to move someone who does not fit in their current team. A project team is an exciting place to work and you want creative, enthusiastic people with a strong sense of responsibility and commitment. A successful team consists of a carefully designed mixture of the right skills and personalities – people who can work together without dissension and conflict. You select people for your team because you value and respect their ability to do a good job under pressure and not because you like them or they are popular!

Numerous tests and models are available to help you understand the different personality types and how each behaves in a team. These instruments will help indicate which of these are better suited to programme and project work; they can also guide you on how to communicate effectively with the different personalities you meet. If possible, make use of these techniques when selecting your team members. Time spent on this activity now will be rewarded with an effective team and raise your chances of success.

A balanced team encouraged to mature its working norms quickly can overcome overwhelming difficulties and achieve what appears at times to be a 'mission impossible'.

BUILDING YOUR TEAM

Clearly, you face many potential difficulties in getting a project team working well. Do not despair. Many are normal in team development and often predictable. Team size can add to complexity if the team is large (more than five or six members). Pay particular attention to avoiding:

- confusion over any aspect of the project;
- unclear responsibilities;
- unclear lines of authority;
- uneven workload distribution;
- unclear task assignments;
- unclear overall objectives;
- failure to identify stakeholders;
- communication breakdowns;
- mistrust between team members;
- personal objectives unrelated to project work;
- lack of commitment to project plan;
- lack of real team spirit;

- lack of concern about quality;
- a climate of suspicion;
- lack of direction;
- conflict and personality clashes;
- rigid attitudes.

There is no secret to success, no magic dust to sprinkle around to remove these difficulties if they occur. Take positive actions to minimize the problems and act promptly when necessary. You sometimes have to take unpopular decisions in the interests of the project. Test your team at intervals with the simple test given in Figure 4.6. Check that team working improves as the project progresses – it's not about luck, it's just hard work!

> Successful teams don't just happen; they have to be built through effective leadership and commitment.

SUMMARY

- Clarify your project organization:
  - Who is your sponsor?
  - Are all programmes and projects sponsored?
  - Are all programmes and projects prioritized?
- Clarify and understand defined responsibilities:
  - the programme steering team;
  - the sponsor;
  - the programme manager;
  - the project manager.
- Confirm your authority for the programme or project.
- Recognize the importance of stakeholders.
- Focus on the dimensions of leadership:
  - identifying and managing stakeholders;
  - managing the project's dynamic life cycle process;
  - managing the performance of yourself, the team and the stakeholders.
- Select your core team carefully; use selection instruments.
- Take positive actions to build the team:
  - Regularly review performance.
  - Test team working.
  - Encourage participation.
  - Celebrate and reward high performance.

HOW IS YOUR TEAM DOING?

Answer each statement with a ranking in the range 1 – 5

The team knows exactly what it has to get done:
Disagree strongly   1   2   3   4   5   Agree strongly

The team members are encouraged to offer ideas and suggestions:
Disagree strongly   1   2   3   4   5   Agree strongly

The team members are encouraged to express their opinions freely and share information:
Disagree strongly   1   2   3   4   5   Agree strongly

Each team member has a clear idea of his/her role and responsibilities in the project:
Disagree strongly   1   2   3   4   5   Agree strongly

Everyone in the team is listened to with interest:
Disagree strongly   1   2   3   4   5   Agree strongly

Everyone in the team is involved in making and taking decisions:
Disagree strongly   1   2   3   4   5   Agree strongly

Team members do not feel threatened by exposing their true feelings:
Disagree strongly   1   2   3   4   5   Agree strongly

The team members respect each other and encourage each other in their work:
Disagree strongly   1   2   3   4   5   Agree strongly

Teamwork enables personal development and ranks it as important:
Disagree strongly   1   2   3   4   5   Agree strongly

Your score:
9 – 15   This seems to be a group, not a working team.
16 – 33   Teamwork is good: ask the team members if they agree with your scores. Identify areas for improvement and work on them.
34 – 45   Ask the team members if they agree with your scores. If they do, keep up the good work. Watch out for any slippage and react promptly.

Figure 4.6 Test your team working

Checklist 5 gives some key actions for effective leadership throughout the project.

CHECKLIST 5: ACTIONS FOR EFFECTIVE LEADERSHIP

Throughout the programme or project:

- Build trust and inspire good team working:
  - Focus on behaviour and problems, not the person.
  - Maintain the self-esteem of others.
  - Keep relationships constructive.
  - Keep the team well informed at all times.
  - Encourage ideas and suggestions.
  - Involve them in decisions.
  - Clearly define roles and responsibilities for all project tasks.
- Create a team identity:
  - Clarify purpose and objectives.
  - Confirm understanding and acceptance.
  - Set clear personal targets.
  - Recognize and praise effort.
  - Celebrate team achievements.
- Encourage personal development:
  - Assess individual abilities and experience.
  - Assess training needs.
  - Coach individuals to enhance skills.
  - Appraise individual performance.
- Seek continuous improvement:
  - Evaluate team processes and practices.
  - Evaluate team performance.
  - Encourage creativity and innovation.
  - Devalue tradition and find better methods.
  - Reward success.
- Resolve conflict and grievances promptly:
  - Treat team members with respect.
  - Encourage active participation.
  - Listen to the team's views.
  - Support problem solving constructively.
- Champion and support the team:
  - Help the team to reach consensus.
  - Support team decisions.
  - Look after the team's interests.
  - Give guidance and assistance on request.

Part 2

The programme and project processes and techniques

In Part 1 the focus was on understanding the environment for successfully selecting and controlling the portfolio of programmes and projects. In Part 2 we shall explore all the processes required to start up, define, plan, launch and execute a programme or project successfully through to closure and completion. These processes for each of the life cycle phases are the same for:

- a programme;
- a project within a programme;
- a stand-alone project (one not related directly to any programme);
- a sub-project of any project.

To avoid confusion, throughout Part 2 you will find reference only to projects for all the processes, procedures and checklists. Where there is a specific variation to a process or procedure for a programme or sub-project this is indicated. In general, the life cycle and phase gates described in Part 1 are valid for all programmes, projects and sub-projects.

5

Starting up: ideas and opportunities for projects

As we have seen earlier, projects are derived from many sources, but it is important to establish a clear purpose that aligns to the strategic needs of the organization. This does not preclude unforeseen opportunities being grasped to satisfy customer needs. Often the start-up of a new project is confusing and 'fuzzy' because of:

- unclear direction;
- uncertainties about what is really required on the part of everyone interested in the outcomes;
- confusion because people cannot stand back and take a holistic view;
- the unknowns about how to get some results;
- failure to assess costs effectively;
- lack of a clear idea, which can be defined, of benefits;
- lack of clear information on the resources available;
- lack of a clear idea about how long it will take.

You are enthusiastic and keen to dive in and get going and show some activity. It is prudent to review just what information you can now assemble to ensure that the project does not set off in the wrong direction.

If the PST exists in your organization then your direction from now is more clearly defined as your first task is to prepare an initial proposal and business case to submit for acceptance. The first steps are to answer some basic questions.

THE FUNDAMENTAL DATA NEEDS

Who is your sponsor?

Are you clear who is sponsoring your project? It may be the person who gave you the idea or opportunity and asked you to look into the possibilities. The sponsor, you will recall, is the person accountable for the project – the person who is held to account for a successful outcome. This may be your line manager or a manager or director one level higher in your organization, but this is not always the case. If you do not have a sponsor then you need to find someone in the management team who you consider is the most likely person to have enthusiastic interest to support the idea at a PST meeting. The PST may choose to appoint a different sponsor in the future.

Who is the customer?

Your next step is to identify who really is your potential lead customer and who is your main contact, since you must start to build a working relationship with this individual. Many projects have multiple customers, even inside the organization. Each customer has personal perceptions of what he or she would want from your project and these perceptions will frequently generate hostility and conflict. You need to use all your skills of diplomacy to influence such a group and identify the needs and expectations of each customer.

One way to reduce the problems multiple customers create for you is to get them to agree that one of the group takes the role of *customer representative*. The customer representative is the key individual – preferably not a committee –who has the necessary authority to take decisions affecting the project. Where there is no PST, your organization may prefer to appoint a *project board*, although for reasons given earlier this is really best avoided. The purpose of such a group is to make sure that the departments that will be affected by the project and its outcomes are all represented as a collective customer. However, in such situations the chairperson of the project board is given the authority to act on behalf of the board when necessary and this person effectively becomes the sponsor.

Who will use the results?

Although the customer wants the results from the project, the customer is often not the person or group of people who will actually use the results on a day-to-day basis. You will need to have contact with the potential *end users* or a small representative group of the end users to check that you understand their needs and concerns about how the results will be used.

With the assistance of the customer, identify the end user representative who will be your future contact if the project goes ahead. Eventually you may decide to include this person in your project team. On larger projects a *user group* is often appointed, comprising four to six people.

Who are the key stakeholders?

Apart from the sponsor and customer there are other key stakeholders who may have an interest in this project. Checklist 2 in Chapter 4 gives you a good starting point for identifying the other stakeholders so you can approach them for their input to the business case. Some will be supportive but you may find some who for various undisclosed reasons will oppose the whole idea. At this stage your skill in managing the stakeholders is likely to be well tested as you try to gather information to help you prepare your proposal.

WHAT ARE THE CONSTRAINTS?

The constraints limit all project activities. In today's business environment it is rare for you to have unlimited resources, funding and time to complete the work. The project may yield significantly reduced benefits if you provide the results at a time when the requirements or the market needs have changed dramatically.

If you are intending to develop a new product, the date of availability to the sales team is critical to acquiring a significant market share and beating the competition. If the sales team cannot satisfy their customers and break promises, they risk losing important accounts. The organization's credibility and reputation will suffer. It is always difficult to recover frustrated customers and convince them such things will not happen again. It is known that a few months' delay in getting a new product to the marketplace can lead to a huge reduction in the profit yield. The customers will buy a competitive product even if yours is better when it eventually arrives. You are then too late to grab a major share of the market without incurring heavy advertising expenditure.

As we have discussed earlier, business needs are continually changing. Even with an internal project, late completion may lead others to conclude that the whole effort was a waste of time, because of new requirements. Project 'drift' sets in and you will face what seems like a never-ending project, trapped into acquiring the reputation of being 'the project manager with the endless project'.

You must make sure even at this early stage that as many constraints as possible are identified. The customer(s) will decide how much they are prepared to pay for the project, and this forces a cost constraint on the budget. Do remember that until you plan the project effectively, no budget is accurate. Any budget set at this early stage is derived through inspiration or from historical comparative data.

Constraints usually fall into categories:

- market – share, competition, time to market or full implementation;
- financial – project cost, capital costs, materials, revenue and resource costs;
- time – time to deliver the results, the critical date when the results are needed;
- quality – the scope, specifications and standards to be achieved.

You need to explore each with your potential customer to gather the information you need to guarantee success. You will find that the customer will often be unable to answer your questions, arguing that it is part of the project work for you to uncover the answers. If you make any assumptions now, these may ultimately become constraints, so do ensure that all assumptions are recorded.

WHAT DATA DO THE PROGRAMME STEERING TEAM REQUIRE?

The inputs to programme and project selection were reviewed in Chapter 3. You must collect this data using whatever help you can get. This can occupy much time, and it is often valid to ask your sponsor to give you some additional support by assigning a small team to you. This team may not stay with the idea or opportunity if it is approved to start up as a programme or project at a later date. Any data you collect at this stage are tentative because of the lack of detail. Your aim is to put together only enough information to convince the PST that the idea or opportunity is worth taking further for detailed investigation after the primary screening. The key information you must focus on includes:

- expected deliverables;
- expected 'cost to market';
- expected 'time to market';
- potential financial benefits;
- potential market benefits;
- potential internal benefits to the organization;
- potential risks.

The 'cost to market' is a preliminary assessment of the expected total cost of carrying out the work to realize the expected benefits. The 'time to market' is the expected period of time from final approval at Phase Gate One through to final completion and availability to the marketplace. In some circumstances the marketplace may be the organization itself, particularly for projects providing new company-wide systems. With this type of project, run-up time to full operation may need to be highlighted as a separate period downstream of completion, with an assessment of the cost of implementation.

PREPARING THE INITIAL BUSINESS CASE

When you consider you have sufficient information, prepare your initial business case. Most organizations have a standard format for this type of document. If none exists, you can use the following suggested list of headings for your report:

1. opportunity statement – concise description of opportunity;
2. solution statement – concise statement of proposed solution (deliverables);
3. alignment to current business strategy;
4. business benefits – information statements;
5. organization benefits – expected gain in working practices, etc;
6. market analysis information – current and potential future markets;
7. competitive position;
8. financial summary – cost–benefit analysis for a three- or five-year period;
9. technology – development and manufacturing philosophy;
10. resource requirements – preliminary assessment of people and skills needs;
11. expected constraints;
12. potential risks;
13. expected time to market;
14. legal – any legal implications.

You can add any other sections as required, but do remember that this should not be a voluminous document. Keep the whole proposal concise and focused on factual data where possible – probably limited to a maximum of 10 pages. The PST members do not have the time to read many long documents at this initial stage.

When you have finalized the proposal, contact the PST administrator to arrange for you to present the proposal to the next PST meeting. Make sure you brief your sponsor before the meeting – you need the support! If you are asked to make a presentation to the PST, then once again do keep it concise – 10 minutes and 10 slides is a good rule, allowing you one minute to talk through each slide.

Present your proposal to the PST and request approval to pass through Phase Gate Zero.

THROUGH GATE ZERO TO GATE ONE

When the PST accepts your proposal, Phase Gate Zero is passed and you enter Phase Zero, where a detailed business case must be prepared. At this stage the PST has decided that it considers that the opportunity is valid and is keen to proceed further. You will be given authority to form a small core team to work on preparing the information required. You may also be given a target date to complete the work.

The PST administrator is responsible for entering the new programme or project on the programme register with the agreed priority ranking.

Your next task is to take the approved initial proposal and expand its content with significantly more detail. This involves several key steps:

1. Identify the customer needs and expectations.
2. Derive the preliminary schedule.
3. Assess the resource needs.
4. Derive a budget.
5. Prepare the financial case.
6. Finalize the business case.
7. Submit the business case to the PST.

The small team you have formed is charged with the responsibility of deriving the data required, but you will almost certainly need to seek help from many other departments. The financial data will almost certainly be required in a standard format, and persuading the finance department to assist in the preparation of the data creates a possible future ally.

You should always approach this stage of the work with a conviction that the opportunity will be approved at the next submission to the PST.

Identify the customer needs and expectations

Defining the needs of the customer starts off a process that will ultimately allow you to produce deliverables specifically designed to meet the customer's expectations. Once you have established a clear understanding of the needs, you can develop the requirements that drive the planning process.

Regard this as the preparation of the foundations of the project. Failure to give this activity appropriate time and effort will have a continuing impact on the project throughout its life. You can develop a superbly detailed plan but it never compensates for misunderstood needs or poorly specified requirements to satisfy those needs. As a consequence, the control you initiate to keep the project on track will never yield data that interests your customer, because the plan is increasingly perceived as inadequate.

You must make a particular effort to:

- understand the customer(s) – find out what makes them tick;
- understand the environment in which the customer(s) must operate;
- use political skills – not all customers are equal and some needs cannot be addressed for political reasons;
- demonstrate your technical competence and your awareness of the technical needs of the customer(s);
- convert ill-defined needs into practical solutions;
- keep an open mind and a creative approach;
- analyse the mixed signals you receive through personal influences on needs;
- attempt to expose the hidden expectations.

Your purpose at this stage is to turn the information you receive into a clear *statement of needs* that the customer can accept with no ambiguity. Avoid two potential traps. First, do not offer gold when silver is adequate: avoid striving for technical perfection beyond current capability or known state of the art. Simplicity is often more effective. Confirm that the customer understands the risks of going for leading-edge solutions. Second, avoid bias filters: it is easy for you to ignore needs for which you cannot think of an easy solution because they are outside your experience or knowledge.

Working with your customers can be frustrating. At times you will need to exercise all your communication skills to achieve a good, open relationship enabling the project to move ahead to achieve the agreed objectives. Deriving the needs statements yields a product of a partnership between you and your customer. This places an obligation on your customer to enter into the partnership with a serious intent to contribute openly and not sit on hidden agendas.

Try to persuade your customer that it is beneficial to adopt a total life cycle approach for the project. Such an approach starts with needs and requirements and ranges through planning, execution, handover and full implementation.

The project does not end with closure and handover. You must check that the critical period after this phase is defined clearly for maintenance and service activities to ensure that the customer agrees who is responsible.

CHECKLIST 6: IDENTIFYING CUSTOMER NEEDS

Establish the current reality:

- What happens now?
- Is there an accepted process?
- Is the process or procedures written down anywhere?
- Who owns this process?
- Is responsibility at each step clearly defined?
- Is responsibility shared at any point in the process?
- How do the process procedures interface with other processes?
- Where are the decision points in the process?
- Who has authority to take decisions at each step in the process?
- Why is a change necessary now?
- What are the difficulties now that have promoted the need to change?

Identify needs and requirements:

- What changes are identified?
- Are these just a 'quick fix' or are they a quantum leap?
- What does the customer believe is needed?
- Do all customers agree?
- Have the fundamental needs been separated from wishes?
- Are predetermined solutions being proposed already?
- Has the end users' perception of needs been identified?
- Have the needs been listed as primary, secondary and hopes?
- Has this list been prioritized and agreed with the customer?
- Can you turn the information into a clear statement of needs?
- Can you use the needs analysis to derive a statement of requirements?
- Does the customer agree with your statement of requirements?

After discussions with the customer(s) you should have enough information to derive the *statement of needs*. This is the basis of the *statement of requirements*, which clearly states what deliverables are required to satisfy the customer needs.

The customer contract

You start to build a relationship with your customer through the work of establishing needs and expectations. After PST approval at Phase Gate One you have an obligation to turn this relationship into a form of contract. Often this is not a formal document signed by all parties but is an informal understanding. You may consider it appropriate to document some form of agreement on the obligations of yourself and the customer, focused on achieving the desired outcomes.

Many projects acquire a reputation for poor management when the reality is poor customer performance in fulfilling their obligations. Success is possible only if everyone involved fulfils their responsibilities, and the customer(s) cannot claim it as their right to act in complete independence. You must meet the requirements of the schedule. This is only possible if the customer(s) act promptly when necessary in resolving issues and giving approvals. Delays and cost over-runs occur too easily if customer response is slow. A slow response suggests that the customer is not particularly interested in getting the results of the project on time.

Derive the preliminary schedule

The statement of requirements has given you the list of deliverables to be achieved. With your team you must now derive a preliminary plan. If you are familiar with planning techniques, this will not present you with any difficulty. If you need to review the process then jump to Chapter 7. Your objective at this stage is to plan at high level in sufficient detail to determine the time needed to achieve a satisfactory completion. This will normally mean planning the key stages but neglecting all the tasks in each key stage. The output from this effort will be an estimate of the time required for each of the remaining phases of the project.

It is sufficient to present the PST with a 'phase schedule' only in the business case. Ensure that you have the next level of detail to back up the information provided to the PST – you may be questioned on the detail!

Assess the resource needs

The resource needs are estimated from the key stage plan you have derived. Pay particular attention to highlighting any skills required for the project that do not currently exist in the organization. When appropriate, consult across the organization widely when deriving estimates. These data will be used to derive financial and cost information, so it is important to spend time to achieve realistic estimates. Assemble the resource data by listing both skills, job type or role and grade if appropriate to enable accurate costing.

Derive a budget

Managing the finances of a project is often regarded as being just as important as managing time. The financial plan you develop now will almost certainly become the operating budget for the project. You now have an estimate of the resource costs and to these you must add any other costs you expect to be incurred:

- material costs;
- equipment costs;
- other capital costs;
- external sub-contract costs;
- service and testing costs;
- support costs (eg accounts department);
- preliminary marketing costs;
- overhead costs.

The operating budget should be prepared to give a cost for each phase of the project. As this may be required in a standard format, I would suggest that you involve the finance department in the preparation of the budget.

Prepare the financial case

The financial case must demonstrate the true worth of carrying out the project. Your organization will normally use specific financial data to justify any activity. The data required vary from one business to another and you should consider providing a five-year plan. This may include:

- total development costs;
- forecast manufacturing costs;
- forecast sales volume;
- forecast sales costs;
- forecast income from sales;
- forecast profit before tax;
- cash flow;
- discounted cash flow.

These data can be used to provide the essential financial measures:

- net present value (NPV);
- internal rate of return (IRR);
- return on investment (ROI);
- time to breakeven.

The financial section will receive close scrutiny by the PST, so take care to ensure that all the data included are sufficiently robust to allow a 'GO' decision to be made.

Finalize the business case

Now you can take the initial proposal and expand this into a full business case using the information already derived. Add any additional information you have discovered to support the market analysis made earlier. Where possible provide data in graphic format, as this is easier to review and digest. Some examples are given in Figure 5.1. Notice that resources are given in 'full-time equivalents' (FTEs) as some people may be assigned for only part of their working week to work on project tasks. A similar method can be used for the forecast schedule you have derived, using forecast phase completion dates as the key dates.

If appropriate, use the same section headings as the initial proposal. This allows comparisons to be made when necessary. It is important to highlight clearly any assumptions you have made and the basis of your reasoning.

If appropriate, include contingencies for any aspect of the financial case. Remember that contingencies are only for the unexpected occurrences, ie risks. They are *not* for compensating poor and inaccurate estimating and things you forgot to include. If a contingency is included for a specific risk and it does not subsequently occur, the contingency is not available for something forgotten! Normally the sponsor must authorize the use of contingency moneys in the future.

PRESENTING THE BUSINESS CASE TO THE PROGRAMME STEERING TEAM

When you are ready to present the business case, inform the PST administrator, who will set a date for the submission and advise you what method of presentation is preferred. Once again, if you adopt a slide presentation, do keep it concise and focused on the data essential to persuading the PST to make a 'GO' decision.

When the PST accepts your business case, Phase Gate One is passed and you enter Phase One, where the project passes to *definition*. The business case should contain much of the information required for the work of definition. As the project is now active, some parts of definition require more detail to be added.

At this stage the PST has decided to proceed with the project either immediately or at some future date. It will agree a priority ranking for the programme or project relative to existing active programmes and projects on the register, and this will be recorded on the programme register. You will be given authority to form the project core team and start work. Occasionally you may find that your work on the project is over and another project manager is assigned.

PROJECT COSTS

Forecast total project cost	PHASE £000's	Forecast costs for subsequent phases at the end of Definition Phase	Forecast costs for subsequent phases at the end of Planning Phase	Forecast costs for subsequent phases at the end of Execution Phase	Forecast costs for subsequent phases at the end of Closure Phase
	DEFINITION				
	PLANNING				
	EXECUTION				
	CLOSURE				

RESOURCE COSTS

Forecast total resource cost	PHASE £000's	Forecast costs for subsequent phases at the end of Definition Phase	Forecast costs for subsequent phases at the end of Planning Phase	Forecast costs for subsequent phases at the end of Execution Phase	Forecast costs for subsequent phases at the end of Closure Phase
	DEFINITION				
	PLANNING				
	EXECUTION				
	CLOSURE				

RESOURCE REQUIREMENTS

Forecast total resources FTEs	PHASE total FTEs	Forecast for subsequent phases at the end of Definition Phase	Forecast for subsequent phases at the end of Planning Phase	Forecast for subsequent phases at the end of Execution Phase	Forecast for subsequent phases at the end of Closure Phase
	DEFINITION				
	PLANNING				
	EXECUTION				
	CLOSURE				

Figure 5.1 Presentation of data in the business case

Remember, the business case plus any qualifications and amendments added by the PST is now your 'project charter' and becomes a key working document for the project. Regular reference to the contents is essential in the future, as your performance will be measured against the forecasts it contains. Your next step is to organize the kick-off meeting for the project.

THE KICK-OFF MEETING

You must now ensure you have secured the release of the core team members you select for the project. If the PST authorized the release, your job is considerably easier, but be prepared to enter into negotiations with other managers to get people released from their current activities. The business case should have identified the key people with a close interest in your project and you should now prepare them to attend the kick-off meeting. The purpose is for you to understand what they expect from the project and allow them to confirm that you have a clear picture of the results they require at completion.

The project sponsor should chair and open the meeting to explain the strategic context of the proposed project. Explain why the project is important now and how it is prioritized in relation to other active projects. Your purpose is to gain as much information as possible at this stage by asking questions. If you are fortunate, the customer will have prepared a briefing document. Validate the contents at this meeting to check you have a clear understanding of the requirements.

PROJECT KICK-OFF MEETING

PROJECT: PRISM
VENUE: Meeting Room 4   START TIME: 10:30
DATE: 5 May 2003   FINISH TIME: 12:30

PURPOSE: Project Inception Meeting to establish relevant information for project definition

AGENDA
I. Introduction
2. Project background and assumptions
3. Project context
4. Project approach and strategy
5. Project objectives
6. Identification of constraints
7. Business case
8. Communication
9. ACTION POINTS

ATTENDEES:

John Foster	Sponsor (Chair)
David Johnson	Customer
Alison Williams	Customer
Angela Kimball	Customer
Alex Wimborne	End user representative
Anthony Barrett	Project manager
Jane Foxbury	Team member
Jim Fawcett	Team member
Alan Davidson	Team member
Amanda Hunt	Team member

Please confirm your attendance.

Figure 5.2 Typical agenda for the kick-off meeting

Issue an agenda for the meeting beforehand to give attendees time to prepare. The customer and end user may bring two or three people to the meeting, but it is better to keep the group size down to a minimum where possible. Look at the example agenda format in Figure 5.2. Note that the agenda does not include 'Any Other Business' because this can frequently lead to open-ended discussion, diversion and, ultimately, loss of control of the meeting.

This meeting is the first time you collect together the new core team with your stakeholders. It is an opportunity for you to demonstrate your ability to lead the project team. Good preparation is important to achieve the meeting's purpose. It is important that everyone gets a clear understanding of the task ahead. A list of typical questions that should all be answerable at this stage is given in Checklist 7.

CHECKLIST 7: THE PROJECT KICK-OFF MEETING

Background

- Why is the project necessary?
- What is the overall problem or opportunity being addressed?
- Has the current situation been explored and understood?
- Has a statement of requirements been derived from the needs list?
- Is this an old problem?
- How long has it existed?
- Who wants to change things?
- Have previous attempts (projects) been made to address this problem?
- What information exists about past attempts to fix things?
- What assumptions have been made?

Context

- How does the project align with current organizational strategy?
- Does the project form part of a programme of projects?
- Will the project form part of a chain of linked projects or a programme?
- What is the timescale of the project?
- Is there a business-critical date by which it is necessary to get the results?
- Will the results be of value to another customer or another part of the organization?

Approach

- Have all the needs been identified and analysed?
- Has a statement of requirements been agreed?

- Are there predetermined solutions?
- What are these solutions?
- Is there a best option and a least worst option?
- Is there enough time to explore more than one option?
- Are there known checkpoints for project review?
- What specialized skills are expected to be required for the project work?

Objectives

- Are the project's primary deliverables known?
- What does the customer need, want and hope to get from the project?
- Can these deliverables be clearly defined and specified?
- Does the end user agree with these deliverables?
- What does the end user need, want and hope to get from the project?
- What are the project's perceived benefits?
- Have these benefits been quantified?
- Has a project budget been fixed?
- Is capital investment necessary?
- Has a capital expenditure request been initiated?
- Is time used for project work to be measured and costed?
- How were the costs derived?
- Has a cost–benefit analysis been carried out?
- Has a financial appraisal been carried out to establish payback?

Constraints

- Have the project's constraints been identified?
- Is there a time constraint for all or part of the deliverables list?
- Are there any financial constraints (eg manufacturing cost, project cost)?
- Is there a financial payback constraint?
- Are there any known technical constraints (eg new or untried technology)?
- Are there known resource constraints?
- Is the project team to be located together on one site?
- Is part of the work to be carried out at another site?
- Is part of the work to be carried out by sub-contractors or suppliers?
- Is there a preferred list of approved sub-contractors and suppliers?
- What existing specifications and standards are to be applied to the project?
- Are there any legal constraints that might affect the project work?
- Are there any security implications?
- Are there any operational constraints (eg access to production areas/ test equipment, etc)?
- Are there any health and safety constraints?

PROJECT DOCUMENTATION

You are not alone – no one likes having to record information in a regular and organized manner. Project work produces a large quantity of data and it is important that you record essential material. One of the greatest time-wasters in project work is repeating the recording of information in different formats and the problems created in its interpretation later.

Start off your project by avoiding the 'I'll do it my way' syndrome. Insist that the team members keep all essential project records on a standard set of templates derived specifically for the purpose. Throughout this book at the appropriate time, you are given examples of standard templates. All the templates suggested can be designed on a computer and networked for ease of completion from blank masters.

Some are more important than others, and it is your decision which to use. Whichever you use, having standard templates ensures that everyone involved with the project records data in a consistent and disciplined manner without re-inventing forms every week. In addition you get the right information recorded (and in the appropriate amount) for the project file to support your control system, which aids progress in reporting to the PST and project evaluation at completion. Expect an adverse reaction from people when you suggest using standard templates. It is viewed as 'form filling' and a chore. Stress the importance of keeping everyone informed about what has happened in the project and that it is in their interests to get into the habit of keeping accurate records. Nobody can carry all the plans and information in his or her head!

The first of the standard templates is the *project organization chart*, which lists all those involved with the project, plus their line manager, location and telephone number. This is an important communication document for information, and records agreed commitments of individuals assigned to the project team. Review the document regularly and keep it up to date. Set up a distribution list now, identifying who gets which documents. Distribute copies to all those who need to know – both participants and non-participants.

The project file

Set up a project file for all the documentation related to the project. This file is the permanent record of the project and requires a disciplined approach to administration. Even if you personally prefer to use a paper-based system, some of your team may like to keep all their records on a computer-based file or folder. This makes the distribution of information easier if you have a network. It also makes access and retrieval relatively easy. There is a potential difficulty with using the computer to store all the

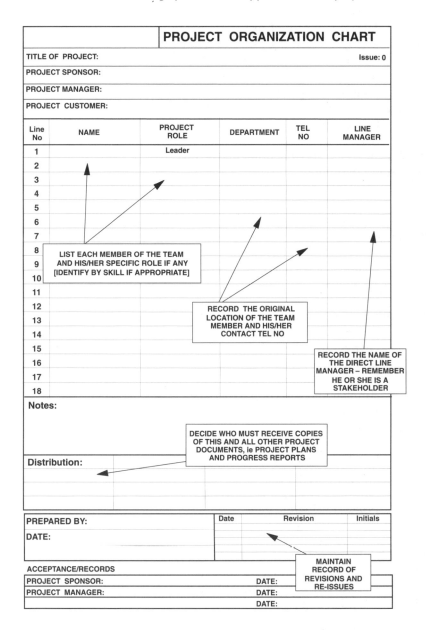

Figure 5.3 Project organization chart

project data. If you cannot restrict access to your data, people can make changes without informing you, and create confusion. Take precautions to prevent unauthorized access, or modification of project documents, and inform the team of their limits on the system. If you have concerns about reliability, always keep a hard copy of the project file.

Organize your project file into sections for the different stages of the project; for example:

- Business case and amendments by the PST.
- Project definition:
  - project organization;
  - stakeholders;
  - project brief.
- Project plans and schedules:
  - project risk management;
  - responsibility charts;
  - schedules;
  - work plans.
- Project execution and implementation:
  - project status reports;
  - changes to project plans;
  - action plans for corrective action;
  - cost control data;
  - supplier and sub-contractor data;
  - records of meetings.
- Project closure:
  - closure checklist;
  - handover checklist;
  - acceptance process;
  - follow-on and post-project responsibilities;
  - project evaluation data;
  - completion report.

Divide it into more detail if necessary. You are responsible for updating the file at regular intervals and it is a good habit to do this once a week. Always let others know where to find the file; it is most frustrating to search for a file that is hidden away!

The project logbook

It is a good discipline to open a *project logbook* at the start of your project. The purpose is to provide you with somewhere to record all events, agreed actions and forward planning ideas. The book is an A4 bound, lined book and *not* a loose-leaf file or folder. Record events with essential relevant data such as:

- date;
- time;
- who is involved;
- key points or content.

Events to record include:

- telephone calls – incoming and outgoing;
- faxes – incoming and outgoing;
- letters – sent and received;
- memos – sent and received;
- e-mail – sent and received;
- purchase instructions issued;
- contracts signed;
- action plans agreed;
- problems encountered;
- solutions derived;
- decisions taken – and how implemented;
- reports issued;
- meetings – sponsor, team, third party, one to one.

The logbook is *not* a personal document; it is an addendum to the project file. When using a logbook:

- Use every page and number them sequentially.
- *Never* remove any pages.
- Start each day with a new page.
- *Always* write in pen, ballpoint or felt tip, *never* pencil.
- Write on every line.
- Rule out all unused lines at the end of each day and sign the page at the bottom.
- Do not allow anyone else to write in the logbook – not even the project's sponsor.

The logbook is particularly valuable for recording events concerned with third parties such as suppliers and contractors. When conflict and differences occur, the logbook provides a record of events that often takes the heat out of an argument. The record can have a legal status if a dispute eventually ends up in the hands of the legal profession!

THE PROJECT BRIEF AND SPECIFICATION

The kick-off meeting you have just completed will have been the focal point of all the initial work associated with the project start-up. The purpose of that meeting was to enable you and your team to understand the expectations of your customer and agree the requirements derived in the *statement of requirements*. The data you collect are enough for you to draw up a preliminary statement of the project objectives and the associated specifications.

This step is often the most difficult, because you must now formulate in realistic terms just what the project is about and has to achieve. This is the foundation of project definition, which we will examine in more detail in Chapter 6.

The *project brief* is a document that summarizes all the relevant facts about the project and is therefore a source of definitive information. The contents include:

- the project's origins – a need or opportunity statement;
- the project's rationale – why is it necessary now?
- the benefits of the project – to the customer and your organization;
- the project budget if known at this stage;
- the current timescale and deadlines – subject always to detailed planning later.

This document is ideally just one piece of paper, but for larger projects it often takes the form of a report with many different sections. If you have a good business case document, the project brief provides a convenient summary of key data. It forces you and the team to focus on real facts and not hopes or wishes. Unfortunately, during the start-up of most projects there is too much expression of hopes and the 'wish list'. You have to resolve this conflict to sort out what you can achieve in practice with current technology, experience and knowledge compatible with the statement of requirements.

Project specification is a term applied to many different types of documents and can include almost anything. Here the term 'specification' describes any document that is an obligatory statement of procedures or processes that apply to the project. It is a statement of policy for the project.

These specifications can range from technical descriptions to quality standards, or even organizational policy documents such as contract purchasing guidelines. When you come to define your project you will collect all the relevant specifications together in the project *scope of work statement*. This document is often referred to as the *SOW* and directly relates to your project brief to support the factual information included for approval by your customer.

All these documents can sometimes be combined into one, termed the *project charter*.

SUMMARY

The key steps may be summarized in a flow diagram (Figure 5.4). Checklist 8 summarizes the key leadership actions during the project selection phase.

CHECKLIST 8: KEY LEADERSHIP ACTIONS DURING PROJECT SELECTION

- Identify your *project sponsor*.
- Identify your *customer*.
- Confirm needs and expectations.
- Identify the end users of the project's outcomes.
- Start to build a relationship with these people.
- Determine the project's constraints.
- Agree a date for a kick-off meeting.
- Select your core team.
- Hold an initial team meeting.
- Explain the project's background and context.
- Explain the overall objectives of the project as you know them at present.
- Confirm the team's understanding of the objectives.
- Share your own enthusiasm for and commitment to the project.
- Listen to what the team members have to say.
- Answer their questions if you can.
- Promise answers to questions you cannot answer now.
- Explain the project phases and the process you intend to use.
- Empathize with their concerns about other commitments
- Explain your intention to have separate one-to-one meetings with each team member.
- Agree dates for the first of these meetings.
- Set up an initial programme of team meetings, say for the next four weeks.
- Explain the kick-off process and confirm their attendance at this meeting.
- Open the project file.
- Prepare for the kick-off meeting with the team.
- Hold the kick-off meeting and record outcomes in the file.

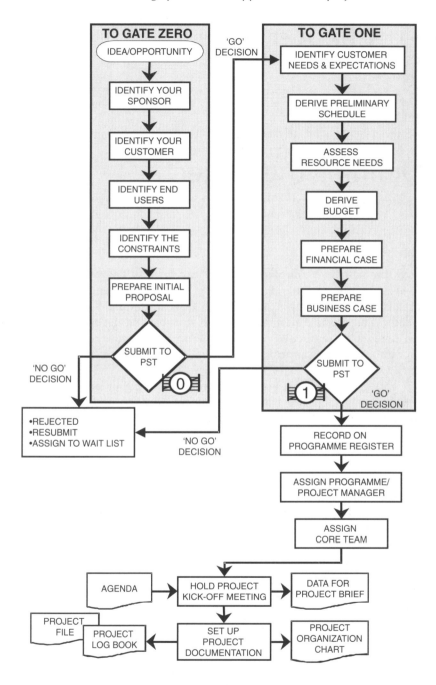

Figure 5.4 Process flow diagram: opportunity selection through Phase Zero

Chapter 6

Defining the project

Now that you have completed the start-up process, you have collected all or most of the data needed to define your project and start the real journey towards success. You should now understand why it is often asked, 'What is the difference between start-up and definition?' The first is a data-gathering activity. The definition is the process of turning the data into something more solid and realistic, something that is no longer just a wish or a hope.

If you decide to build your house on some land already bought, you start by establishing the ground conditions. You then design the building and decide the type of materials you are going to use and the overall size and layout of the property. This process of gathering data enables you to design the appropriate foundations to support the building safely. It often takes longer than the actual building operation. The designs you derive are then submitted to statutory authorities to ensure they satisfy various mandatory regulations. Failure to provide your house with adequate and firm, well-defined foundations approved by the authorities will inevitably lead to structural failure of the building and incur possible legal or other consequences – the building may collapse!

The same is true for your project. You have spent a considerable amount of time and effort to gather all the relevant data in the start-up process to design the foundations of your project. The *project brief* is the summary document that contains the foundation design for your project. It is supported by numerous other documents as appropriate to the project.

Failure to give adequate time to this activity and derive all the relevant data for these foundations will lead to a poorly defined project with a considerably reduced chance of achieving a successful outcome. The consequence of poor definition of the foundations is a project plan that is derived from incorrect or even misleading information. Like the building that collapses because of its poor foundations, your plan will soon start to fail and be discarded as a useless document. Your project goes out of control and you may suffer further serious consequences and criticism.

> A clear definition of your project is critical to success: a large number of projects (more than 75 per cent) are perceived to fail as a consequence of poor or unclear definition.

WHAT IS NECESSARY TO DEFINE A PROJECT?

Apart from the business case, five essential documents are required to define a project effectively:

- a statement of requirements;
- a stakeholder list;
- a project brief;
- a scope of work statement;
- a risk assessment.

All these documents must be approved before you start the planning process. You are effectively returning the project definition to your customer, saying:

> We have listened to you and understood what you need and require. We have examined these requirements and concluded what we believe we can realistically deliver to satisfy these needs. Now we are telling you what we understand we are going to provide for you with this project. Please approve these definition documents as they are the basis on which we will derive a plan and schedule for you to approve later.

The approval or 'sign-off' process is essential to maintain customer and sponsor commitment to your project.

THE STAKEHOLDER LIST

When you start the definition process, the first step is to return to the simple question: 'Who has an interest in this project, now or in the future?'

We identified these people in Part 1 as *stakeholders*, and some of these people you have already identified as *key stakeholders*:

- the customer;
- the end users;
- the sponsor;
- the line managers of your core team members.

With your team you must now try to identify who has now or potentially in the future will have an interest. Refer to Checklist 2 in Chapter 4 for guidance on the questions to ask. Consider that the list could include:

- the finance department;
- the sales and marketing department;
- consultants;
- contractors;
- suppliers;
- other divisions or sites;
- the public;
- other agencies or statutory bodies.

In some projects where your customer is internal, there may be another party in the supply chain such as an end client with users.

All these people have an interest, which means they have an agenda of their own for the project. Although the controlling interest may be perceived as that of your customer, you cannot afford to ignore all others with an interest. They may consider that their level of interest is enough to justify their having a voice to which you must listen. Failure to do so at this stage may lead to conflict, disruption and interference later. This group of people are the stakeholders; all have strong feelings about their stake in the project and will make these feelings known to you probably when you least expect it!

Derive a complete list of the stakeholders as you now see them and record them on the *project stakeholder list*, a typical template for which is shown in Figure 6.1. Making this list is not a single activity; regularly update and reissue it. This is a communication document to keep informed everyone who has an interest in the project. The list is also your database for further analysis as discussed earlier. But why, you ask, is this really so important? So far, you have concentrated on the customer and the sponsor for inputs to the project definition. As we saw in Chapter 4, all stakeholders need to be consulted for their inputs to give a wider perspective of, first, the project's real needs and requirements, and second, what is realistically achievable in the timescale demanded. You use these additional data inputs in your work of defining the project. At this stage of the project you may fail to identify all the stakeholders, so review the list at each team meeting or project progress meeting, adding any newcomers as identified.

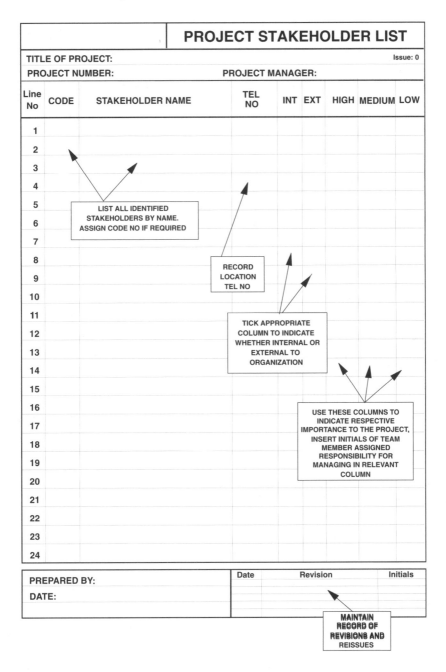

Line No	CODE	STAKEHOLDER NAME	TEL NO	INT	EXT	HIGH	MEDIUM	LOW

PROJECT STAKEHOLDER LIST

TITLE OF PROJECT: Issue: 0
PROJECT NUMBER: PROJECT MANAGER:

LIST ALL IDENTIFIED STAKEHOLDERS BY NAME. ASSIGN CODE NO IF REQUIRED

RECORD LOCATION TEL NO

TICK APPROPRIATE COLUMN TO INDICATE WHETHER INTERNAL OR EXTERNAL TO ORGANIZATION

USE THESE COLUMNS TO INDICATE RESPECTIVE IMPORTANCE TO THE PROJECT, INSERT INITIALS OF TEAM MEMBER ASSIGNED RESPONSIBILITY FOR MANAGING IN RELEVANT COLUMN

PREPARED BY:
DATE:

Date | Revision | Initials

MAINTAIN RECORD OF REVISIONS AND REISSUES

Figure 6.1 Example of a project stakeholder list

THE PROJECT BRIEF

From the business case and the kick-off meeting you held earlier you have derived most of the data for this document. Now you must ensure there is no amendment necessary as a result of consulting with any other stakeholders you have identified. A suggested template for a typical one-page document is shown in Figure 6.2. This contains a number of sub-headings:

Project title

Give your project a relevant title for identification purposes. If appropriate, also identify the project number recorded in the *programme register* for financial budgetary control purposes. Indicate whether the project is part of a programme and identify the programme number.

Overall objective of the project

It is appropriate to write an overall objective statement of about 25–30 words that describes the desired results of the project.

Project manager and project sponsor

Identify yourself as the project manager and identify the *sponsor*.

Planned start date for the project

The planned start date is the date when the real work of definition started after PST approval of Phase Gate One. This may not be the day of approval, depending on the availability of the team and yourself. In some organizations the planned start date may be set as the date when you expect to start planning if the project definition is accepted and the project approved to continue after Phase Gate Two.

Required finish date

State the date when the project is required to end with handover to the customer. This should be clear to you from the kick-off meeting, particularly if it is a business-critical date for strategic reasons. The date may be subject to change after planning is completed.

Project deliverables

Identify the primary deliverables that will be seen from the project through its life cycle. These are tangible outputs from the project that must be capable of being measured.

Apply the SMART test to ensure that each deliverable is:

- **S**pecific – it is clearly defined, with completion criteria;
- **M**easurable – understood metrics are available to identify delivery;
- **A**chievable – within the current environment and skills available;
- **R**ealistic – you are not trying to get the impossible with many unknowns;
- **T**imebound – is limited by a delivery date based on real need.

At this stage only five key deliverables are required, although after planning many more intermediate deliverables may be apparent.

Project benefits

List the benefits you have identified for your organization from the earlier investigative work you have completed in preparing the business case. All benefits should be quantified; preferably they should be measurable in financial terms: cost savings, increased turnover, contribution or profitability in a specific timescale. If in doubt, apply the SMART test to benefits.

Project strategy

State whether you intend to examine more than one route to success: explore alternatives, carry out a further feasibility study, set up a cross-site team, involve the customer in the team or anything else relevant to your approach to the project. These data may have been recorded in the approved business case.

Project skills required

Identify the skills required for the project work, particularly highlighting special experience and technical skills you expect to need. Indicate if certain skills and expertise will be purchased from outside the organization.

Relationship with other active projects

Most organizations have many projects active simultaneously. Does your project interface at some point with another, either depending on it for inputs or providing outputs to another project? Is this project part of a programme? There are certain to be some critical interface dates that are mandatory for your project. Failure to recognize these interfaces can lead to both projects failing to meet completion on time.

Project cost

If the cost is known from the business case or a budget exists from earlier studies or feasibility work then state the cost. If not, either give an estimated cost or leave blank until planning is complete. The relevance of cost depends on whether time is measured and costed or whether only capital expenditure is to be recorded here.

Risk management

You are asked to indicate whether the *project risk log* and *risk management forms* are attached to the document for approval. (See later in this chapter.)

In this document you have collected together all the known relevant facts upon which to base a decision to proceed. It may be supported by another key document that contains the detailed specifications.

THE SCOPE OF WORK STATEMENT

As the name implies, the *scope of work statement* (SOW) is a narrative description of the project objectives in more detail, giving more information about each deliverable and benefit identified. What is more important, the document must identify the boundary limits of the project, clearly stating what is *not* going to be done as part of the project.

The SOW is also a very convenient place for you to record all the constraints identified earlier and any assumptions made, whether before, during or after the kick-off meeting. These assumptions may have profound implications later during the project work.

The SOW is where the applicable specification list is recorded:

- internal product specifications;
- external product specifications;
- mandatory standards imposed by legislation;
- process specifications;
- customer specifications;
- standard operating procedures;
- purchasing procedures;
- quality standards;
- testing specifications and procedures;
- sub-contract terms and conditions imposed on third parties.

Your purpose is to make sure that everyone knows from the outset what standards and specifications apply to your project. The document also identifies, first, where the actual documents can be found for reference, and second, what exceptions, if any, apply to any specification for your project.

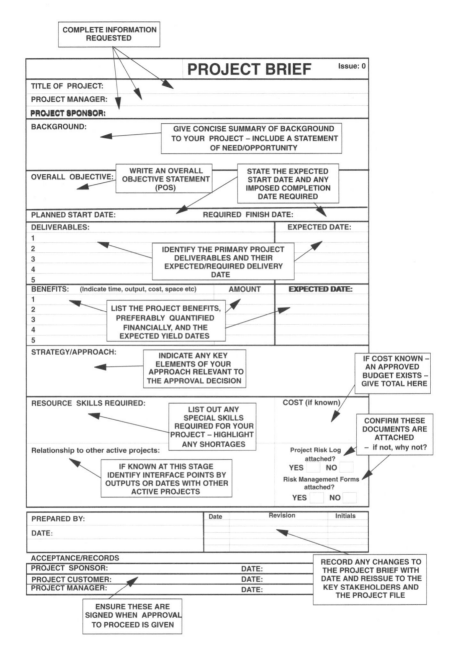

Figure 6.2 Example of a project brief document

If necessary, you can also use the SOW to record for reference purposes any other relevant documents that have been issued previously relating to the project; for example:

- the business case;
- cost–benefit analysis studies;
- feasibility reports;
- studies carried out by consultants;
- project evaluation reports from previous projects.

In practice, similar projects often generate similar SOW statements, so this is an opportunity for you to create a standard template. This is not a form; it is a detailed document that is kept as a master document. For each subsequent project the master need only then be edited and amended as appropriate for any project.

RISK MANAGEMENT

There is uncertainty in all projects, and *risk management* is the means by which this is systematically managed to increase the probability of meeting the project's objectives. Every procedure in this book is really a risk management technique. Some are designed to reduce the chances of delay and late delivery. Others are designed to avoid cost over-run and avoid unavailability of resources. The purpose of this disciplined approach is to identify and contain the risks and minimize the impact on the project. So what is a risk?

> A risk is any uncertain event that, if it occurs, could prevent the project realizing the expectations of the stakeholders as stated in the agreed business case, project brief or agreed definition. A risk that becomes a reality is treated as an *issue*.

A risk always has a cause and, if it occurs, a consequence. Risks can have positive or negative consequences. Success is dependent on maintaining a high commitment to risk management procedures throughout the project. At the definition phase of a project it is valid for an initial risk assessment to be conducted. It will save you much wasted effort chasing an impossibly risky outcome and divert effort towards more beneficial projects with lower risks. Two fundamental types of risks are always present: 1) project risks – associated with the technical aspects of the work to achieve the required outcomes; and 2) process risks – associated with the project process, procedures, tools and techniques employed, controls, communication, stakeholders and team performance.

As project manager you have the obligation, working with your team, to:

- identify and evaluate potential risks;
- derive a response strategy and action plans to contain the risks;
- implement the actions and monitor the results;
- promptly resolve any *issues* arising from risks that happen.

There are two primary components of the process: assessment and monitoring. Some risks should have been identified in the business case and, if appropriate, response strategies for these may have been derived. If you are only conducting a feasibility study at this stage, then each option must be examined for risk, as the results could influence subsequent decisions.

Why is risk management necessary?

Once you have developed a realistic project schedule and detailed plan, the project's progress is measured against this plan. This schedule is your road map to success, and anything that interferes with the progress will seriously damage your chances of success. Unfortunately, even with the best-prepared plan things can and will go wrong from time to time. These problems affect the schedule, leading you to recovery planning to overcome the problem and recover any time lost in the problem-solving process. Many of these problems can be anticipated in advance. How many times have you heard someone say, 'I could have told you this was going to happen.' You probably feel like taking some violent action when you hear such comments, probably because they contain a ring of truth! Use hindsight to question your own foresight in such situations. Could you have anticipated the problem? This is why it is necessary to carry out risk assessment – to anticipate what might go wrong and take action to avoid the problem.

The risks that happen become the issues that you must promptly resolve to maintain the integrity of the project schedule. It is good practice to prepare *risk mitigation plans* for known major risks, taking early action to avoid the risk occurring.

There is always the possibility of unforeseen risks leading to unexpected issues. Provided you are prepared to react promptly, you can still take the necessary actions to hold on to schedule dates. Identify the signals or triggers that suggest a risk is likely to happen and keep the team always alert to the possibility of any risk becoming a reality.

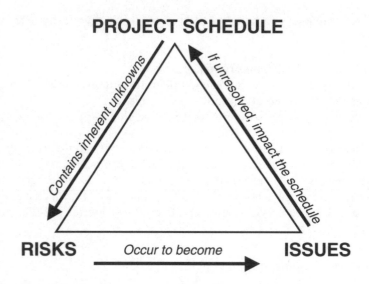

Figure 6.3 *Risks* and *issues:* impact on the project schedule

What are the benefits?

Some people regard risk management as being negative. In fact, it has many benefits:

- The serious threats to your project can be predicted before they happen.
- Mitigation plans can be derived and implemented immediately.
- Contingency plans can be derived in advance.
- Valuable data for negotiating with suppliers are obtained.
- The process creates clearly defined 'ownership' for risks to ensure they are monitored.
- It helps to create a 'no surprises' environment.
- It encourages decisive leadership rather then crisis management.

Risk management does have a cost, but in most situations this is significantly less than the cost of correcting the subsequent issues when a risk occurs.

When is it necessary?

Risk management is a *continuous process* throughout the life cycle of the project and you must maintain awareness of risk in the minds of all the members of your project team:

- It should be started at the definition phase, or earlier if possible.
- It is essential to establishing the project brief.
- Compile a complete list and record it on the project risk log.
- Review and add to the list at regular intervals as the project moves forward.

Review the project risk log at regular intervals, normally monthly at project progress meetings unless decided otherwise by the sponsor at the start of the project. You need to focus this review on the following aspects:

- Identify any change in the potential impact or probability of identified risks.
- Identify any new high risks that have changed from being previously regarded as lower-ranking ones and subject them to closer examination and risk mitigation plans.
- Derive contingency action plans for damage limitation.
- Add any new risks identified to the list and assess these for impact and probability.

Any risk entered on the list is *never* removed, even if the time when it could occur seems to have passed. It could occur again later!

The list of risks from any project is a source of valuable learning data for future projects and is a useful data source for deriving checklists. Data from past projects of similar work content are useful sources of risk management information.

RISK ASSESSMENT

Any project has risks at the outset because of the many unknown factors, some of which you will remove during the planning stage. The risk could be due to external or internal factors. In practice, risks disappear and new risks appear as the project progresses, so regularly review potential risks. Adopt the view that 'anything that can go wrong will go wrong'.

Risk assessment requires answers to some key questions:

- What exactly is the risk and what are its parameters?
- How serious is it as a threat to the project?
- What could be done to minimize or avoid its impact on success?

Call your team together and hold a brainstorming session to identify as many potential risks as possible. Think of anything that could go wrong and hinder the project's progress. Include all perspectives by involving the sponsor, customer and other stakeholders in the process.

You may find that others may perceive some of the risks identified as so insignificant they can be ignored. Test the validity of any risk by asking some simple questions about its possible impact on the project:

- Cost – does the risk have a cost impact?
- Schedule – does the risk have an impact on the preliminary schedule?
- Scope – does the risk have an impact on the project deliverables and quality?

If the answer to all these questions is 'no' then ask if it is really a risk to your project. However, take care: apparently insignificant risks can grow into significance later and become 'project killers'.

Checklist number 9 gives you some typical questions to ask in risk assessment. Some of these are applicable only after the planning phase.

CHECKLIST 9: Questions for risk assessment

YES	NO	
☐	☐	Has the project manager's authority been established?
☐	☐	Is the core team appointed?
☐	☐	Does the core team understand the project's purpose?
☐	☐	Have the project's stakeholders been identified?
☐	☐	Have stakeholder management responsibilities been allocated?
☐	☐	Have the project's objectives been established?
☐	☐	Have the project's benefits been identified and quantified?
☐	☐	Are there clear deadlines and a project timescale?
☐	☐	Is there a known business-critical date for completion?
☐	☐	Is there a scope of work statement?
☐	☐	Are the project's boundary limits clearly established?
☐	☐	Is there an impact if the project fails?
☐	☐	Are the right skills available in the team/organization?
☐	☐	Can the project brief be accurately derived?
☐	☐	Have all the project constraints been identified?
☐	☐	Are there identifiable consequences of late completion?
☐	☐	Has the project brief been approved?
☐	☐	Have all key stages been clearly identified?
☐	☐	Have key stage dependencies been established and agreed?
☐	☐	Are the key stage durations agreed and accepted?
☐	☐	Is the project schedule realistic and achievable?

☐ ☐ Have key stage responsibilities been allocated and accepted?
☐ ☐ Are the resources realistically available?
☐ ☐ Have workload priorities been clearly established?
☐ ☐ Have line managers accepted and committed their staff involvement?
☐ ☐ Have all resources required given commitment to their responsibilities?
☐ ☐ Has the plan been developed to a low enough level for effective control?
☐ ☐ Have key stakeholders signed off the project plans?
☐ ☐ Are project procedures established and understood?
☐ ☐ Has a milestone schedule been established?
☐ ☐ Have performance measures been derived?

Any questions to which the answer is NO must be examined further to establish the consequences and, if they are significant, contingency action plans must be derived.

YES *NO*
☐ ☐ Is there an impact of doing nothing?
☐ ☐ Are staff or organizational changes possible/expected during the project?
☐ ☐ Are business requirements likely to change during the project?
☐ ☐ Is new technology involved?
☐ ☐ Are new techniques to be employed?
☐ ☐ Are new suppliers/contractors to be used?
☐ ☐ Is the project dependent on another project?
☐ ☐ Are there possible constraints on third parties?
☐ ☐ Can third parties impose constraints on the project work?

Any questions to which the answer is YES must be examined further to establish the consequences and, if they are significant, contingency action plans must be derived.

Having identified all the risks, you need to decide a *risk response strategy*. This involves separating the identified risks into three types. The key steps in the process are shown in Figure 6.4.

Review the risks, making sure none are repeated, and then separate them into three lists:

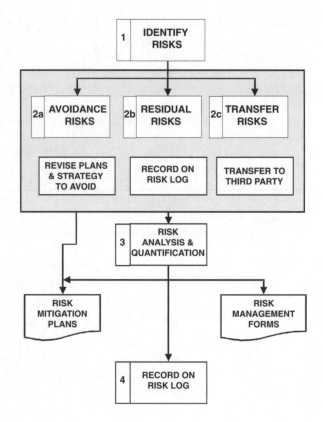

Figure 6.4 Steps in a risk response strategy

- *Avoidance risks* – risks that you can clearly see can be avoided by revising your approach to the project. You may have to revise the initial schedule derived for the business case.
- *Transfer risks* – risks that could possibly be transferred to a third party for management and monitoring, such as suppliers and contractors.
- *Residual risks* – risks that can be managed and monitored within the project team.

Avoidance risks can take considerable time to correct. As this may involve significant revision, after making the necessary amendments to the business plan you must review the residual risks on your list. Some may disappear and some new ones may appear.

If you revise the business case, you must include the revised version as part of your submission to the PST when seeking approval of the project definition.

When you are satisfied with the list of residual risks, record them on a *project risk log*. A typical example is shown in Figure 6.5. Then attempt to establish two characteristics for each risk: 1) What is the probability of its happening – based on currently available data? 2) What is the likely impact on the project if it happens? This assessment can only be subjective, based on the previous experience of you and your team, but you should attempt to reach a consensus for each risk identified.

Remember that *anything* that could go wrong and threaten the project is a potential risk and must not be ignored.

Constraint or risk?

Do not confuse constraints with risks. Constraints are fixed and imposed on the project either from the outset or later, knowingly or unknowingly. You usually have little control over these constraints so you have to live with them and find ways to work around them to achieve a successful outcome. Constraints help you bring the project to 'ground zero' and the real world rather than end up with a 'mission impossible'.

Constraints usually fit into three types:

- known at the outset – financial, time limitations, quality or scope;
- changes during the project – scope, budget, logistics or resources;
- hidden – from invalid nodding agreement to some aspect of the project.

A constraint is always a constraint, and too many will condemn your project to a sure disaster unless you can remove them by changing your strategy.

QUANTIFYING IDENTIFIED RISKS

When you have derived your list of risks, work with your team, using their experience to decide for each risk:

- The *probability of occurrence* on a scale of 0.0 to 1.0. A probability of 0.0 is low, meaning that the risk is most unlikely to materialize. At the other end of the scale, 1.0 is very high – essentially meaning a certainty that it will happen.
- The *impact* on the project if it does happen. Here, a probability of 0.65–1.0 is HIGH, implying a significant effect on the schedule and project costs. A figure of 0.3–0.64 means a MEDIUM impact – a less serious effect on the schedule, some effect on costs. A figure of 0.0–0.29 means LOW impact – some effect on schedule, little effect on costs.

PROJECT RISK LOG

Issue 1.1

	Page ___ of ___	Date	
		Version	
		Prepared by:	

TITLE:

SPONSOR:

MANAGER:

PROJECT No:

Planned start date:

Planned end date:

Risk rank	Risk No:	Risk category	RISK TITLE	Date raised	Activity ID	Cost impact £000's	Risk type T/A/R	DATA P	DATA I	DATA S	Status ACTS	Risk owner	RMP Y/N	RMF Y/N

Notes:

1. Record the Risk Category as (U) Unacceptable, (H) High, (M) Medium, (L) Low
2. Indicate expected cost impact of risk if it occurs as 'Cost Impact £000's' if known.
3. In DATA column enter Probability (P), Impact (I) and Risk Score (S).
4. Identify current status as (A) active and (C) completed or Cancelled (T), Suspended (S).
5. Indicate (Y) yes or (N) no in RMP and RMF columns to indicate if Risk Mitigation Plan / Risk Management Form has been derived.

Figure 6.5 Example of a project risk log

Remember, this should be a team consensus decision using all the available information at the time. Generally there is a tendency to de-rate a risk by confidence that it can readily be dealt with if it does happen. A word of caution, though: it is better to up-rate a risk to ensure that closer monitoring is carried out.

Once a set of risks has been assessed for impact and probability of occurrence you can categorize them using a matrix (Figure 6.6) with the parameters of *probability* and *impact on the project*. Each risk is located in the relevant box in the matrix by the intersection of the impact and probability ratings assessed. Number each risk on your *project risk log* and use these numbers in the matrix to derive a category for the risk.

Risk category

Assess the current category of all risks identified at the outset and subsequently during the project using the category matrix (Table 6.1). The definitions are given below for HIGH, MEDIUM and LOW categories:

- HIGH: major impact on the project schedule and costs. Serious consequent impact on other, related projects. Likely to affect a project milestone. Must be monitored regularly and carefully. Review action plans.
- MEDIUM: significant impact on the project with possible impact on other projects. Not expected to affect a project milestone. Review at each project meeting and assess ranking. Monitor regularly.
- LOW: not expected to have any serious impact on the project. Review regularly for ranking and monitor.

IMPACT ON THE PROJECT				
		LOW 0.0–0.29	MEDIUM 0.3–0.64	HIGH 0.65–1.0
PROBABILITY	0.65–1.0	*medium*	*high*	*unacceptable*
	0.3–0.64	*low*	*high*	*unacceptable*
	0.0–0.29	*low*	*medium*	*high*

Figure 6.6 Risk category matrix

If the project contains nearly all HIGH risks at this stage then a review of the business plan may be necessary. An alternative strategy may be required to reduce the level of risk and the likely impact.

Actions you must take

Any risks that clearly fall into a cell in Figure 6.6 labelled *unacceptable* must be closely analysed in more detail. If they could cause project failure, decide whether some changes to the project brief are necessary to reduce the level of risk. If you can do something now to reduce the ranking then you must derive and implement an action plan. No project should continue with such risks remaining. Derive and agree a *risk mitigation strategy* with clear actions and action owners to avoid the risk now. Ensure you track the implementation of these plans through to completion. In an ideal world the actions should be completed before you launch the project. Highlight any outstanding *risk mitigation plans* not completed when you seek PST approval to proceed through Phase Gate Two. An example risk mitigation plan is shown in Figure 6.7.

High risks should be examined to derive contingency plans to contain the possible damages. Use a standard template *risk management form* for deriving these action plans. A typical template is shown in Figure 6.8. The same approach can be used for all or selected medium risks if required.

If you decide to change the ranking of a risk at any time, record the change. If the change is to HIGH then record the revised ranking on the project risk log and then reissue the document to the key stakeholders. The increased rating of the risk then requires a *risk management form* to be completed.

> Risks change with time as the project work progresses, so review all risks and their ranking at regular intervals.

Risk score

The risk score gives you a convenient way to derive a ranked list of all the risks in order of priority. The risk score is determined from the probability and impact values assigned earlier for each risk:

Probability Impact = Risk Score

The risk scores can then be used to rank the order of risks. This helps you monitor the potential threats to the project more effectively. Record the risk scores on the risk log. The highest risk scores should appear at the top of the list on the project risk log. Clearly, an electronic version of the risk log makes this task easier in practice.

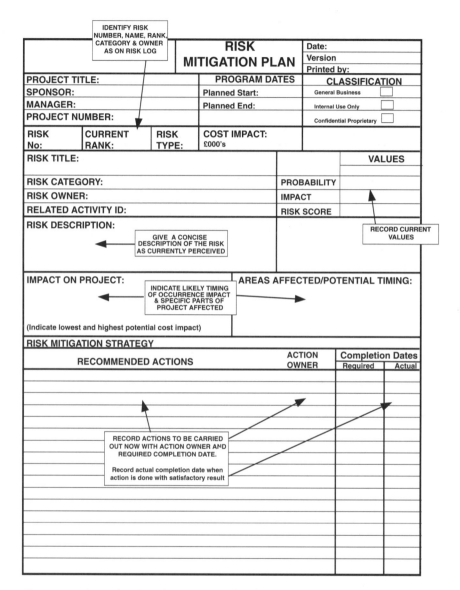

Figure 6.7 Example of a risk mitigation plan for risk correction

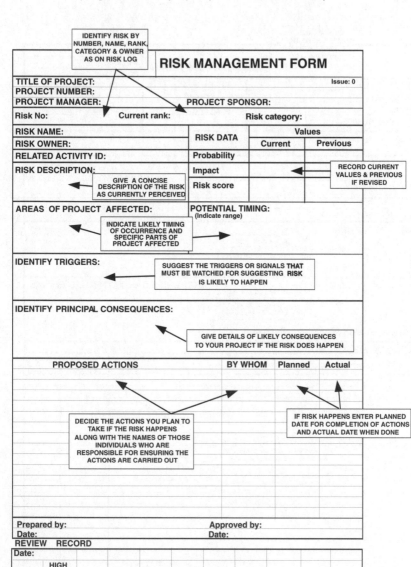

Figure 6.8 Example of a risk management form for action planning

When you are conducting a risk review later in the project, the risk scores are adjusted if the probability and impact values are revised.

Risk ownership

The most important part of the risk management process is to assign an owner for every risk on the risk log. Do not take ownership of all the risks yourself. Assign risks to each member of your team and, if appropriate, to the sponsor and other stakeholders. Record the name of the owner on the risk log.

The responsibilities of the risk owner include:

- ownership of the risk for response tracking and monitoring;
- completion of the risk mitigation plan or risk management form;
- deciding and allocating owners of actions in the action plan;
- agreeing completion dates of agreed actions with the action owners;
- presenting the risk mitigation plan or risk management form to the project manager for approval;
- monitoring progress and validating that actions are completed on time;
- reviewing the results of action plans and adding more actions if necessary;
- informing the project manager of progress with action plans;
- issuing a final version of the risk mitigation plan or risk management form when all actions are completed satisfactorily.

Ownership of a risk involves both responsibility and accountability. The owner is accountable to you as the project manager for getting the action plans completed. It is essential to ensure you give the risk owner the necessary authority to achieve a result. Similarly, if you assign any risk to yourself you are accountable for the action plans to the sponsor.

RISK MONITORING

Once risks to the project have been identified and action plans derived then these must be monitored to make sure prompt action is taken when appropriate. Because any risk can change its characteristics with time, control of risk involves, first, monitoring risks and reporting the actions agreed, and second, monitoring valid identified risks for any change of probability and impact.

Remember that risks that happen become issues that must be resolved promptly to avoid any time-related cost impacts on your project. Risk monitoring is assisted by the use of *risk triggers* in the schedule. These are marked on the schedule a short period before a particular risk is expected to occur. This alerts the risk owner specifically to watch out for signs of the risk occurring, and can reduce the probability of occurrence.

Creating a *look ahead watchlist* can also help monitoring. Review the risk log and identify the risks that are expected could occur in the next four weeks. List these and ask the team particularly to watch out for any signals that one or more of these are about to occur. Do warn the team that this should not distract from their normal vigilance in watching out for new risks.

The full risk management process is shown in Figure 6.9. We will consider monitoring further in the context of project control in Chapter 9.

Issues

An *issue* is a risk that has become a reality and needs to be resolved promptly. The relative importance of the issue and its impact dictate who will take corrective action. Some issues will need to be escalated for decisions to the sponsor. Very serious issues are escalated to the senior management of the organization. You are responsible for ensuring that issues are dealt with promptly at the appropriate level, and although you must monitor risks and outstanding unresolved issues, the sponsor also has a part to play in the management of risks and issues.

Issues are most expected to occur during the execution phase of the project, although often they do happen earlier in the project's life cycle. The process of managing issues is the same whenever they occur, as will be discussed in more detail in Chapter 9.

GETTING YOUR PROJECT DEFINITION APPROVED

The final step in the definition process is to present your documented definition to the PST for approval to pass through Phase Gate Two. Before you take this final step, check that you have done everything necessary to define the project fully and clearly – see Checklist 10. To prepare for this submission inform the sponsor and your customer that the definition is complete and request them to review the documentation and approve the content. The PST will expect confirmation that this has been done before it gives its decision that the project can go on to the planning phase.

Getting agreement and approval is often best carried out in a meeting to enable you to explain any decisions you have taken following the earlier kick-off meeting. The documents you are presenting comprise:

- the *business case*, with any revisions made;
- the *project organization chart*;

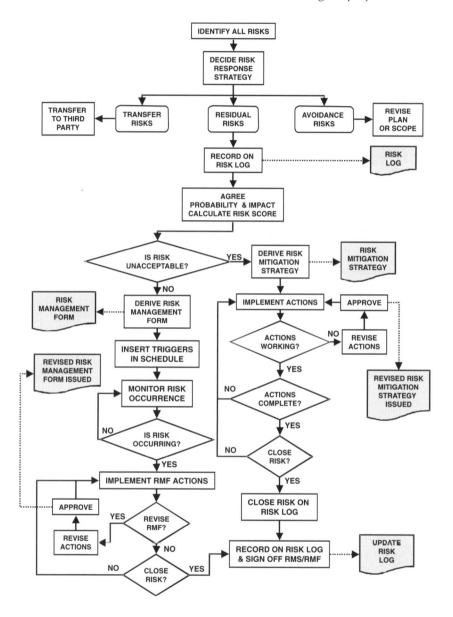

Figure 6.9 Process flow diagram: risk management process

- the *project stakeholder list*;
- the *scope of work statement*;
- the *project risk log*;
- the *risk mitigation plans* for UNACCEPTABLE and/or HIGH risks;
- the *risk management forms* for HIGH risks;
- the *project brief*.

If the project is of a confidential nature then you must show how all project documentation is to be kept secure and ensure that all documents display appropriate security classification codes.

It is good practice for the sponsor to sign all documents as approved, acting on behalf of all stakeholders. The customer must, of course, indicate acceptance of the project definition by also signing the project brief.

You can then inform the PST administrator that you are ready to present your project to the PST, requesting approval of the project definition and authority to pass Phase Gate Two. *Do not* allow your team to assume that approval is a foregone conclusion and start work on the planning phase. This could be a costly error if the PST decides to suspend or cancel the project.

Once you have made your presentation and satisfied the PST to give a 'GO' decision you are in a position to start planning your project.

CHECKLIST 10: DEVELOPING THE DEFINITION

Ask:

- Is the project organization clearly established?
- Are roles and responsibilities at all levels understood and accepted?
- Have project accountability and authority statements been issued?
- Has a project organization chart been prepared and issued?
- Has the project stakeholder list been prepared and issued?
- Have all the key stakeholders been identified?
- Have stakeholder management responsibilities been allocated in the team?
- Has a project need/purpose/opportunity statement been agreed?
- Has all the relevant background information been collected?
- Has an overall project objective statement been agreed?
- Are the corporate and strategic context and priority of the project understood?

- Is the customer clearly identified?
- Is a client project team involved?
- Are the project boundary limits clearly established?
- Is there a business-critical date for the completion of the project?
- Have the project deliverables been clearly identified?
- Have the project benefits been established or revised from the business plan?
- Have the project approach and strategy been agreed?
- Has a preliminary resource skill analysis been carried out?
- Is the project related to other projects?
- Is the impact on other projects understood?
- Have the project risks been identified and quantified so far?
- Have all avoidance risks been identified and assigned owners?
- Have risk mitigation plans been prepared and actioned or completed for all avoidance risks?
- Have all transfer risks been identified and handed over to appropriate third parties?
- Have risk mitigation plans been prepared and actioned or completed for UNACCEPTABLE risks?
- Has a project risk log been prepared listing all residual risks?
- Have all risks on the project risk log been ranked by risk score?
- Have risk management forms been prepared for HIGH risks?
- Has a scope of work statement been prepared?
- Have all assumptions made so far been documented clearly?
- Are existing communication procedures acceptable for the project?
- Has a project brief been prepared ready for approval?
- Has the business case been revised to reflect any agreed changes?

SUMMARY

The key steps of project definition are shown as a flow diagram in Figure 6.10. Checklist 11 summarizes the key leadership actions for the definition phase of the project.

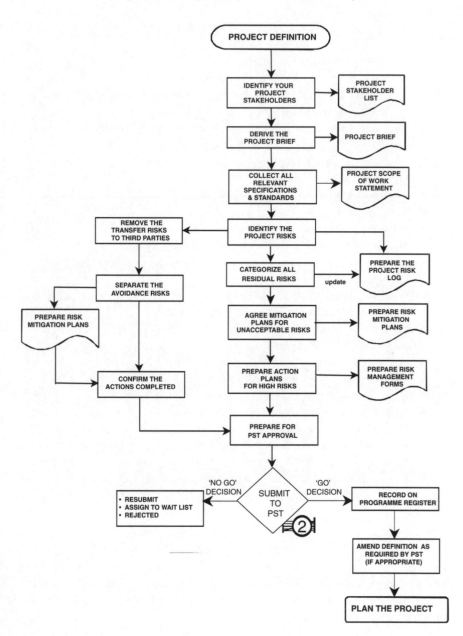

Figure 6.10 Process flow diagram: project definition

CHECKLIST 11: KEY LEADERSHIP ACTIONS DURING PROJECT DEFINITION

- Project stakeholders:
  - Confirm needs and expectations.
  - Confirm the statement of requirements.
  - Clarify the project's purpose and context.
  - Establish authority and accountability.
  - Confirm the project's deadlines.
  - Confirm the project's constraints.
- Project tasks:
  - Confirm the key stakeholders.
  - Identify the project deliverables.
  - Identify the project's benefits.
  - Decide the project strategy/approach.
  - Establish the project budget.
- Project team:
  - Involve the team in project definition.
  - Hold regular team meetings.
  - Clarify the project objectives.
  - Encourage ideas and suggestions.
  - Listen to the team's views.
  - Involve the team in the decision process.
- Team members:
  - Identify special training needs.
  - Hold regular one-to-one meetings with team members.
  - Encourage participation.
  - Reinforce motivation with responsibility.
  - Understand personal objectives.
  - Review skills and experience.
  - Resolve conflicts promptly.

7

Planning your project

Successful projects do not just happen; you have to do a host of things to make them happen. You have made a considerable effort to get your project clearly defined and approved by the PST; now it is essential for you to plan the work in a logical and structured manner. It is a certainty that by this stage the business case will have been amended to state clearly the expected end date and dates for all expected deliverables. Unless particularly difficult issues occur you must adhere to these dates. Some of your colleagues may suggest that you can just plan as you go along; well, try it and see how often you have to do rework and see your project go through cycles of stop–go–stop–go. Yes, you may eventually reach the end of the project, but at considerable cost to the organization and your health! Consider the stress induced in your team members struggling to keep the work moving without any clear idea of when each piece of work should be completed or how it links into the next piece of work.

Planning is a process of creating order out of apparent chaos, made complex by the environment in which you are operating, where you continually face change. In its simplest approach, planning is just a process of asking questions:

- What actions need to be taken?
- When are these actions to be taken?
- Who is going to take them?
- What equipment and tools are required?

WHAT IS NOT GOING TO BE DONE?

The answers to these questions lead you to consequential questions, but your purpose is to convert the contents of the project brief to a form that everyone understands. The objectives for you and your team are to achieve the results on time, to the budgeted cost and to the desired level of quality. Project planning is carried out so as to:

- reduce risks and uncertainty to a minimum;
- establish standards of performance;
- provide a structured basis for executing the work;
- establish procedures for effective control of the work;
- obtain the required outcomes in the minimum time.

You are rarely confident enough to plan all the detail work of your project at this stage. Too often the outputs from early work do not give expected results and you have to take this into account to plan the detail of the following work. If the plan is fully detailed, you must spend time replanning and reworking the earlier planned detail. This difficulty is always with you but can be overcome to a large extent by using the right tools and techniques. Planning is a dynamic and continuous process to enable you to remain proactive throughout the project. You finish planning only when you finally close the project file.

WHO NEEDS TO BE INVOLVED?

The short answer is you and your project core team together. Before you start your first planning session, review the skills and experience of the team members. If you can identify any shortcomings in skills, knowledge or experience needed for planning, seek to fill the gaps now by inviting other people to join your planning session. Invite experts from other departments to join you, stressing that this is not committing them to project work later and that you value their inputs to your efforts. If they can add value, invite specific stakeholders to assist you. Persuade your sponsor to attend and open the planning session, explaining the project's strategic context, relevance and priority. Planning is essentially a participative activity that motivates your team, contributes to team building and creates team 'buy-in' to the plans derived. Such commitment is essential to success. Producing a plan yourself and then seeking agreement from everyone else is a long process that does not create a sense of commitment in your team. It becomes 'your plan' and not 'our plan'.

WHERE DOES PLANNING START?

The question of where planning starts is often subject to debate and argument. The options are, first, top down – identifying the principal blocks of work involved; and second, bottom up – identifying all the tasks to be carried out. A third option – working backwards from the completion date – is often suggested but is subject to huge risks at this stage.

The top-down method suffers from the disadvantage that the blocks identified are likely to be based on functional activities that may only be few in number. This creates a significant loss of potential concurrency of the work – activities that can be carried out in parallel. As a result, the blocks are arranged in series.

The bottom-up approach suffers from the disadvantage that it takes a long time to identify all the tasks to be carried out and a huge number can be identified. You are then faced with the difficulty of arranging them in the right sequence for optimum time in a project schedule. In addition, you almost certainly forget or miss some tasks.

Before we go any further, some terms have been introduced that need defining:

- *task* – a (relatively) small piece of work carried out by one person;
- *activity* – a parcel of work of the project comprising several tasks, each of which may be carried out by different people;
- *concurrent activities* – activities (or tasks) that are designed to be carried out in parallel, ie at the same time;
- *series activities* – activities (or tasks) that are designed to be carried out one after another, each strictly dependent on completion of the earlier activity.

As an example, producing a report is an activity but it comprises many tasks:

1. gathering data from different sources – in parallel;
2. analysing data;
3. writing the first draft;
4. editing the draft;
5. preparing the graphics: charts and diagrams;
6. preparing the final draft – in parallel with 5;
7. producing the final copy for reproduction;
8. reproducing and issuing the report.

It may even be possible to break down some of these tasks into yet more detail (or sub-tasks) if different people are involved in writing different sections of the report.

Successful planning is a mixture of both approaches to reduce the difficulties and arrive at a plan that has sufficient detail to maximize concurrency. A hybrid approach is to start by identifying the *key stages* of your project.

IDENTIFYING THE KEY STAGES

The essential process in planning is to use the collective experience and knowledge of your project team and others invited to the planning session to identify the work as a list of tasks to be done. This is carried out in a brainstorming session to derive a long list of tasks. Write everything down on a flip chart, and when carrying out these sessions remember to follow two basic rules: 1) quantity before quality – even if the same tasks appear more than once; and 2) suspend all judgement – disallow any critical comments.

The list derived is not ordered or ranked with any priorities at this stage and may seem to be a complete jumble from which no sense will ever appear. When everyone feels they have run out of ideas for tasks, you can suspend the brainstorming activity. There are now several flip chart sheets containing many tasks. The next task for the team is to reduce the long list. The first step is to clean it up by removing obvious duplicates. Then start to cluster together those tasks that are clearly related together (as in our earlier example of the report), either in series or in parallel. Aim to reduce your task list to a reasonable number of activities, preferably in the range 30–60, depending on the size of the project.

These are the *key stages* of your project from which everything else is developed. The forgotten tasks lose significance for the moment as they are hidden away in the key stages, and you can return to the detail later. This approach generally helps you identify most of the possible concurrency now and gives you an activity list of a size that is relatively easy to manipulate. You may find that later you will split key stages into two or more to improve the accuracy of your plan. In practice your clustered list of activities will be at least 90 per cent accurate, or frequently even better. Do not steamroller this step; it is the basis on which all subsequent planning is carried out, so spend time to save time later!

Using the key stages

Once the key stages are known and agreed, you organize them into a logical sequence to maximize concurrency. There are some traps here for you. First, avoid considering real time or dates yet. Second, avoid assigning people or functions to the key stages. Both will lead you to create errors in the project logic.

The next step is to derive the *project logic diagram*. This is done using a technique known as *taskboarding*. Write each key stage on a separate small card or Post-it note. Use these as parts of the project 'jigsaw' to build the picture. Arrange them in the right logical order either on a table, using a whiteboard or simply on the office wall. This is achieved by taking each key stage in turn and asking, 'What must be completed before I can start this work?' Start with the first key stages that come out from a card labelled 'START'. Continue working from left to right until all the Post-it notes have been used. Connect all the Post-it notes with arrows to show the logical flow of the project from start to finish.

The advantage of this technique is that everyone can be involved. The graphic impact of the diagram developing makes each member of the team question and debate the validity of the logic as it grows. An example of a logic diagram is shown in Figure 7.1.

Note that the logic diagram is continuous; that is, every key stage has at least one arrow entering (an input) and at least one arrow leaving (an output). To ensure integrity of the logic this rule must be maintained, otherwise the plan will contain errors. Of course, it is not unusual to find more than one arrow depicting dependency entering and leaving some key stages.

Note also that the basis of the logic is that a new activity cannot logically start until all immediately previous activities finish. If you find on reviewing the logic that a following task can start earlier than the end of the previous key stage, it must be split to show that earlier dependence. For example, from the logic diagram shown in Figure 7.1, the 'design phase 1' has been split into two to allow 'purchase orders' to start before the end of 'design phase 1', to give the result shown in Figure 7.2. The basic rules for deriving the logic diagram are given in Checklist 12.

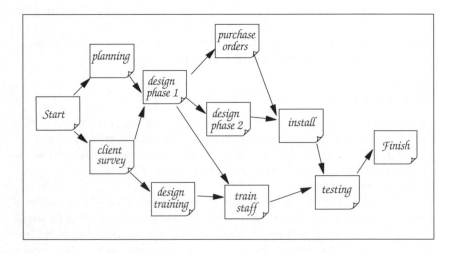

Figure 7.1 A simple project logic diagram

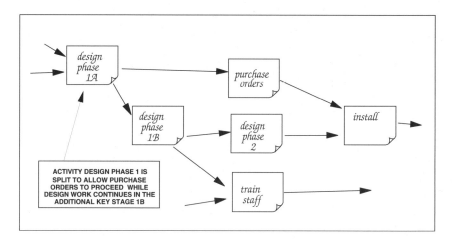

Figure 7.2 Splitting a key stage to improve project logic

CHECKLIST 12: DERIVING THE PROJECT LOGIC DIAGRAM

- Time flows from left to right.
- There is no timescale on the diagram
- Place a START Post-it note at the extreme left of the sheet.
- Place a FINISH Post-it note at the extreme right of the sheet.
- Make sure you have prepared a separate Post-it note for each key stage.
- Start each KEY STAGE description with a verb (present tense).
- Do not attempt to add durations for the key stage yet.
- Use different-colour Post-it notes for different functional activities if appropriate.
- Locate the Post-it notes on the sheet in order of dependency – debate each one.
- When all Post-it notes are used up, validate the dependencies – try working back.
- Show the dependency links as FINISH to START relationships initially.
- Do not take people doing the work into account – doing so can produce errors.
- Do not add in responsibilities at this stage
- Draw in the dependency links with straight arrows in pencil.
- Avoid arrows crossing as it leads to confusion.

- Label each key stage with an alphanumeric code: AB, AC, AD, AE, etc. Do not use I or O in order to avoid confusion with one or zero.
- When you are satisfied it is correct, *record the dependencies*.
- If appropriate, tape the Post-it notes down on to the sheet, then roll it up for filing.

Though you have derived the diagram, it is worth considering keeping a record of all the dependencies you have agreed. You may use this information to input to project management software later to prepare the schedule. When recording dependencies, record only each immediate predecessor key stage number to any particular key stage.

THE PROJECT WORK BREAKDOWN STRUCTURE

The work breakdown structure (usually referred to as the *WBS*) is a convenient means of graphically presenting the work of the project in a readily understandable format. The use of a hierarchical form of structure is surely familiar to most people and is shown in Figure 7.3. It is easy to prepare: the project key stages form the highest level of the WBS, which is then used to show the detail at the lower levels of the project. You know that each key stage comprises many tasks identified at the start of planning, and later this list will have to be validated. Expanding the WBS to the lower levels is the process of multi-layer planning that you will use throughout the project.

The WBS has many uses apart from just showing the work structure. Note that:

- The WBS does *not* show dependencies other than a grouping under the key stages.
- It is not time based – there is no timescale on the drawing.

Now that you have identified the key stages and the WBS for your project, the next step is to insert some time estimates into the plan. However, there is one intermediate step that is worth considering at this stage.

ALLOCATING RESPONSIBILITY

Each of the key stages of the project needs to be owned by one of your team members. This allocation of responsibility is essential to make sure the work is done on time, and your objective is to distribute the work fairly

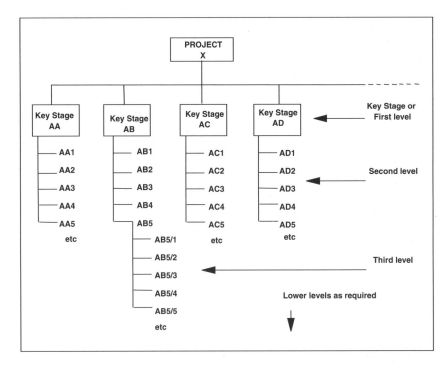

Figure 7.3 The work breakdown structure (WBS)

and evenly among the team. You must persuade each member of the team to accept the role of *key stage owner* for one or more key stages. Occasionally it may be a departmental representative who accepts responsibility for the work to be completed on time. This person is responsible within his or her department for the processes used to achieve the results desired.

The key stage owner accepts the obligation for his or her key stage to confirm that:

● the work required is identified at task level;
● the dependencies are clearly identified;
● the estimates of durations are accurate;
● the work gets done on time to the quality needed;
● the work conforms to quality assurance procedures and requirements;
● regular monitoring is maintained;
● regular accurate status reports are issued;
● you are promptly alerted to problems and issues.

> Each key stage can have only one owner even if that person assigns some of the tasks involved. Split or multiple ownership leads to confusion and no ownership.

Ensure that your team members have:

- the necessary authority to get the work done;
- a strong sense of commitment to the project;
- the tools for the job;
- the essential environment for quality to be maintained;
- access to the right skills for the work;
- the visible support of both yourself and the sponsor;
- a clear understanding of the performance expected of them.

Allocating responsibility is not a matter of random choice or an auction; you must heed the current circumstances of each individual. Some guidelines are given in Checklist 13.

CHECKLIST 13: SOME GUIDELINES FOR ALLOCATING RESPONSIBILITIES

Consider:

- individual capabilities;
- depth of knowledge;
- previous relevant experience;
- speed of working;
- accuracy of past work;
- creative ability demonstrated previously;
- problem-solving ability;
- personal time management ability;
- personal development objectives;
- individual work style – team or loner;
- current workload – other projects;
- current functional workload;
- capacity to do the work on time;
- previous performance record;
- personality conflicts;
- who can provide advice, support and back-up;
- whether additional training is necessary now or in the future.

Consider also whether:

- the tools and equipment are available;
- the essential technical skills exist;
- any special training is required.

Record the allocated responsibilities

Keep a record of the responsibilities you have allocated. This is a key communication document for everyone involved, including the line managers of the human resources assigned to the project. As the plan develops, more names are added as the extended team is identified for parts of the detailed work. A suggested format is shown in Figure 7.4.

This document lists the key stages and the name of the individual responsible for the work involved in that key stage. Also, note that the template includes the name of the individual consulted for advice, who may be an expert in the organization – not necessarily yourself. At this stage of planning you do not have the data to complete the 'Duration' or 'Planned finish' columns. Issue the document to all those on the list and anyone else you consider needs to know.

Your reason for allocating these responsibilities is to assign the estimating of key stage durations to those people in your team who are most likely to have the appropriate experience.

WHAT IS AN ESTIMATE?

An estimate is a decision about how much time and resource are required to carry out a piece of work to acceptable standards of performance. This requires you to determine:

- The 'size' of the task or group of tasks, as determined from measurements if possible.
- The amount of 'effort' required to complete the work. How can the work be broken down? Can it be divided between two or more people? Effort is measured in project time units: hours/days/weeks.
- The level of risk involved.

Once the effort is known then optimize the resource needs, taking individual capacities or available time into account to determine the levels of effort required from each.

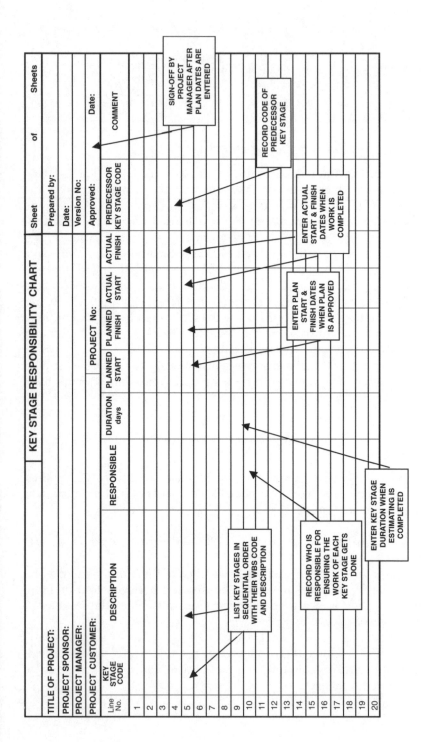

Figure 7.4 Example key stage responsibility chart

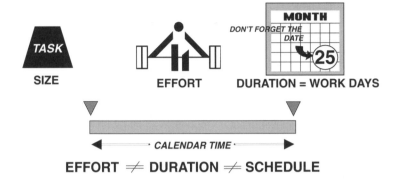

EFFORT ≠ DURATION ≠ SCHEDULE

Figure 7.5 The relationship between effort, duration and schedule

Effort is a direct measure of the amount of a person's time needed to do a piece of work, in normal workdays. Unfortunately, that person will often have other, non-project activities to complete, which will reduce his or her capacity to do the work. At a capacity of 50 per cent, the work will take at least double the number of workdays. In practice it takes longer, because of the 'back-track' effect due to the breaks in the flow of the work. Effort is measurable as continuous work with no interruptions.

Duration is a conversion of effort taking into account the number of people involved, their capacities and an allowance for non-productive time. It is often more convenient to use full-time equivalents (FTEs) in working out how many people are needed for any part of a project.

Since duration is measured in real working days, it is never the same as the schedule, which has to take into account:

- days not available for project work;
- non-working days – weekends;
- public and organization holidays;
- staff holidays.

The first step for you is to derive some realistic durations and then apply these to a calendar to derive a schedule.

ESTIMATING THE DURATIONS

As the duration of each key stage is the real time it will take to complete the work, this is usually the most difficult part of the planning process. Unfortunately, there is an abundance of 'good advice' in most organizations about how long a piece of work will or should take. The process appears to be one of part art and part science, which is hardly surprising since you are really trying to predict the future! So far no one has produced a reliable crystal ball! The sources to help you derive accurate estimates are limited:

- the experience of others;
- the expert view;
- historical data from other projects.

There is no substitute for experience. If similar work has been done before then you can ask others for their own previous experience and adjust the data for your project. It is a reasonable way to start, but always take a cautious approach.

The data you collect this way will often hide important relevant information. No one will easily admit taking longer than the plan predicted for a piece of work – particularly if slippages caused problems. Also, with the passage of time, people's memories have a habit of remembering only the good news. If good plans and records exist, review these to determine what actually happened compared to what was planned to happen. Take more than one opinion if you can and remember that no two people ever do the same piece of work at the same pace. The equation relating effort and performance is different for us all.

Who are the experts? There may be a few – or so they believe! Always ask questions about how reality compared with original estimates for some work. Check that the nature or content of the work did not change. You soon discover who is above average at estimating accurately – the expert(s) you desperately seek. Since it is relatively rare for work to be identical between different projects, apply your *adjusting factor* to arrive at a realistic duration for each of the activities. Keep a record of how you derived the estimates in case you are wrong, then you can improve your estimating skills.

People problems

Ask anyone how long a piece of work will take and you are likely to be given a shrug and a smile and a wildly inaccurate answer. This is because people do not ask themselves some simple questions:

- Do I really understand what is involved?
- Do I have all the necessary skills and tools for the work?
- What else must I do at the same time?
- What is the priority of the project work compared with that of other work?

- When is it really needed by?
- Can I break the job down into chunks to do at different times?
- Can I predict what I will be doing when this project work needs to be done?
- Will I be taking any holiday during the time concerned?
- Do I have any other obligatory commitments during the time concerned?
- What does my manager know about my future commitments that I do not know yet?

The reality is that the majority of people are not productive 100 per cent of the time! As much as 20 per cent of their working week is taken up by:

- meetings – particularly ones they need not attend;
- general interruptions:
  - visits to desk and others – wanderlust;
  - equipment failure;
  - reading journals and e-mail;
  - searching for information;
  - giving support and advice to others;
- commitments to routine functional work and other projects;
- unforeseen events;
- seeking advice from others;
- communication failures;
- personal organization;
- engaging in conflict;
- inability to say 'no' to others' requests.

Consider also:

- project complexity:
  - specifications: adequacy, unfamiliarity;
  - new quality standards;
  - unclear understanding of the technology;
  - new technology: always has a learning curve for confidence;
- team size and location of the team members;
- anything else you can think of.

The answers to these and other similar questions are often ignored in deriving an initial estimate, leading to considerable problems later. Rash promises are assumed to be realistic and inserted into the plan.

CONTINGENCIES

The purpose of contingencies is to attempt to quantify the extent of uncertainty in the estimating process that make up the project plans. *Contingencies are not intended to cover changes to the project definition or objectives after they have been agreed with the stakeholders, nor are they intended to cover estimating errors or tasks not included originally.* If such changes occur then the contingencies are rolled forward and adjusted. Ask:

- What factor can you use for adjusting people's estimates?
- Is that factor global for all estimates or different for different types of work and for different people?
- Should you expose your adjustment factor(s)?
- What limits must you use in applying contingency?
- Should you multiply some estimates by an additional weighting for:
  - team size;
  - team experience (in individuals);
  - team working history of this team;
  - project complexity;
  - the project's use of new techniques or technology?
- If so, what should it be?

Adjust the base estimates using these additional factors when appropriate. One other contingency that can be considered is referred to as *scope contingency*. This may be required when some parts of the project include uncertainty about what must explicitly be done. Scope contingency is used only when you as the project manager specifically authorize its use through the *change management process*. Usually the contingency involves the release of extra funding for the work, so you must have clearly delegated authority to use the contingency.

You take the final decision as to what figures for durations you intend to insert into your plan. These lead you to calculating the total project time, with a projected completion date. Obviously there is a balance between the desired project completion date and the projected or forecast completion date based only on estimates. The former may well appear to be almost impossible and quite unrealistic, the latter insupportable and good justification for cancelling the project! Somewhere in the middle there is an acceptable solution and only attention to detail and all the experience you can gather will help you to find it. Always record any assumptions you have made in deriving the durations.

TIME-LIMITED SCHEDULING AND ESTIMATES

There is always a conflict when a completion date is imposed on a project before any work on estimates is carried out. This imposed date is outside your control completely, so you then attempt to compress estimates to fit the plan. To a limited degree this is acceptable as a target, but too often this process moves you into a totally unreal situation where you are faced with 'mission impossible'. You must still prepare realistic estimates to derive a clear case and state:

- what you can deliver in the time;
- what you cannot deliver in the time;
- why you can meet only part of the objectives of the project.

You can then use your skill as a negotiator to arrive at an agreed solution!

Since the major portion of all project costs is frequently the time expended, the accuracy of estimates is a key factor in achieving project success. Historical data can be valuable even from parts of previous projects as an initial guide. Analysis of the actual proposed work is essential if accurate estimates are to be derived. Even then, people seem habitually to underestimate the time needed for execution of work. There are some people, however, who have an intuitive ability to visualize the work involved and give accurate estimates. Identify and make good use of them!

Some practical guidelines that can be used are as follows:

- Schedule full-time team members at 3.5–4.0 working (productive) days per week (to allow for holidays, absences, training courses, etc).
- Include management time where appropriate as an additional 10 per cent.
- In planning, avoid splitting tasks between individuals as far as possible.
- When tasks have to be split between two individuals, do not reduce time by 50 per cent – allow time for communication and co-ordination.
- Take individual experience and ability into account.
- Allow time for cross-functional data transfer and responses.
- Build in time for unscheduled urgent tasks arising on other non-project activities.
- Build in spare time for problem solving and project meetings.
- Include appropriate contingencies at *all* levels of planning.

Any estimate is only as good as the data upon which it is based, so, as with project risks, accept that they may change with time as more data become available to you. As the project continues, always review and validate the durations you have used. For each key stage keep a record of:

- the estimates you have finally decided on;
- any assumptions made during estimating;
- where contingencies have been added;
- how much contingency has been added.

Now, with durations agreed, you can analyse the logic diagram for its critical path.

IDENTIFYING THE CRITICAL PATH OF YOUR PROJECT

Critical path techniques have been in use on projects now for some 30 years, having proved their value as a tool for project scheduling and control. The fundamental purpose is to enable you to find the shortest possible time in which to complete your project. You can do this by inspection of the *logic diagram*.

Enter the durations on to your Post-it notes in the logic diagram for each key stage. Begin at the START note and trace each possible route or path through the diagram to the FINISH note, adding the durations of all the key stages in the path. The path that has the highest number – that is, the longest duration – is the *critical path* of your project and represents the shortest time in which it is possible to complete the project. All other paths are shorter. All the *key stages* on the critical path must, by definition, finish on time or the project schedule will slip.

For example: referring to the previous logic diagram (Figure 7.6), the available paths are:

1. Start – planning – design phase 1 – purchase orders – install – testing – finish: 37 days.
2. Start – planning – design phase 1 – design phase 2 – install – testing – finish: 42 days.
3. Start – planning – design phase 1 – train staff – testing – finish: 36 days.
4. Start – client survey – design phase 1 – purchase orders – install – testing – finish: 56 days.
5. Start – client survey – design phase 1 – design phase 2 – install – testing – finish: 61 days.
6. Start – client survey – design phase 1 – train staff – testing – finish: 46 days.
7. Start – client survey – training design – train staff – testing – finish: 42 days.

So, the *critical path* is number 5 in the list of available paths.

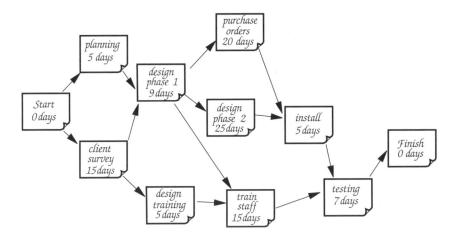

Figure 7.6 The logic diagram with durations inserted. Note: durations are in consistent units

This is where reality hits you – is the project total time what your customer actually requires? If it is a long way out, do not worry yet, as most project managers expect this to happen. Remember, your estimates are based on people's perceptions. Your job is to attempt to compress the time to a schedule that, on the one hand, is real and achievable and, on the other, satisfies your customer. To do this you need to make use of another valuable tool of project management: *Programme Review and Evaluation Technique* (PERT). This tool allows you to analyse the logic diagram to confirm:

- the critical path – confirmation of your inspection;
- the start and finish times of all the key stages;
- the amount of 'spare time' available in the non-critical key stages.

All these data are very useful to you for optimizing the project schedule and, more importantly, for the control of the project work once this starts.

THE PROGRAMME EVALUATION AND REVIEW TECHNIQUE

The PERT method of critical path planning and scheduling is the most commonly used technique for project management control. It is based on representing the activities in a project by boxes (or nodes) that contain essential information calculated about the project. The interdependencies between the activities are represented by arrows to show the flow of the project through its various paths in the logic diagram. The PERT diagram (sometimes referred to as a network) is identical to the logic diagram you derived earlier, each Post-it note for a key stage representing a node.

The conventional data stored in the node box are as shown in Figure 7.7. The four corners of the node box are used to store the *four characteristic times* for the key stage. These are calculated times using the durations derived in estimating; remember to keep all durations in the same units.

The lower middle box contains the *total float* for the key stage. This is the spare time in the key stage that allows you to take decisions about the actual start time or extending the duration within limits.

In Figure 7.7 the earliest start time is day 12 and the latest start time is day 16. This gives an option to start the activity anytime between day 12 and day 16. The four-day difference is the spare time associated with the activity. Starting anywhere in this time zone will not affect the total project time provided the activity is fully completed by the latest finish time of day 26. Say you were to start the activity on day 12 as the earliest planned date. If the time taken becomes extended from 10 days to 14 days, you use up all the spare time but maintain the total project time. If, however, the duration becomes extended to 16 days – two days more than the available spare time – you will extend the total project time by two days.

Obviously, this process applies to every key stage and lower-level activity in the WBS. If every key stage takes longer than the available spare time, the project will be very late. If the spare time is calculated as zero then that key stage is termed *critical* and is one of those on the *critical path*.

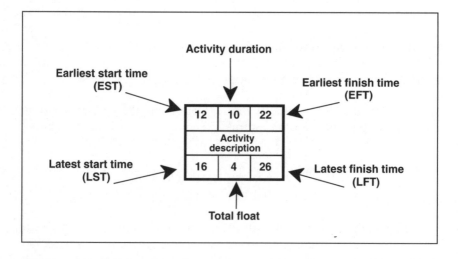

Figure 7.7 The PERT node box

The PERT technique is founded on calculating this information to permit you to take such decisions and control the project.

The default or normal relationship used is FINISH-to-START (see Figure 7.8). Under certain circumstances it is valid to impose constraints with the START-to-START or FINISH-to-FINISH relationships between activities.

You can impose a forced delay using a LAG between the START or FINISH of a predecessor activity and the START or FINISH of one or more successor activities.

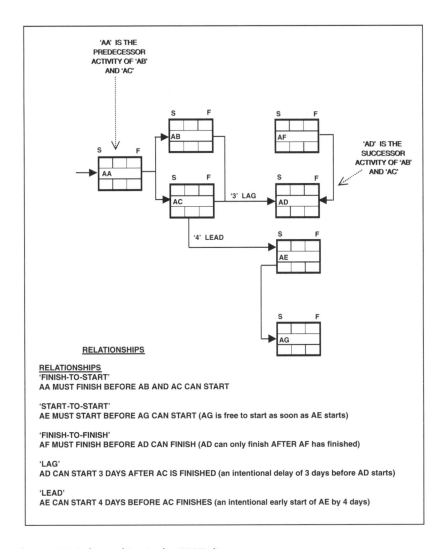

Figure 7.8 Relationships in the PERT diagram

The forced start or LEAD is used to start a SUCCESSOR ACTIVITY before the PREDECESSOR ACTIVITY is completed.

Lags and leads should be used with care; it is easy to become confused and introduce errors. Split an activity instead of using leads to keep the diagram relatively easy to read and understand.

ANALYSING THE LOGIC DIAGRAM

The analysis of the diagram is a simple logical process extending the initial calculation you made earlier to locate the *critical path*. Two steps are involved: 1) adding durations from start to finish – the *forward pass*; 2) subtracting the durations from finish to start – the *backward pass*. Figures 7.9–7.11 illustrate the technique.

As you can see, the calculations involve only some simple arithmetic and you can easily carry out the analysis on the actual Post-it notes you used to derive the logic diagram. In this way you and your team can quickly calculate the total project time and find those areas of the project where float time exists.

USING THE PERT ANALYSIS DATA

At this point in the planning process you may be looking at a plan that is giving you a total project time considerably longer than you really want. Do not despair – yet! Do not allow yourself to be tempted to go back and amend your time estimates. The next step is to convert the PERT data into a graphic format that is easier to work with and understand. This is the *Gantt chart* – a very useful tool for project work originally devised by Henry Gantt early in the 20th century. At the time it was devised, Henry Gantt could not have truly envisaged just how valuable his invention would become for project managers.

The Gantt chart and its various parts are shown in Figure 7.12. The chart allows you to show a listing of all the key stages of the project, their durations and, if required, who is responsible. The chart is divided into two sections: a tabulated listing and a graphic display on which each key stage is represented by a rectangle. All the rectangles are located on a time-scaled grid to show their position in the schedule. It is useful to have both a project timescale bar and a calendar timescale bar across the top of the chart. This allows you to include the non-working days such as weekends and holidays. The key stages are listed on the left-hand side by convention, in order of their occurrence in the logic diagram (working from left to right). List activities in such an order that the rectangles will appear on the

STEP 1

Decide the time each activity or key stage will take and enter these DURATIONS on to the logic notes or BOXES.

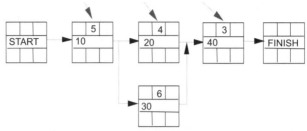

STEP 2

Number each box from START through to FINISH, working from left to right – numbers or alphanumerics.

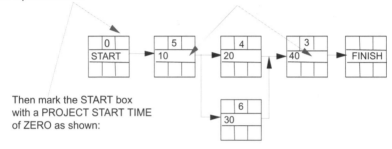

Then mark the START box
with a PROJECT START TIME
of ZERO as shown:

STEP 3

Transfer this TIME figure to the next box in the logic diagram:

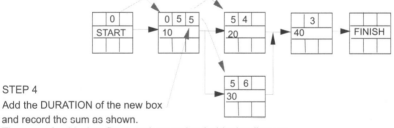

STEP 4

Add the DURATION of the new box
and record the sum as shown.
Then transfer this time figure to the next box(es) in the diagram.

STEP 5

Repeat STEP 4, working through the LOGIC DIAGRAM from left to right.
When 'paths' meet, ensure you record the HIGHEST NUMBER into the next box.

Figure 7.9 Analysing the project logic diagram – 1

The completed FORWARD PASS analysis now looks like this:

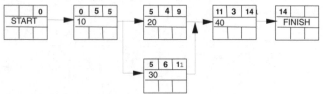

So, we can conclude that the earliest time this small project can finish is 14 units of time. The whole process is now reversed.

STEP 6
Transfer the finish time to the bottom corner of the box as shown.

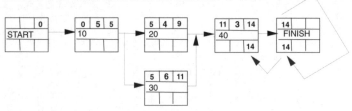

Then copy this same time figure to the lower right-hand corner of the predecessor box.

STEP 7
Subtract the activity DURATION from this time figure and enter the result in the lower left-hand corner of the same box.

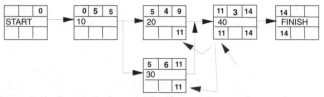

Then copy the result time figure to the lower right-hand corner of any predecessor boxes as shown above.

STEP 8
Continue step 7, copying the LOWEST TIME FIGURE to the next predecessor box where paths merge in the reverse pass.

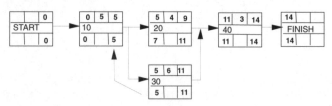

Figure 7.10 Analysing the project logic diagram – 2

The analysis of this logic diagram is now complete and the CRITICAL ELEMENTS can be clearly identified.

STEP 9

Look at each box in turn and identify those where the DIFFERENCE between the time figures in the UPPER and LOWER left-hand corners is EQUAL to the difference between the time figures in the UPPER and LOWER right-hand corners.

THESE BOXES IN YOUR DIAGRAM ARE THE CRITICAL ELEMENTS AND FORM THE CRITICAL PATH OF THE LOGIC DIAGRAM.

DIFFERENCE = 0   DIFFERENCE = 0

A CRITICAL ACTIVITY

STEP 10

Finally, enter the above-calculated DIFFERENCE in the lower MIDDLE part of the box. This is the spare time or FLOAT TIME.

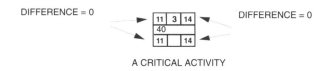

Then calculate the FLOAT times for all the boxes in the diagram:

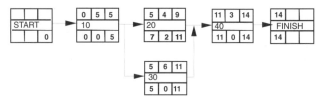

The LOGIC DIAGRAM analysis is now complete. Record the data in tabular format.

TERMINOLOGY

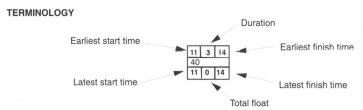

Duration

Earliest start time

Earliest finish time

Latest start time

Latest finish time

Total float

Figure 7.11 Analysing the project logic diagram – 3

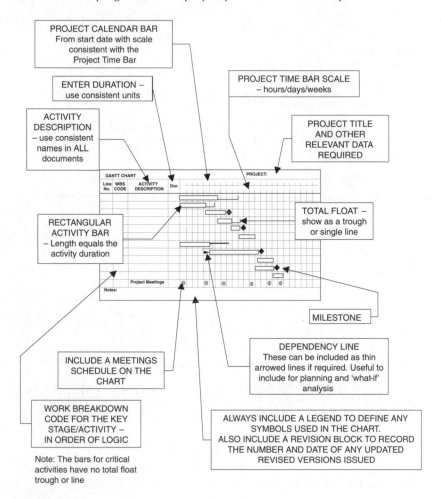

Figure 7.12 Gantt chart

chart to give a perception of flow. This is from the top left-hand corner to the bottom right-hand corner where project completion occurs.

You will note that the float time is also shown on the chart as a trough extension to those rectangles or *bars* (the common term) on the right-hand end, ie at the finish end of the bar. When you initially draw any Gantt chart the float is *always* drawn at this end. The limit of float is the limit of the time available if the schedule is not to be threatened and, possibly, the whole project extended. Of course, critical activities have zero float and you can choose to highlight these with the use of colour.

The dependency links you have established in the logic diagram are not usually drawn on the Gantt chart, because they might cause some confusion in reading the document. However, you can include them and this is readily done by using carefully drawn arrows on the chart, between the start and finish of the dependent activities (ignoring the float zone).

Eventually you will use the Gantt chart to include some other useful information by adding some symbols to the diagram, but do not use any more than is essential. Essential data usually include:

- milestones – special checkpoints usually indicated by a triangle or a diamond symbol;
- project meetings – indicated by a filled circle or dot;
- project reviews (ie financial/audit) – indicated by a filled square.

Remember to give a legend describing what the symbols mean!

The initial Gantt chart you produce at this stage is then optimized to reflect what you can achieve with available resources balanced with customer desires. This frequently involves compressing the schedule to reduce the time for the project. If there are no resources to do the work in the time scheduled, the Gantt chart is a useless document expressing hopes and wishes! Analyse the resource requirements for the tasks in the plan and then optimize the schedule.

These steps may involve considerable reiteration to arrive at an acceptable solution – a process in which project management software is very powerful. Small changes in the schedule are rapidly reflected in the chart and the logic simultaneously recalculated automatically. This allows you to carry out 'what if' analysis, viewing the impact of changing anything in your plan in a host of different ways. You can explore all available options you can think of to derive a finally acceptable schedule. This process is necessary to convince your customer and the sponsor just what is realistically possible provided clear commitments of resources are made. Obviously, this process is much more time-consuming manually. Project management computer software today allows you to carry out this process rapidly and easily without losing data.

ANALYSING YOUR RESOURCE REQUIREMENTS

You must now ask your key stage owners to validate the task list in their respective key stages using the techniques used earlier for the key stages. Many of the data will have been generated earlier, but now need some closer analysis, particularly for the initial key stages.

Identify the resources most likely to be assigned the work and then, working with them as an extended team:

- Review the initial task list.
- Add to the tasks where necessary.
- Analyse for the 'often forgotten tasks':
  - documentation;
  - approval times;
  - testing planning and development;
  - project reviews and gathering the data;
  - project meetings;
  - replanning and planning reviews;
  - customer meetings;
  - user group meetings;
  - negotiations with suppliers;
  - expediting and purchasing administration;
  - training;
  - inter-site travel and communication;
  - updating project file records.

Suggest that each key stage owner draws up a complete list of tasks, and then produces a responsibility chart for each key stage. Then he or she can estimate the durations of all the tasks in the key stage using the same techniques as before. With the key stage owner, identify the actual people who will carry out the work and confirm their commitment and availability. When you identify resources, remember to review:

- their previous experience;
- their individual capabilities;
- their technical knowledge;
- the accuracy of their work;
- their speed of working;
- their capacity to do the work.

Use the same techniques as before to derive the logic diagram for all the tasks inside each key stage. Then determine its critical path and the total float available in the tasks. Some of these tasks may be assigned milestone status later. This enables you to produce a Gantt chart for each key stage. As the project continues, you develop a complete family of such charts that are all expanded views of the primary or overall *key stage Gantt chart*. In this way, a detailed plan of the work for a particular part of the project is clearly defined by the people doing the work, and it minimizes misunderstandings about responsibility. At the same time, these people can confirm:

- that the work can realistically be completed on time;
- resource capacity and availability;
- the commitment of the line manager(s) to providing resources.

You now have the data to update the WBS. However, another advantage of this method is that the detailed work of a key stage does not need to be derived until a week or two before the work starts. This allows the planning to incorporate any unexpected outputs from earlier key stages. In this way you continuously work to hold your plan dates, seek the required resources and optimize your schedule to meet the total project time desired.

OPTIMIZING YOUR SCHEDULE

The schedule is always based on the calendar, taking into account the non-working days during the project. Before attempting to optimize, review the project brief to check that nothing is forgotten and the plan is aligned to stated objectives. The process of optimizing a schedule is a team activity to create acceptance and commitment to the desired total project time.

Optimizing is conducted at two levels: *project* and *business case*. At the project level, optimization involves taking decisions by consensus to maintain a balance between:

- the schedule – time;
- the resources available – cost;
- performance – scope and quality.

The options available are fairly limited when optimizing trade-offs between these three to arrive at a solution. There is no perfect plan; only the best solution based on available information at the time. The options are as follows:

- Review original estimates – realistically.
- Review assigned durations – remove or reduce contingencies added.
- Seek more or different resources.
- Seek to get current resource capacities increased – more time available.
- Re-evaluate the dependencies in the logic for the key stages.
- Review relationships – initially you used FINISH-TO-START; now examine whether other types give an improvement (see Figure 7.8).
- Introduce LAGS and LEADS – with caution, though.
- Split key stages to get more concurrency.
- Examine to ensure that reinvention is minimized.

Although it is sometimes tempting to use activity float times in optimizing, it is better to keep this option up your sleeve. Float time is not to be seen as an opportunity to stretch an activity to fill the available time. If you allow this to happen, you create another critical activity by convention, so it is easy to turn everything critical by using up all floats.

> It is preferable to tell your team that float time is used only as a last resort with your consent (during the execution phase) to enable recovery planning when things go wrong.

Re-estimate the project

Are you an optimist? You face the prospect of reviewing all your assumptions made during estimating durations and making amendments. You may feel you have a deeper understanding of the project now and you could reduce those estimates that were more pessimistic. Unless you have new information to justify improved accuracy this is really wishful thinking and you subject your team to the risk of imposed durations. If you can reduce estimates you reduce cost and possibly schedule time, but carefully examine the consequences. The golden rule is 'avoid reducing estimates and, if you must, do so only in exceptional circumstances'.

Do not succumb to demands by the customer or stakeholders to reduce estimates to show a better result for them. If you have given time to deriving accurate estimates, re-evaluation reinforces your data and gives little advantage.

Change task responsibilities

It is relatively easy to change task responsibilities, particularly with project management software. The first step is to look carefully at the critical path. As this dictates the total project time, if you can move resources from non-critical key stages to the critical key stages you can reduce the total project time. Remember, the non-critical key stages have float time so they get done later anyway. Moving resources should not affect the project cost, but be aware of the potential risks of doing this: an overrun of a critical key stage could impact on the non-critical key stages owing to lack of resources and change the critical path!

Just adding people to a key stage does not automatically proportionately reduce duration. Having more people increases the communication problems and may even cause confusion leading to loss of efficiency and higher costs. The consequent effects on the non-critical key stage are similar. Moving people is fine if you have enough of the right skills available, and the non-critical key stages must have sufficient float available to allow you to reduce their float times. Always ensure you do not use more than 60 per cent of available float in this activity.

You have another option available: to add more people, but this will increase the project cost. The reduction in schedule time is a trade-off against increased cost, and if this is not too significant, it may be acceptable to your customer and sponsor. However, it is better to review the assignments initially to see if you can reallocate the key stage responsibilities, or get your key stage owners to reallocate task responsibilities within each key stage.

Moving people around could improve performance and reduce time without affecting cost significantly. Replacing people with others having more expertise may help reduce time, but possibly increase cost. However, yours is not the only active project and the demands on the time of high performers may exceed their availability.

Crashing a schedule

When a high-priority project is looking as though it cannot meet delivery time requirements there is a temptation to 'crash the schedule'. This means compressing the critical path to shorten the whole project. The consequences are significant cost increase and the probability that the critical path will change, making the exercise complex. Any inaccuracy in the estimates will rapidly become visible when work starts.

If you do try to crash the schedule, derive a schedule of the impact on cost as shown in Figure 7.13.

Crashing a schedule can impact performance, affecting the quality of the work done and ultimately the deliverables. This is usually not an acceptable option. Another consequence is the need for people to work longer hours and overtime costs, which may not proportionately improve output.

Do not confuse crashing with fast-tracking. Fast-tracking involves overlapping activities that are traditionally done in sequence. This technique can be used sometimes on parts of a project but involves considerable risk of extending the schedule and cost.

Revising the business case

If attempts to optimize at the project level do not produce the desired result, you must resort to reviewing the business case. This requires the authority of the customer and sponsor and possibly other stakeholders. The obvious start point is the revision of the deliverables, either quality or quantity. Reducing the quality of the deliverables may reduce the market potential so a complete re-evaluation of the initial requirements must be conducted. If you consider you are proposing to build a battleship when compliance to requirements only needs a frigate, you could improve the value of the deliverables.

				CRASH IMPACT SCHEDULE				
PROJECT TITLE:						**PROJECT No:**		
PROJECT MANAGER:						**Prepared by:**		
PROJECT SPONSOR:						**Date:**		
CUSTOMER:						**Version No:**		
Line No:	Key stage No:	Current duration	Current cost £000's	Compressed duration	Compressed cost £000's	Cum. increased cost £000's	Float time left	Priority
1	AA	15	10	8	18	8	0	5
2	AB	10	7	6	11	12	0	2
3	AC	20	16	14	22	18	0	4
4	AD	12	9	9	11	20	3	
5	BA	18	15	13	20	25	0	3
6	BB	6	4	4	6	27	0	1
7	BC	14	12	10	17	32	0	3
8	BD	10	8	8	10	34	5	
TOTALS		105	81	72	115	34		

Figure 7.13 Example crash impact schedule

Reviewing this compliance could eliminate some tasks and/or reduce the estimates of duration. Focus initially on the critical tasks to reduce the schedule time. If the project is over budget, a cost–benefit analysis is necessary to evaluate the trade-offs of each benefit against the cost using the *work breakdown structure*.

If the business case is revised, you must seek approval of the customer and sponsor before resubmitting the business case to the PST for acceptance.

Whatever solution you finally derive, do not forget to update the key stage Gantt chart and review the risks on the project risk log to identify whether any risks have changed category, probability or impact.

With a final Gantt chart produced, you must decide that there is no further improvement needed or it is the best result you can achieve. Before you go through the final steps of tidying up your project plan it is advisable to present this schedule informally to your customer and project sponsor to check whether it is acceptable. If it is not, then you must seek alternative solutions through further optimization. If the schedule is nominally agreed, you can proceed to the final steps of planning before seeking PST approval to launch the actual work.

REVIEWING YOUR PROJECT RISK LOG

Refer to your project risk log and review all the risks identified during the project definition phase. Ask:

- Have any changed status?
- Are there any new HIGH risks? Identify actions on a risk management form.
- Are there any new risks identified from planning?

In reviewing risks it is tempting to avoid having any HIGH risks listed – after all, it saves paperwork, but does it reflect reality? Remember, as project manager you are responsible for project performance. If you knowingly misrank a risk, who are you kidding? It could backfire on you later, so carefully debate the quantifying and ranking of *all* risks with the team and agree a result. Identify the triggers for the risks identified.

Examine your plan to identify possible risk areas (refer back to Checklist 9, p 114):

- tasks on the critical path (and inside a key stage);
- tasks with a long duration (low capacity factors);
- tasks succeeding a merge in the network;
- tasks with little float left (where is the float?);
- tasks dependent on third parties;
- tags and leads;
- START-TO-START relationships;
- tasks using several people (particularly at different times);
- complex tasks;
- anything involving a steep learning curve;
- tasks using new or unproved technology.

If any risks are no longer likely to occur, do not remove them from the log; only remove the status ranking and leave these columns blank.

Prepare risk management forms for any new HIGH risks identified or those that have moved up in ranking, and derive risk mitigation plans where appropriate. These are copied with the risk log appropriately dated as a new issue into the project file and to the sponsor. Assign responsibilities for day-to-day monitoring of risks to the key stage owners. Stress the importance of monitoring for the triggers that could signal a risk becoming an issue. Avoiding a risk is better than a damage limitation exercise later!

> Remember – any risk that happens becomes an issue, and this requires you to take prompt action.

REVIEWING YOUR PROJECT BUDGET

At this point, now that the base plan is complete and you are confident you have an acceptable schedule, review the project budget. Begin by updating the project WBS with all the lower-level detail – or at least as much as you can at this stage. This is the easiest way to work out the cost of each, based on:

- capital equipment costs;
- resource direct costs – based on cost rates;
- revenue costs for the project team: materials, expenses, etc;
- indirect costs – chargeable overheads, etc.

With the costs of each key stage identified you can produce an *operating budget* as a cumulative amount aggregated against the schedule time. This is the real budget for project control purposes. If it varies significantly from the original *approved budget* as shown in the business case or one you were given by the sponsor then this variance must be investigated and the conflict resolved. If an increased cost is identified then the customer will need to be consulted for approval. Prepare for this discussion by deriving some alternate options as you did when optimizing the schedule earlier. The operating budget must be submitted to the PST for approval when you seek authority to pass through Phase Gate Three to project execution.

Generally, a small increase in cost has far less significant impact on the benefits than an increase in project time, particularly for new products. Keep a record of all costs for control measurement and variance analysis as your project proceeds.

INTERMEDIATE PHASE GATES

Larger projects with high work content or several sub-projects generally take a longer time to complete. Although you will conduct regular project reviews, the PST also needs to understand the true status of the project as you proceed. The intermediate phase gates during the execution phase provide an opportunity for the PST to conduct an intermediate review. Intermediate phase gates can be fixed at significant points in the schedule:

- when particular sub-projects are due to complete;
- when a particular project in a programme is due to complete;
- where a major sub-contract is due to complete;
- where one or more intermediate deliverables are expected.

In fact, any significant event in the life cycle can be designated an intermediate phase gate. I suggest that you propose the dates for these gates in consultation with your sponsor and then include these in your schedule. For each intermediate phase gate you should clearly indicate:

- date of the gate in the schedule;
- what is expected to be achieved and the completion criteria;
- the budget cost of the work done at the gate.

The PST treats these intermediate phase gates as being of equal importance to the primary phase gates. When you approach an intermediate phase gate, you are required to make a presentation to the PST that at least includes:

- what has been achieved;
- the budget cost of the work done at the gate;
- the actual cost of the work done at the gate;
- the progress of the whole project;
- a report of current risk level;
- outstanding issues and actions to resolve;
- forecast dates for remaining intermediate phase gates;
- forecast dates for project completion.
- forecast project cost at completion;
- any variances to the business plan.

The project essentially comes to a temporary halt until the PST approves the opening of an intermediate phase gate. Occasionally the 'GO' decision may not be given if any part of the work completed is considered unacceptable and rework is required. It is more likely that you will be given a conditional 'GO' decision to continue the project. If costs are starting to escalate seriously, the PST must consider additional funding requirements or make a decision to delay, rescope or cancel the project.

Ensure that the intermediate phase gates are clearly shown in your plan before seeking approval to proceed to the execution phase. As a guide, set the gates at approximately three- to four-month intervals or at intervals of 25 per cent of the total schedule time.

SEEKING APPROVAL TO LAUNCH YOUR PROJECT

You have now completed the planning phase as far as necessary before launching the project work. At this point, plan documentation comprises:

- a list of key stages;
- the project logic diagram;
- a project key stage responsibility chart;
- responsibility charts if appropriate for each key stage;
- a record of estimates for all the key stages;
- an optimized project Gantt chart for the key stages;
- Gantt charts for the early key stages or, if possible, all of them;
- an updated and reviewed project risk log;
- risk management forms for new HIGH risks;
- a project operating budget;
- an updated project brief if appropriate.

Go through Checklist 14 to make sure you have not forgotten anything! The steps you have taken to arrive at this stage of the project are shown in the flow diagram in Figure 7.14 (p 166).

Call the key stakeholders together for you to present these documents and explain the plan. Request them to approve the plan, which you then 'freeze' as the *baseline plan*. You can now inform the PST administrator that you are ready to present the plan to the PST and request approval to pass through Phase Gate Three and launch the project into the *execution phase*. Up to this point, the financial commitment made by the organization has been principally in people costs. The next phase could involve a significant step change in costs, so the PST will need to review detailed plans and supporting data to come to a 'GO' decision. Do not prepare your presentation until you are sure you have all the data you need to fully justify such a decision.

Do not allow your team to assume that approval is a foregone conclusion and start work on the execution phase. This could be a costly error if the PST decides to suspend or cancel the project.

CHECKLIST 14: A BASELINE PLAN CHECKLIST

Ask:

- Is the project brief still completely valid?
- Is the scope of work statement still valid?
- Has the project manager's authority been confirmed in writing?

- Are all stakeholders identified?
- Does the team understand who manages the stakeholders?
- Is the WBS developed as far as practicable?
- Does the WBS include all project administration tasks?
- Are customer and sign-off checkpoint meetings included?
- Is the critical path established and agreed?
- Are all key stages allocated for responsibility?
- Are key stage owners clear about their responsibilities?
- Is the project risk log complete and up to date?
- Are estimation records in the project file?
- Has a project calendar been established?
- Are resource loadings and capacities optimized and agreed?
- Does the Gantt chart reflect an agreed plan and schedule?
- Has the project's operating budget been derived and approved?
- Does the team include all the skills needed?
- Has action been taken to acquire unavailable skills needed for the project?
- Are the team members working well together?
- Have any conflicts been resolved promptly and effectively?
- Is intra-team communication working well?
- Is the project sponsor performing in accordance with his or her defined role?
- Are there any conflicts with the business plan?

Add additional questions to ask as appropriate.

SUMMARY

Figure 7.14 gives the process flow diagram for the steps in planning the project. Checklist 15 summarizes the key leadership actions to focus on during the planning phase.

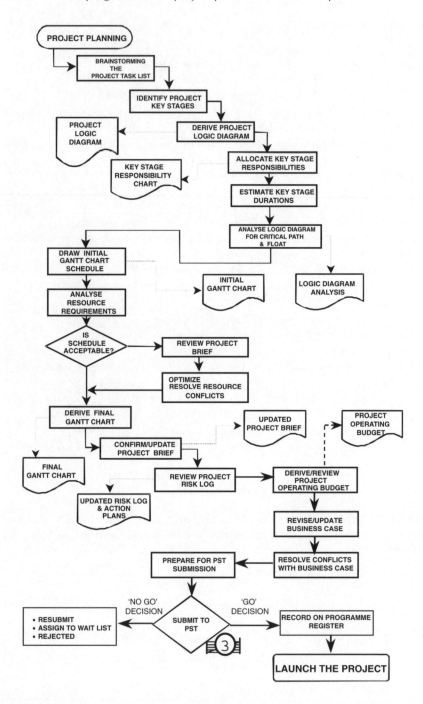

Figure 7.14 Process flow diagram: project planning

CHECKLIST 15: KEY LEADERSHIP ACTIONS DURING PROJECT PLANNING

- Project stakeholders:
  - Gather relevant data.
  - Consult regularly with customer and end user.
  - Involve in planning.
  - Use their skills and experience.
- Project tasks:
  - Confirm any special skills required.
  - Prioritize the work.
  - Decide what planning tools to use.
  - Confirm options.
  - Set standards.
- Project team:
  - Involve in all aspects of planning.
  - Encourage creativity.
  - Structure as appropriate.
  - Focus on short-term priorities.
  - Encourage consensus.
  - Confirm roles.
  - Explain all decisions.
- Team members:
  - Encourage participation.
  - Uncover past experience.
  - Listen so as to understand.
  - Respond to questions.
  - Agree personal targets.
  - Maintain enthusiasm and commitment.
  - Coach and develop skills.
  - Confirm responsibilities.

8

Launching your project

Congratulations, the PST has approved your plan and schedule, so now you are ready to start the project work. If the PST has given you a qualified 'GO' decision, you must take account of any changes required. There are still a few activities you need to give some attention to before you hit the 'GO' button. You produced a final Gantt chart for the key stages and analysed this for your resource needs when you optimized the schedule to meet the customer requirements. At this stage these resource requirements are not really a commitment. Certainly you may have received some promises from individuals and even their line managers but you cannot continue with the work on the basis of mere promises. You need to take such statements a stage further to be sure resources are available to you just when the plan tells you they are required. If the sponsor has adequately stressed the context and priority of the project, you can rely on this being clearly understood by all line managers providing resources and you will not be let down! The PST's approval will have been communicated to all departments by the PST administrator, which will help you get the commitment you now need.

Are you really that confident? The key stage owners for the early key stages should have identified all the tasks to be carried out in each. This task list is the basis of ensuring that you get the commitment you need.

ESTABLISHING KEY STAGE WORK PLANS

Consider what happens when you assign some work to someone. The first thing most people do is to work out how and when they are going to do the work, even if it is only a simple 'to do' list. There is no reason why you cannot do this for them. Ask the key stage owners to verify their task lists, making sure they have not forgotten any tasks. If appropriate, even get them to work out the logic diagram for the key stage using the same techniques as you used earlier. Then record the task list on a *key stage work plan chart* (see Figure 8.1).

You will notice that this template records some important information for the key stage under consideration:

1. the key stage code as recorded on the WBS;
2. the key stage schedule START and END dates, whether the key stage is critical and the calculated float;
3. the duration of each task in the key stage using consistent units;
4. the amount of float in each task if this has been calculated;
5. the name of the person responsible for carrying out the task;
6. the planned START and END dates for each task;
7. a record of the actual START and END dates for each task.

Once the work plan is complete, confirm that all the tasks:

● are allocated to someone for responsibility;
● have plan start and end dates;
● are realistic and achievable within the total time planned for the key stage without using the float time or additional contingency.

Then submit the document for sign-off and approval by the key stage owner and yourself. This sign-off also allows you to verify that the task list does not:

● include tasks that you do not want done or consider unnecessary;
● omit some tasks that you consider essential to your project;
● contain any obvious errors of estimating.

If the resources employed are not reporting to you full time, then get the work plan accepted and signed off by the line manager(s) involved as a commitment. Copy the work plans produced in this way to the people involved and their line managers. This reminds them of the contract they have concluded with you.

Of course, the work plan may show that it is not possible to carry out all the tasks within the time allowed for the key stage. You must use your skill as a negotiator and influencer to seek a way to resolve the conflicts you can identify. Take the same approach to optimization as you used when deriving your original Gantt chart. Your choices are limited but usually enough to come up with a satisfactory and acceptable solution:

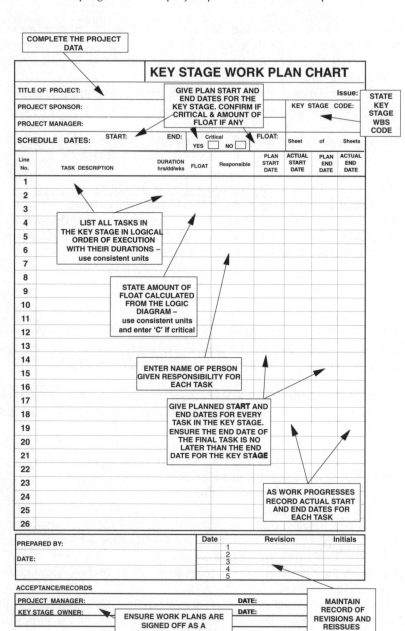

COMPLETE THE PROJECT DATA

KEY STAGE WORK PLAN CHART

TITLE OF PROJECT:

PROJECT SPONSOR:

PROJECT MANAGER:

SCHEDULE DATES: START: END:

GIVE PLAN START AND END DATES FOR THE KEY STAGE. CONFIRM IF CRITICAL & AMOUNT OF FLOAT IF ANY

Issue:

KEY STAGE CODE:

Critical YES ☐ NO ☐ FLOAT:

Sheet of Sheets

STATE KEY STAGE WBS CODE

Line No.	TASK DESCRIPTION	DURATION hrs/dd/wks	FLOAT	Responsible	PLAN START DATE	ACTUAL START DATE	PLAN END DATE	ACTUAL END DATE
1								
2								
3								
4								
5								
6								
7								
8								
9								
10								
11								
12								
13								
14								
15								
16								
17								
18								
19								
20								
21								
22								
23								
24								
25								
26								

LIST ALL TASKS IN THE KEY STAGE IN LOGICAL ORDER OF EXECUTION WITH THEIR DURATIONS – use consistent units

STATE AMOUNT OF FLOAT CALCULATED FROM THE LOGIC DIAGRAM – use consistent units and enter 'C' if critical

ENTER NAME OF PERSON GIVEN RESPONSIBILITY FOR EACH TASK

GIVE PLANNED START AND END DATES FOR EVERY TASK IN THE KEY STAGE. ENSURE THE END DATE OF THE FINAL TASK IS NO LATER THAN THE END DATE FOR THE KEY STAGE

AS WORK PROGRESSES RECORD ACTUAL START AND END DATES FOR EACH TASK

PREPARED BY:

DATE:

	Date	Revision	Initials
1			
2			
3			
4			
5			

ACCEPTANCE/RECORDS

PROJECT MANAGER: DATE:

KEY STAGE OWNER: DATE:

ENSURE WORK PLANS ARE SIGNED OFF AS A COMMITMENT. INCLUDE LINE MANAGER AS APPROPRIATE

MAINTAIN RECORD OF REVISIONS AND REISSUES

Figure 8.1 Example of the key stage work plan chart

- Seek more resource capacity.
- Obtain more resources.
- Review and modify the logic inside the key stage.
- Amend the scope or quality of the work.

Using the *key stage work plan chart* is also a convenient way to record the progress of tasks to completion.

This process may seem at first sight to be time-consuming and onerous, but the people doing the work have to make some sort of plan. You are only asking them to use a consistent and disciplined approach to work planning. You do not need to produce all the key stage work plan charts at the outset, just those for the first few key stages. As the project continues, at any point you can work proactively to prepare more work plans, taking into full account everything that has happened in the project. This is termed 'layering the plan' as the project proceeds. It is more effective and less time-consuming, minimizing replanning of detail due to changes. If the logic diagrams for each key stage are worked out then turn these into individual Gantt charts for the key stages. This family of charts at the second level of planning should align with your overall key stage Gantt chart.

Having satisfied yourself that the early work plans are acceptable, you now need to decide where to locate the milestones of your project.

DERIVING A MILESTONE SCHEDULE

Recall the earlier diagram relating the schedule to risks and issues (see Figure 8.2). Replace 'schedule' with milestones, since these are all the significant events that are due to occur during the execution of the project. Like the lump of stone beside the highway, the *milestone* is a flag or signal at some clearly defined point in the project. That signal indicates that something special should have happened or is about to happen. The milestone is therefore an instrument of control, effectively placing target points in the project schedule for certain events to be signed off as completed.

There are two types of milestone in the plan: 1) key milestones – the phase gates and intermediate gates; and 2) schedule milestones – set to identify a major event in the schedule. The key milestones comprise the fixed phase gates when PST approval is required to pass the gate. The PST can also require additional intermediate phase gates to be inserted in the schedule, particularly during the execution phase, which is expected normally to take the largest chunk of the project time.

What are the schedule events? Really, they can be anything identified as a target that is significant in the project. However, this does not mean that

PROJECT MILESTONES

PROJECT SCHEDULE

Contains inherent unknowns

If unresolved, impact the schedule

RISKS   *Occur to become*   **ISSUES**

Figure 8.2 The risks–issues–schedule triangle

everything is a milestone. Key stages and tasks on the critical path are by their nature types of milestones, so do not make them all milestones. Focus on events that have measurable deliverables.

Some of the common events given the status of project milestones are:

- completion of a key task, eg providing output to third parties;
- completion of one of the project deliverables;
- stage generation of benefits;
- completion of third-party significant event, eg acceptance tests;
- completion of third-party activity, eg delivery of equipment or data;
- a financial audit point;
- a project audit point;
- a quality audit;
- completion of a significant stage of work (possibly a critical element);
- a significant decision point, eg whether to abort the project;
- completion of a project stage to release further funding – called a phase gate.

Each key stage owner must suggest where to locate the milestones in their key stage and agree these in a team meeting. The frequency of milestones in a network must be sufficient for effective control. Record the list of milestones on a schedule and on the Gantt chart. For effective control, *all* milestones must be measurable with clearly established metrics – apply the SMART test.

> Think of the milestones as the 'marker posts' to show the route to the finishing post: project completion. For a successful project you must reach each milestone on time or be prepared to explain why a slippage has occurred.

An example template for the milestone schedule is given in Figure 8.3.

CRITICAL SUCCESS FACTORS

You might be asked to identify critical success factors (CSFs) for your project. These are a means of identifying progress towards a successful outcome. Two types are relevant: *process type* and *project type*.

Process CSFs are those associated with the strategy you employ to achieve success. These include the tools, techniques, processes and procedures you use to define, plan, execute and complete the project on time, to the budget. Therefore, they include the following:

- The project's objectives, deliverables and benefits are defined.
- A sponsor is appointed and sustains support and commitment to the project.
- The stakeholders are regularly consulted and kept informed of project status.
- An appropriate team is formed and the right skills are utilized.
- A carefully crafted and scheduled plan exists and is kept up to date.
- Everyone understands control procedures for monitoring and tracking progress.
- The WBS is maintained accurately as you continue to layer the plan.
- Project sign-off and approval processes are maintained.
- Project risks are regularly reviewed and monitored.
- Project issues are resolved promptly at the appropriate level of management.
- Reporting and communication procedures are established and working well.

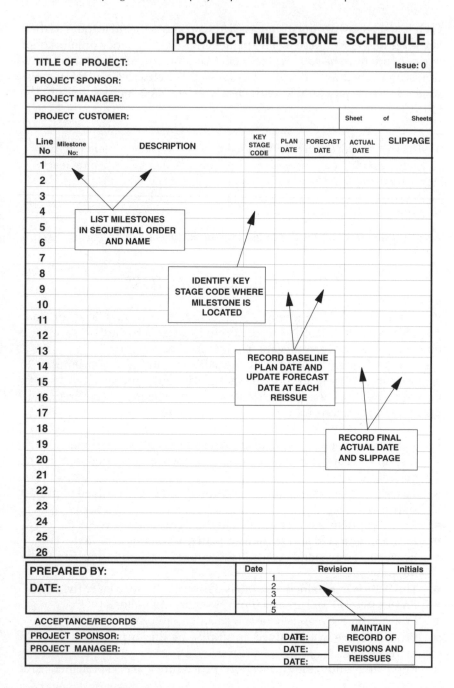

Figure 8.3 Example project milestone schedule

Project factors are derived from the list of deliverables and benefits, particularly if the latter start to produce a yield before completion. Do not select all deliverables as CSFs; rather, select just three or four. Identify those for which you can easily derive some metrics and agree how to measure progress. Although the budget is regarded as a measurable factor, it is only one way of measuring progress and does not always signify success!

Whatever you select as a CSF, check that it is acceptable to your key stakeholders – the customer and your sponsor – as they can use this as a means of measuring performance.

ENSURING EFFECTIVE COMMUNICATION

Communication in project work is the glue that holds everything together! Poor communication is a major source of conflict and slippages, so give this serious attention before you start the project work. Ask yourself:

- who needs to know;
- what they need to know;
- how much they need to know;
- how often they must be informed.

Establish distribution list(s) as appropriate but avoid generating large volumes of paper that few will ever read. The focal point for all communication is you. You must decide the ground rules you will impose on everyone involved to get prompt feedback of the prevailing situation with the work in progress. Effective monitoring and tracking of the project is dependent on good communication in the team, between you and the team and your key stakeholders. You need prompt feedback about:

- current progress of the active tasks;
- problems encountered with the work;
- problems anticipated with work waiting to be done;
- technical difficulties being encountered.

Reporting in a project environment requires you to have a continuous awareness of what is happening and what is due to happen next. Promptly identify any problems that interfere with progress. You must be promptly alerted of potential changes to the plan that become apparent as a result of work in progress. Lay out the ground rules for an *early warning system*; it can save a great deal of rework later and reduce the risk of replanning causing project delays. Agree the ground rules with your team so they all accept they are not being asked to do things they consider unnecessary. Stress that you intend to operate an 'open door' policy – even if you do not have an office door! You are always willing to make time available to discuss difficulties and give help and guidance.

Your open door policy effectively means that you:

- are always ready to listen to their concerns and difficulties associated with meeting the schedule requirements;
- want regular verbal reports as well as documented reports of the project's progress;
- want to be informed promptly of any risks identified;
- need to be told if anyone anticipates a problem or risk occurring – however trivial it may appear to be.

Work with your team to create a climate for regular sharing of information in the interests of continuous improvement. Evaluate performance, not to apportion blame when things do not go according to plan but to learn and improve performance.

> Maintain everyone's focus on achieving the project's objectives on time, to the budget and to the quality desired by your customer.

PROJECT STATUS REPORTS

Your key stakeholders expect to receive regular status reports. Decide the frequency of these with your project sponsor. In practice, status reports are an administrative headache for many people. Some will avoid reports completely if possible; others will write a note of just a few lines. Some people are delighted to spend a whole afternoon compiling a thorough and detailed report blow by blow of everything they have done. It is an opportunity for literary abuse or verbosity, so set the standard and quality you require. In today's electronic environment it is tempting to use e-mail and copy to almost the whole organization! Tell the team members what you expect of them irrespective of the methods employed. Long reports are often only scanned and not fully digested, with key issues being lost among the jargon and detail. Try to avoid jargon if reports are likely to go to people who have a different jargon dictionary from you and your team. Define clearly any jargon you do use so there is no opportunity for misunderstandings to occur later.

The PST will require you to present a status report at each intermediate phase gate. Ask yourself just what you need to clearly define the current status of the project. Tell the team how you want these reports given and their frequency.

At any point in the project you want to know:

- what has been completed;
- what has not been completed and why;
- what is being done about the incomplete work;
- what problems remain unsolved;
- what needs to be done about these unsolved problems;
- what difficulties are anticipated in the work waiting to be done;
- what risks have occurred and the actions taken to resolve them.

It is appropriate to use a single-page standard template for reporting the project's progress. You could use the key stage work plan charts, although these are not focused enough for control purposes.

The *project status report* (Figure 8.4) highlights progress using the milestones fixed earlier. The essential inputs to the report are:

- a concise summary of overall progress;
- a list of milestones due to be passed since the last report and their current status, ie passed on time, late, etc;
- a list of milestones due in the next reporting period, with their expected dates;
- actions set in place to correct any slipped milestones;
- forecasts for the project's completion based on current information;
- reasons for any revision to earlier forecasts to completion;
- changes to the project risk log and the project milestone schedule;
- any issues outstanding for resolution.

No one likes to hear bad news, but the sooner it is exposed, the quicker you can react to limit the damage and take corrective action. You can use this template at any level in the project. Ask your key stage owners to use it to report progress on each key stage in this way. Similarly, you can use the same template to report to the key stakeholders.

Agree the frequency of reporting with your project sponsor. If you are not confident of the veracity of any report, you can soon investigate at a more detailed level. At least you are keeping the formal paper volume to a minimum.

Remember that issues arise from risks that actually happen, even if you failed to identify them as risks. The managing of issues will be discussed in detail in Chapter 9.

Throughout the project, make sure everyone understands who is responsible for carrying out the separate parts of the project and give your support and guidance whenever it is needed. This includes securing the help of others when necessary in the interests of the project. Good

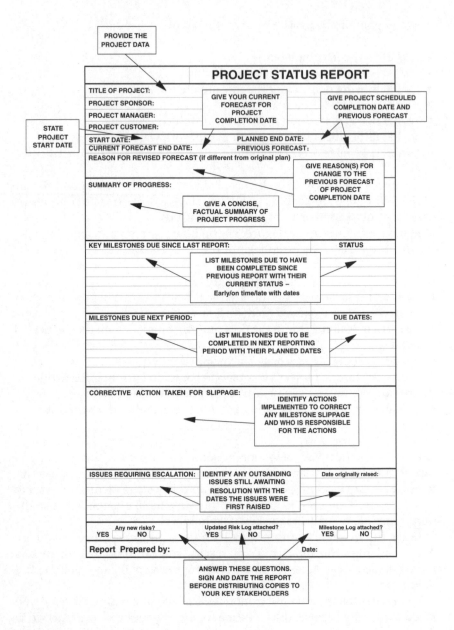

Figure 8.4 Example of the project status report

teamwork is directly related to effective and regular communication. The other element of communication you must consider is the meetings schedule.

DERIVING A MEETINGS SCHEDULE FOR YOUR PROJECT

The subject of meetings and making them effective is a topic that has received a huge amount of attention, and numerous works exist to guide you. You must now decide what meetings are essential to the project process:

- one-to-one meetings with the project sponsor;
- one-to-one meetings with your team members;
- project progress meetings with the team;
- problem-solving meetings;
- meetings with particular stakeholders;
- project review meetings with the stakeholders.

All are necessary at different frequencies throughout the project, but do not convene a meeting unless you have good reason and a clear purpose. The one-to-one meetings are very important in order to maintain close contact with your sponsor and the members of your team. They are the only way you can really get to know these people as individuals and give and receive information at a personal level. This contributes to the creation of a motivating climate in your team, encouraging open communication and sustaining the focus on the project's success. It is also the forum for discussing problems and resolving issues of a more personal nature that impact on the performance of the project work.

Apart from giving guidance and support, you may need to coach team members sometimes, recognize their efforts and take action to promote personal development. These are all things you must do to build a successful project team. Set up a schedule in your diary for regular one-to-one meetings (say monthly) with each team member. Decide with your sponsor how often you should meet, and enter these meetings in your diary. Allow 30–45 minutes for these informal one-to-one discussions.

Problem-solving meetings tend to be *ad hoc* as problems arise, involving specific people, which may not mean the whole team. Consider including other experts, invited to give help and advice. Do not mix problem solving with progress or team meetings, as the discussion easily gets out of control and the meeting becomes diverted from its purpose.

Agree a schedule of project progress meetings, preferably throughout the whole project, showing the schedule dates on the key stage Gantt chart. This does not mean you must necessarily hold such meetings. It does mean that everyone knows they must be available to attend and not interpret any schedule date as an opportunity to take a day's holiday! If you have nothing to discuss, cancel or postpone any meeting. Decide the frequency to suit your needs and the size of the project. Weekly short meetings at the start or end of a week are good for small to medium-sized projects if all the team are on the same site. If your team is multi-site, the frequency is likely to be monthly, so you must confirm you have opened other communication channels where appropriate – e-mail or video link meetings.

Project review meetings with your stakeholders are less frequent and are not to be confused with PST reviews. Reviews with the stakeholders usually involve you in preparing much more material to present formally to the group. Ideally, limit these meetings to three or four in a 12-month period. The PST can require a review at any time apart from the phase gates.

MANAGING PROJECT CHANGES

Yes, you are certain to face changes as the project proceeds! Manage change – don't let change manage you. However carefully the plans are prepared, there are certain to be some aspects of the work that produce unexpected surprises. Few projects get completed exactly as planned. Rigid schedules and budgets rarely work, and since change is inevitable, managing the impact of change is a key aspect of managing the project. Uncontrolled change can sink the whole project. Minor changes appear during effective monitoring and are controlled by prompt reaction and taking corrective measures. Significant change is much more serious and must have a closer scrutiny before implementation is permitted. These changes can come from anywhere. A customer or end user can request a change because of changes to their needs or their working environment. A serious technical problem may signal a major change, causing replanning of the project and modifying the objectives.

Any change that is expected to create a replanning activity and affect the total project time as currently scheduled must be handled in a formal manner. The primary elements of change management to consider include:

- the source of the change request;
- the benefits from making the change;
- the consequences of doing nothing at this stage;
- the cost impact of making the change and the effect on the operating budget;
- the effect on project constraints;

- the effect on resource needs;
- whether there is an increase or decrease in project risks;
- the effect on the objectives and scope of the project.

Major change can have a demotivating effect on the team unless it is something they have sought in the interests of the project. Large changes are not implemented until after careful consideration of the consequences for the project, and even for other active projects. A major change on one project could have serious impact on the resource availability for another project. The customer and the sponsor must approve all major change before action is taken to replan. In most situations some work is necessary to examine alternative solutions and their impact on the schedule before an agreement is reached with the customer.

> Change management is the process through which changes to cost, schedule, scope or benefits are identified, evaluated and approved or rejected.

Sources of change

Changes to any project can come from many sources, including:

- changes to business needs or requirements driven by the customer, sponsor or other stakeholders;
- changes to the market conditions;
- changes to the business;
- issues arising during the project;
- technical failures or deficiencies;
- potential enhancements identified during the project work;
- errors or omissions discovered by the team doing the work.

Change is a modification of the original baseline project environment set by the business case and your plans that has been approved by the PST at Phase Gate Three. One of the most significant problems you will encounter is *scope creep*. This is due to a large number of apparently very minor changes or additional requirements being added as you proceed. The cumulative impact of these changes is often hidden until a point is reached when the effect on the schedule is suddenly visible on the horizon. Danger signals start to light up and then you have a major damage limitation exercise on your hands. The problem can be avoided sometimes by collecting a group of minor changes together and adding them to the project as one change.

It is essential to keep your team alert to such creeping changes to minimize the consequences. Delaying some changes to a later follow-on project as future enhancements may be an option you can use.

Issues arising during the project execution must be resolved promptly and may lead to changes to the schedule or, in extreme situations, may change the business case. Then the impact assessment could highlight that the project is no longer viable and should be cancelled. This is always a difficult decision to make but should not be treated as a failure. On the contrary, a decision to cancel at the right point in time before excessive costs are incurred should be treated as a success.

The change management process

Since change can have such disastrous effects on your project, it is most advisable to institute a formal process to identify, assess and track performance of implementing change. A flow diagram of the process is shown in Figure 8.5. The essential steps are:

- Identify change and record it on the project change log.
- Analyse the change for impact on the project, and record on the change request form.
- Seek acceptance as appropriate from key stakeholders.
- Modify as appropriate to obtain acceptance or outright rejection.
- Seek approval from the project manager or sponsor as appropriate.
- Sign off the change request form for implementation to proceed.
- Record approval on the project change log.
- Inform the originator of the decision.
- Implement actions to effect the change.
- Track implementation.
- When the change is completed satisfactorily, record the fact on the project change log.
- Sign off the change request form to show that the change is closed.

Agree authority levels for accepting and approving change requests with your sponsor. A change does not always need immediate implementation and may be delayed or have other conditions attached. Once a change is completed satisfactorily, the project documentation must be updated and, if appropriate, the business case revised accordingly.

The project change log

It is important that you maintain a complete record of all the changes that occur in your project. Not all the changes that occur are considered

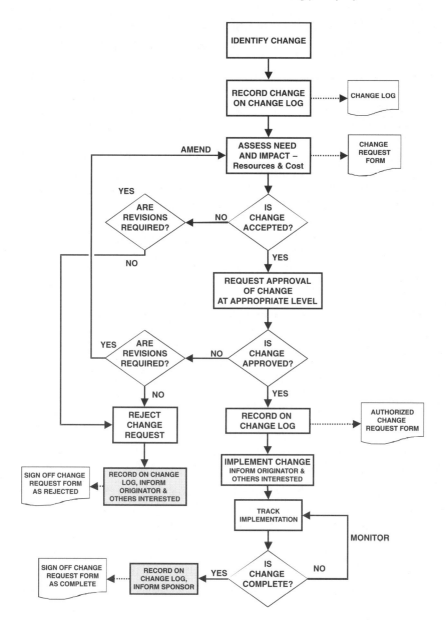

Figure 8.5 Process flow diagram: change management

essential, and some are rejected, but you should still record them for later reference and evaluation. An example *project change log* is shown in Figure 8.6.

All possible changes must be recorded, and none is deleted from the log even when rejected or closed. The log gives a summary of changes and the subsequent actions taken with appropriate dates. The status at any time is readily available as:

- open (O) – change in process either under analysis, awaiting approval or under implementation;
- closed (C) – change implementation completed satisfactorily;
- rejected (R) – change rejected as unnecessary.

Ensure that all the team members are involved in change management and understand the process.

The change request form

All changes that occur are analysed and the results recorded on the *change request form*. An example is shown in Figure 8.7. The form summarizes all the key information needed to help the approval process to arrive at a decision.

Apart from recording the key elements of the impact of the proposed change, the form records any risks identified from making the change and records the decisions made on acceptance or rejection, approval, implementation and closure of the change.

Accountability for change decisions

All proposed changes must be reviewed and a decision made by someone. The PST can proscribe the level of decision making. Table 8.1 gives an example of the approvals required in a change process.

It is good practice to have these levels of authority detailed in the business case to avoid any confusion later. If the impact of a change in one project has a serious consequence on another interdependent project in a programme then the sponsor should bring this situation to the attention of the PST.

Avoid the clever stuff!

It is too easy to be swamped by changes in a project, and particularly changes that are clever enhancements to the results. Unless these are really required by the customer, don't do it. Yes, it looks good and clever,

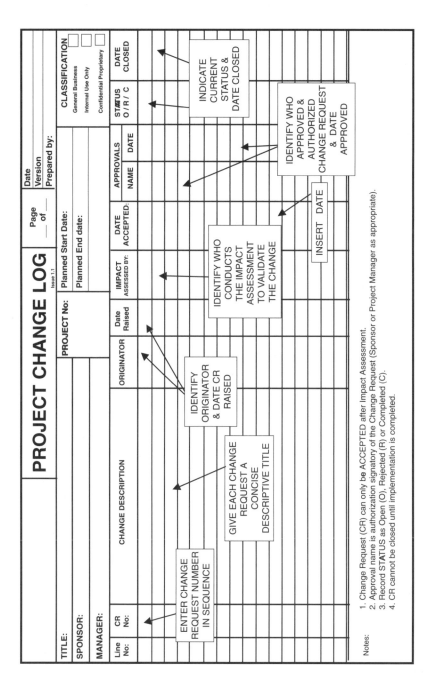

Figure 8.6 Example project change log

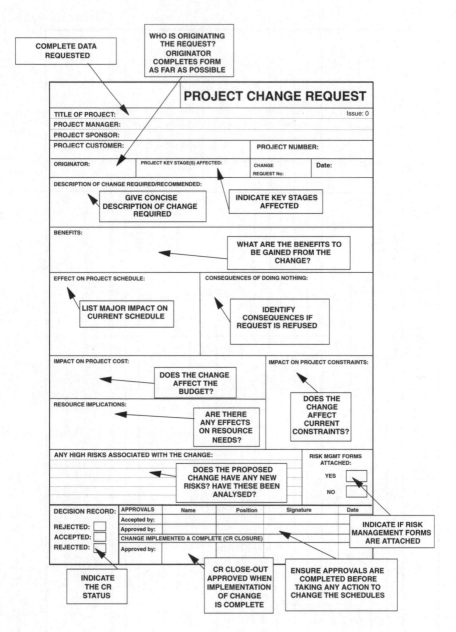

Figure 8.7 Example change request form

Table 8.1 Approvals that may be required in a change process

Impact of change	Approval required by Programme	Project in programme	Stand-alone project	Sub-project
No impact on schedule, cost or scope	Programme manager	Project manager	Project manager	Project manager
Some impact on schedule or costs – within scope of agreed contingencies	Programme sponsor	Programme manager	Project sponsor	Project manager
Significant impact on scope, objectives and benefits and affecting the business case – may be beyond sponsor's authority	Programme steering team	Programme steering team	Programme steering team	Programme/project sponsor or Programme steering team

but always consider whether there is a cost impact for giving something that is not essential. Remember that the cost implication applies not just during the project but also, possibly, in the manufacture phase. The sales-people will be delighted with extra features to help them sell your product, but that does not mean the customer will be delighted and prepared to pay more.

HOLDING A LAUNCH MEETING

Now you have prepared everything you need to launch the project. The final steps after completing the baseline plan include:

- incorporating any changes required by the PST;
- preparing work plan charts for the early key stages;
- deriving a milestone schedule for the project;
- deciding a progress reporting process with the templates everyone must use;
- agreeing a meetings schedule.

This launch meeting is a milestone in your project. It is the point from which all project work starts. Your purpose is to get together all the important people who are involved with your project and explain the plans in some detail. Decide whom you want to attend:

- the project sponsor;
- the customer;
- other key stakeholders – line managers providing you with resources;
- the project team.

Prepare yourself and your team well for the meeting. This is an important opportunity for you to explain the plan and the areas of high risk to achieving success. You are looking for acceptance from all those present that the project is well planned. You must convince them that with their co-operation you can achieve the objectives. Consider preparing a document package containing:

- the project organization chart;
- the project stakeholder list;
- the key stage Gantt chart;
- the key stage responsibility chart;
- the project brief;
- any other relevant information.

You can issue this information pack to participants at the meeting to help gain their commitment. No one can then later complain that they do not understand the project plan or what you are trying to achieve. It is an ideal opportunity for team building. The chances of getting the team and stakeholders together in a project are rare and this meeting helps them understand their responsibilities in an organizational context. This is an important event, so make it special – provide some lunch, if your budget allows! This encourages people to mix and talk together and get to know each other – contributing to good co-operation in the future.

CHECKLIST 16: THE PROJECT LAUNCH MEETING

Ask your sponsor to open the meeting, to:

- explain the context of the project in the organization's strategy;
- stress the priority of the project as compared with that of other active projects;
- focus on the importance of co-operation and support at all levels;
- reinforce the communication processes needed for success.

You take over the chair, to:

- introduce the project team;
- introduce the information pack;

- briefly explain the project's background;
- confirm the project's objectives and deliverables;
- identify all the project's benefits;
- explain the baseline plan, focusing on the critical elements, the areas of high risk and the schedule dates;
- set the ground rules for the communication processes, particularly status reporting;
- confirm everyone's understanding of his or her responsibilities;
- accept any relevant ideas and suggestions for improving the chances of success;
- respond to questions; commit yourself to responding to any questions that you cannot answer.

Celebrate the project's launch: provide a buffet lunch!

SUMMARY

The steps you take in the launching of your project are summarized in the flow diagram shown in Figure 8.8. Checklist 17 gives the key leadership actions for this part of the project.

CHECKLIST 17: KEY LEADERSHIP ACTIONS DURING A PROJECT LAUNCH

- Project stakeholders:
  - Confirm acceptance of the schedule.
  - Identify functional roles in its execution.
  - Agree reporting procedures.
  - Agree a meetings schedule.
  - Clarify stakeholders' responsibilities.
  - Confirm resource priorities and commitments.
- Project tasks:
  - Confirm that work plans are completed.
  - Clarify the project's objectives.
  - Explain the plan.
  - Explain the control procedures.
  - Hold a launch meeting.
- Project team:
  - Confirm key stage responsibilities.
  - Agree and approve all work plans.
  - Monitor team co-operation and communication.
  - React to conflict and resolve it.
  - Celebrate the launch with a team activity.
- Team members:
  - Encourage participation.
  - Recognize their efforts.
  - Act on grievances and concerns.
  - Confirm acceptance of short-term responsibilities.
  - Check non-project work commitments.
  - Guide and assist when appropriate.
  - Appraise performance.
  - Review personal targets and objectives.

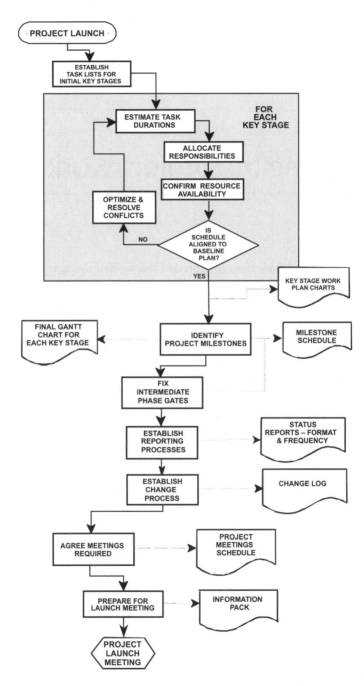

Figure 8.8 Process flow diagram: project launch

9

Executing the project work

After all the enthusiasm demonstrated at the launch meeting, you believe everyone is highly motivated and plunging into the project work. The reality is sometimes the opposite! After all the effort put into planning there is sometimes an 'adrenaline dip' when the team feels it should be doing something but nothing appears to happen! This is where you need to show your skills as a leader. Immediately after the launch meeting, call the team together for a very short team meeting. Give encouragement to reinforce the motivational level in the team. Check that there are no concerns, uncertainties or misunderstandings about the initial scheduled work. Ask them to tell you if any problems occur. Remind them to watch out for new risks and any signals that suggest that a risk is likely to happen and create an issue.

One of the most difficult areas of project work is new information coming in to the team members after the work starts. This is sometimes quite casual, through informal meetings in the corridor, staff restaurant or even the car park. It may come from lower-level sources in the customer's organization. The input is also intentional on occasions and could have profound effects on the work, the schedule and team motivation. Changes to the plan are often started because of this type of information flow. You must guard against any input creating more work than necessary and remind team members to inform you immediately of such situations.

You are asking your team to keep you informed of progress, so when additional information appears, you (and the team members) must question the source:

- Where does the information come from?
- Why was it not exposed before?
- Who has decided it is relevant now?
- Is the information accurate and realistic?

- Is there some hidden agenda associated with the timing?
- What impact does it have on the plan and schedule?
- Does this change the project's objectives, deliverables or benefits?

Project work can be seriously constrained, or even sabotaged, by the subtle transfer of erroneous information to a team member. A complete absence of information when it is due to appear can have similar sinister origins. You are flexible in your approach to the project and always ready to consider changes to your plan when essential. If the information and data essential to the project work are confused by mixed messages from different people in the customer's organization, the result will be conflicts and confusion. Prepare your team for these events because they are certain to occur at some time in the project's life – if you have not experienced them already!

Your *early warning system* is the best way to get feedback about what has happened and what needs to happen. This provides you with the information you need to control the project.

THE PROJECT CONTROL SYSTEM

Control of a project environment involves three operating modes:

- measuring – determining progress through formal and informal reporting;
- evaluating – determining the cause of deviations from the plan and how to react;
- correcting – taking actions to correct.

These form the essential elements of your control system. The plan and schedule are the foundation that determines what has to be done to satisfy the objectives set out in the project brief. Your objective is to regulate the activities, resources and events to achieve the results defined by the plan. Control is associated with the present, so reporting is time-sensitive to enable prompt decisions when deviations occur. If all reporting mechanisms give feedback a considerable time after the event, as a matter of history, then you cannot control your project. The communication processes you designed during the project launch are designed to give timely visibility to significant events.

System design

No amount of time and effort expended on planning, scheduling and resource assessment will compensate for a lack of effective monitoring and a sound *control system*. The purpose of this system is to ensure that you and the team always have the information to make an accurate assessment of what *has happened* and compare this with what *should have happened* according to the plan.

You compare these two inputs to establish whether there is a variance. The best control system is the simplest; making the procedures and collection of data complex only leads to higher costs and an increasing possibility of error. The basic inputs to control are the plan schedule and the actual results observed and measured by the team.

Figure 9.1 shows the essential elements of any control system. The comparison activity should show whether the project is on track and everything is going according to plan. If it is, you can update the project records and charts and report progress to your customer and sponsor. If progress is not to plan then it is important to identify the causes of any problems that are creating delays. Then develop solutions, preferably deriving several options before selecting the best or most appropriate. Prepare and implement an action plan to correct the difficulties and restore the project to the planned schedule. It is essential to measure the impact of action plans to provide feedback in the system and a check that the solution has worked.

Your control system must be capable of providing information on:

- the resource required – its availability and its effective use;
- equipment and machinery required and used;
- materials used, ordered and required;
- the costs incurred to date and forward commitments;
- the time used and float time remaining in active tasks;
- the results achieved – tasks completed;
- a valuation of the results – as expected?

Controlling the project means managing the many problems that arise to maintain the project schedule. You do this on a day-to-day basis through:

- monitoring the work – observing and checking what is happening;
- identifying and resolving the problems that arise;
- tracking the project – comparing progress with the plan and updating the records.

Although these are continuous activities, the schedule is easier to track if you use some additional specific control points. The milestone schedule gives you the clearly defined markers for control throughout the project. Focus the team on these marker points, stressing the importance of maintaining the dates. Tell the team you must know if any milestone date is expected to slip. Remind them that the total float is not spare time for them to use by choice without reference to you.

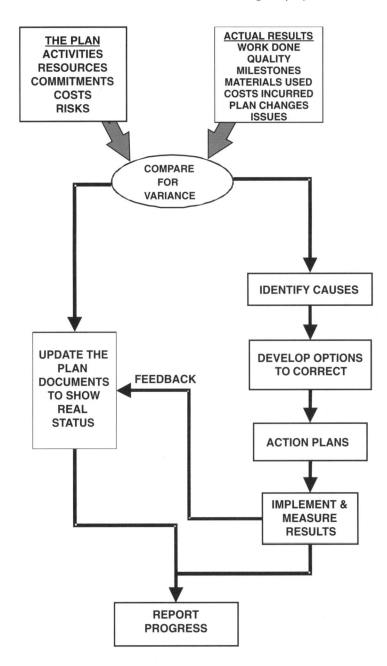

Figure 9.1 The essential elements of a control system

One of the most time-consuming activities in project work is the administration. Good control of any process is dependent on accurate data, so make a special effort to keep the project file up to date. This involves a regular check and update of:

- the project organization chart;
- the stakeholder list;
- the key stage responsibility charts;
- the project brief;
- the key stage Gantt chart;
- the key stage work plan charts;
- the project risk log;
- the milestone chart;
- the business case when significant changes occur.

Depending on the size of the project, you can speed up the administration process using a project management software package – once you are familiar with its many features! Keeping the project file up to date is an obligation you must fulfil. You could be moved to another project at any time and someone else have to take over. Do ensure that the legacy you leave behind is a good one, otherwise you will continually be subject to queries and requests that interfere with your new role.

Controlling a project takes time and effort and is a key part of the project manager's role. Stress the importance of status reports and keep them concise and factual. Use meetings to achieve clearly identified outcomes.

CHECKLIST 18: DESIGNING THE CONTROL SYSTEM

Ask:

- How is the work actually controlled now?
- Do you have budgets for hours and costs?
- Do you have data comparing actual hours/cost with planned hours/cost?
- How is the quantity of completed work measured and compiled?
- Is completed work related specifically to hours used or based on forecasts?
- Are you kept informed of potential delays to milestones?
- How long does reported information take to get to you after the close-off?

- How much time/cost is spent between close-off and receipt of reports?
- What action do you take after reading the report?
- Can you take action based upon information in the report?
- Is reported information reasonably accurate? If not, why not?
- Who receives copies of the report? Why them? Can they take action? Do they?
- Can you list who receives the reports for information only?
- Who could take action to reduce costs, but does not receive reports?
- Has someone been assigned responsibility for each piece of work in the plan?
- Does the system provide a way to reduce key variables such as hours, costs, etc?
- Does the system focus on profit, time, quality, completion or more than one of these?
- Do the system reports and rewards motivate the desired behaviour?
- Does the system allow time–cost–quality trade-off decisions to be made quickly?
- Does the system include an early warning system to identify risks and issues?

MONITORING PROGRESS

Although you have made a particular effort to set up effective communication processes, do not rely on these always working effectively to give all the necessary information regarding progress. Confidence in progress reports comes only from verifying these from time to time. Verifying them obliges you to monitor:

- the status of work being performed;
- the volume of work completed;
- the quality of work performed;
- costs and expenditure compared to those set out in the operating budget;
- the team's behaviour, cohesiveness and performance;
- the stakeholders' attitudes.

You cannot do this effectively from behind a desk; you need to walk about, observe and have conversations! This is your data-gathering process, which if done effectively is far more useful than any written report. Still demand the written reports; they are a valuable discipline for everyone working on the project as well as providing an historical record. Monitoring is a checking activity – talking to the team members and finding out directly how things are going. This is encouraging to the team members and shows you care about them and their work. Too much monitoring is sometimes interpreted as interference, so there is a fine balance between the two extremes. Monitoring is also an opportunity to check that promised human resources are in fact working on project tasks and are not diverted to other activities. Your visibility to the team also creates a climate where you rapidly learn about concerns and difficulties.

Decide the frequency

Are you content to rely on team meetings as the focal point of reporting project progress? This depends on how often you can afford to get the team together and your style of conducting these meetings. You must decide how often you intend to:

- walk about to observe what is happening – daily/twice weekly /weekly?
- hold one-to-one meetings with the customer and the sponsor;
- hold one-to-one meetings with the team members;
- measure the progress of key stage tasks;
- receive local reports – verbal and written – from key stage owners.

Many projects benefit from having regular short team meetings at the same day and time each week. This does depend on the team members' location, and less frequent meetings may be the only way of ensuring attendance. Holding less frequent meetings of the team puts a greater emphasis on frequent monitoring to check that the team members are communicating with each other effectively. Regular monitoring demonstrates your concern for success and reinforces messages about watching out for new risks or anticipating future problems.

Measuring progress is always a difficult area for most people to define. Ask anyone how the work is going and the common response is 'OK. Everything is coming along fine.' The reality is that they probably haven't started yet! If you establish well-defined metrics to measure the progress, you soon know the project's status. Agree the metrics and the frequency of recording with the people doing the work, and stress the importance of using them effectively. Try to determine what tangible outputs come from a task or group of tasks and ask how the people doing the work measure these. After all, they must have some idea of how they are going to confirm when the tasks are completed! These data are essential in order to value the work completed at any point and check that the results achieved are in accordance with the plan. If unusual or unexpected results appear, you need to be informed promptly so that corrective action can be decided. Figure 9.2 gives the essential steps in the normal monitoring process.

Reviewing the project risks

You have a project risk log updated at the close of the planning phase of your project. Throughout the execution phase you must keep a watch for risks that:

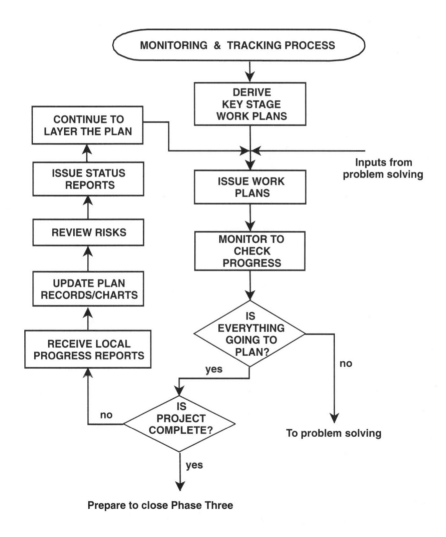

Figure 9.2 The normal monitoring process

- are about to happen – and become an issue;
- are new – they were not identified earlier;
- have changed their category (HIGH, MEDIUM, LOW);
- have revised probability and/or impact leading to a revised risk score;
- are no longer perceived as relevant.

It is useful to carry out a short review of risks at each team meeting. However, make sure the team understands that the steps involved in risk reviews are not confined to a meeting. They are a state of mind and must be part of the day-to-day work of each member of the team. You need to know about new risks anticipated or identified at the time they are recognized. The formal risk review is a team activity to use the experience and skills of the team members. If appropriate, involve others with relevant expertise to help the team.

The review process follows a number of discrete steps using the last issue of the project risk log.

CHECKLIST 19: REVIEWING THE PROJECT RISKS

Steps in the risk review:

- Check whether any risks are no longer valid; remove the category and risk data completely but leave the risk on the list for future reference.
- Use the risk category matrix to verify the categories of all risks on the list; amend the categories by consensus agreement among the team.
- Prepare risk management forms for any risks revised to HIGH.
- List any new risks identified from current work and new work plan charts.
- Use the risk category matrix to categorize new risks.
- Prepare a risk mitigation strategy for any risks categorized as UNACCEPTABLE.
- Implement the action plans promptly.
- Prepare risk management forms for new HIGH risks.
- Ensure that everyone knows the triggers that signal HIGH risks becoming issues.
- Confirm or allocate responsibility for managing the risks on the list.
- Update the project risk log with any revisions to the risk scores and rankings.
- Issue the project risk log to key stakeholders and the team.

After the review, update the project risk log and if necessary amend the order to show revised rankings from the risk scores. Continue to remind the team at intervals of the risks that are particularly relevant at each stage of the work and maintain regular contact with your sponsor for support. You know that risks become issues when they actually happen, and a process for the prompt handling of these issues is essential.

MANAGING ISSUES

The purpose of the issue management process is to make sure all risks that happen are resolved promptly to avoid and/or limit damage to your project.

An issue is defined as:

> any event or series of related events (that may previously have been identified as a risk) that have become an active problem causing a threat to the integrity of a project and/or related projects.

Managing issues is similar to managing the original risks, requiring you to: 1) keep records of all issues that occur; and 2) ensure that action planning is used promptly to resolve the issues.

Issue identification is not the sole preserve of the project manager. Everyone involved with the project has a responsibility to identify an issue and react promptly, if only to inform you. It is valuable to record issues to focus the team and others on learning from the corrective actions taken. It helps to prevent issues recurring on projects in the future. Although your primary concern when dealing with an issue is to get an action plan in place and implemented, a disciplined approach to planning action is important. It is too easy to over-react, 'shoot from the hip' and action the first idea you think of as a solution. This is not always the best solution and ignores the team's expertise in deriving an answer to the problem.

Record issues as they happen on an issue status log, a complete list of all issues raised on the project, giving:

- issue name and source;
- associated risk if identified (by risk number);
- who owns it;
- which parts of the project are affected;
- who is responsible for action plans to resolve;
- a record of current rating;
- when action is complete.

Design a template similar to the project risk log if appropriate. Issues are identified through regular monitoring. An example is shown in Figure 9.3.

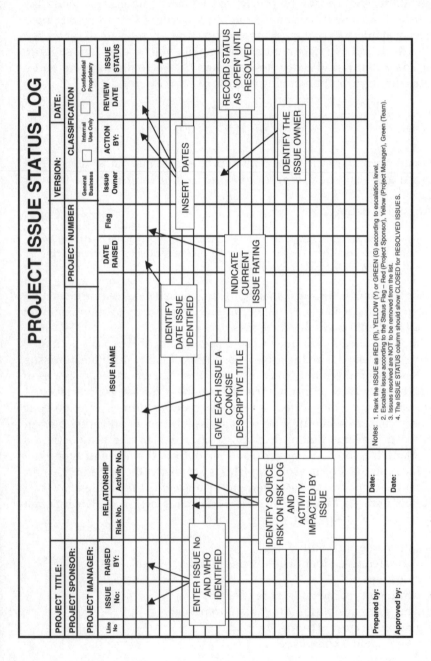

Figure 9.3 Example issue status log

Since you have limited authority, it is unlikely you can resolve all the issues without support from your sponsor, or even higher management. To enable a simple process, the issues are rated using a traffic light system.

Rating issues

Issues raised are rated according to their impact and anticipated consequences by assigning a RED, YELLOW or GREEN FLAG:

- RED FLAG. Major issue having serious consequences for the project. Prompt action needed by the sponsor to implement a decision to resolve. Overdue resolution of outstanding YELLOW flags revised to a RED flag by the project manager.
- YELLOW FLAG. Significant impact on the project and/or other projects. Unless resolved promptly, will cause delays to milestones. The project manager is responsible for resolution. Becomes RED flag if action is delayed for more than five days.
- GREEN FLAG. Consequences are limited to a confined area of the project and are unlikely to affect other projects. Normally they are within the authority of the key stage owner to resolve. Becomes YELLOW if not resolved in five days so as to avoid project slippage.

This initial rating is your responsibility as project manager after a cause and impact analysis. The initial rating gives an immediate indication of the relative importance of the issues on the log. Issues on the log are not arranged in any order of priority. An issue that is outstanding remains outstanding until it is fully resolved and the consequences avoided or corrected.

Any outstanding issues are identified when reporting the progress of the project. You must also ensure that the rating of any issue has not changed. It is important to keep your key stakeholders informed on progress with resolving issues, invoking their active support when necessary in the interests of the project.

As with the risks on the project risk log, no issues are normally removed from the log, even after resolution. The list is a valuable source of learning for future projects.

Escalation of issues

As you do not always have authority to decide all the actions needed to resolve issues arising during project work, it is essential to establish defined responsibilities for the escalation of issues:

- Any issues given a GREEN flag are the responsibility of the key stage owner to resolve.
- Any issues given a YELLOW flag are the responsibility of the project manager to resolve.
- Any issues given a RED flag are escalated to the sponsor to decide the appropriate actions to implement and who should implement them.

In most situations you attempt to resolve the issue or consult your sponsor, and without involving senior management. If the issue is rated RED then it is always referred to the sponsor for a decision. You are close to the problem, so if this happens, expect to be asked for suggested actions to resolve the issue. A convenient way to focus on the essential elements of issue resolution is to use a standard checklist or standard template, particularly for the serious issues rated RED and YELLOW.

It is necessary to modify the issue escalation process for programmes to ensure that issues are not left lurking in a corner and unresolved. The process is shown in Figure 9.4.

Issue ownership

Like risks, all issues must have an owner who is accountable for prompt resolution. Issues can be major roadblocks for the project, so the importance of ownership allocated in the team cannot be over-stressed. Do not take ownership of all issues yourself.

The responsibilities of the *issue owner* include:

- ownership of the issue for resolution and tracking;
- completion of the relevant issue management form;
- deciding additional resolution actions as required;
- allocating action owners for each action in the issue management form;
- obtaining approval of the completed issue management form from the project manager;
- issuing the issue management form to all action owners for actions to proceed;
- reviewing the outcome of all actions;
- informing the project manager of progress with actions and when they are completed;
- issuing the final version of the issue management form to show all actions completed and the issue as resolved and closed.

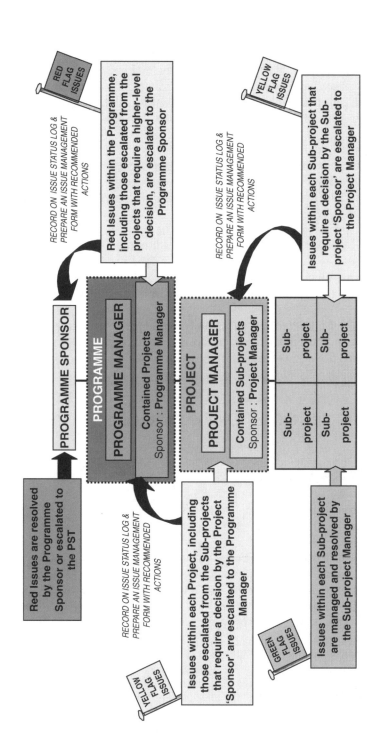

Figure 9.4 The issue escalation process

Issue resolution strategy

The *issue management form* is a typical template (see Figure 9.5) to check that all aspects of an issue are carefully analysed and actions planned to resolve the consequences. This allows you to identify more than one way of resolving the issue, offers senior management a choice of solutions and focuses on:

- areas of the project affected and consequences forecast;
- consequences if not resolved;
- proposed actions to resolve, with cost and resource implications;
- current rating of the issue.

Always confirm that responsibility is clearly allocated for actions planned, to avoid confusion when action is implemented. Finally, check that each possible solution is analysed for potential risks. Too often a 'quick fix' solution may seem perfect in the short term, but introduces additional risks to the project later.

Issue owners, who should carefully analyse an issue for one or more potential solutions, must treat resolving an issue as a high-level commitment. Typical questions to ask are given in Checklist 20.

CHECKLIST 20: QUESTIONS FOR ISSUE OWNERS

For any potential solution, ask:

- Who is affected by the solution?
- How are these people to be kept informed?
- What are the expected consequences of the solution?
- Who could be affected by these consequences?
- Does the plan need to be revised?
- Do issued work plans need to be revised?
- Does the operating budget need to be revised?
- Do project procedures need to be modified?
- Are additional skills/resources needed?
- What timescale is acceptable for implementation of the solution?
- How is the progress of actions to be monitored?
- What measurements need to be made to assess progress?
- What indicators are required to show that further action is necessary?

Ask consequential questions as appropriate.

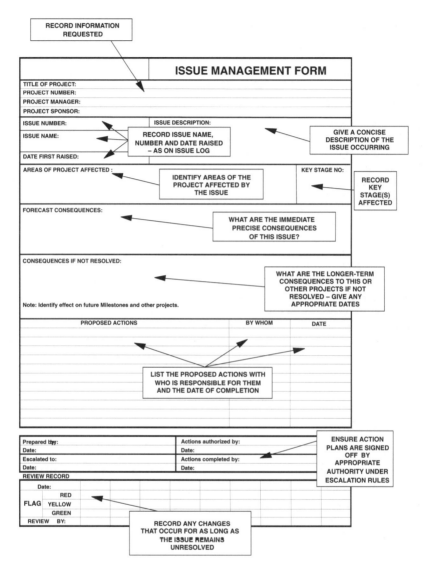

Figure 9.5 Example of an issue management form

Tracking the issue resolution strategy

The issue owner is responsible for tracking the actions listed in the relevant issue management form. Regular contact with the 'action owners' is essential to ensure that agreed actions are carried through to successful completion.

For each action listed, the issue owner needs to establish that:

- the 'action owner' understands the action and accepts responsibility for completing it;
- the 'action owner' has agreed to the 'planned completion date';
- the 'action owner' has a copy of the relevant issue management form for reference;
- the action is completed on time;
- the action effectively has the desired effect;
- no consequential issues (in the sense used here) arise from completion of the action;
- no additional actions are required to secure the resolution effect desired.

The issue owner for each issue is responsible for reporting progress of the issue resolution strategy to the project manager. This needs to be done at weekly intervals, or more frequently if required. This does not preclude any unusual circumstances arising, eg an 'action owner' not carrying out actions, when the project manager must be promptly informed. This type of event may necessitate escalation to a higher authority for immediate resolution.

REVIEWING PROJECT ISSUES

You should conduct weekly issue review meetings with the team to:

- review the current programme issue log entries;
- take recommendations from the issue owners for any revisions to the issue rating for any issue;
- escalate the issue to a higher authority if necessary and revise the rating;
- establish progress with active issue resolution strategies;
- decide revisions to issue resolution strategy actions for any issue;
- decide changes to issue ownership when appropriate;
- approve revisions to any relevant issue management form;
- agree revisions to the schedule when appropriate;
- review the cost impact of any issue when appropriate;
- decide that any issues identified as having their issue resolution strategy successfully completed as 'CLOSED' can be recorded with that status on the issue log;
- identify any risks that appear when an issue is closed and record these on the project risk log;

- record any new issues that have been identified on the issue log and conduct a full issue analysis;
- inform the sponsor and relevant stakeholders of the outcome of the issue review.

When a new version of any issue management form is approved as a result of revisions to issue data or resolution actions, the issue owner must issue the new version to all 'action owners' and any others as decided by the project manager, eg the sponsor and selected stakeholders. The resolution of issues is a primary responsibility for the project manager. The issue management form is revised if appropriate. The date of the review and any change to the rating are recorded: 1) on the issue log; 2) on the issue management form before reissue to the appropriate individuals concerned. If it is necessary to revise the data recorded on the issue log and/or the issue management form at any time, these documents must be reissued as a new version.

When the project manager is satisfied that an issue is resolved, that issue can be marked on the issue status log as CLOSED. Closed issues are *not* deleted from the issue status log and stay recorded for review of the project history. The issue management form can also be approved as CLOSED after recording the date when all actions are completed. Ensure that you report all closed issues in your regular contact with the sponsor and stakeholders. Review the project plan and revise it if required when any issue is closed.

The issue management process is shown in Figure 9.6.

TRACKING YOUR PROJECT

It is essential to keep the project moving along the right track. To achieve this requires:

- that project control and monitoring tools are appropriate to the type of project;
- that the project team performs to the highest standards possible and responds to the changing needs of the project as data are generated by the control system;
- that the stakeholders remain committed to the project and promptly respond to changes perceived to be necessary for the successful completion of the project.

Tracking is the process by which the project progress is measured through monitoring to ensure that:

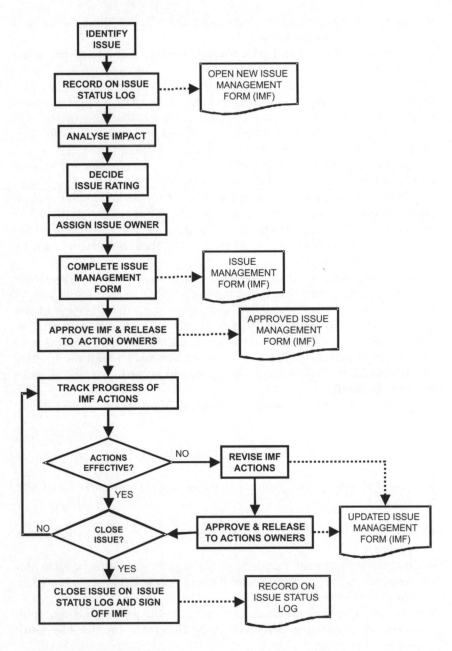

Figure 9.6 Process flow diagram: issue management

- the work is carried out in the right order as stated in the plan;
- planned performance is maintained – to agreed quality standards;
- the team members are well motivated and committed to completing their individual work plans on time and within budget;
- changes to the plan caused by problems or the customer are promptly acted upon;
- the reported progress data are used to update the plan charts and records in the project file.

The process normally involves working with the WBS and the key stage Gantt chart to show the real status of the project – the tasks that are on time and those that have slipped. To do this you must have a starting point or baseline to show the variances.

The baseline for all tracking is the project plan devised before implementation at Phase Gate Three, where all key stages are fixed and responsibilities are clearly defined and accepted by the team members. The final key stage Gantt chart is the project baseline, which remains unchanged throughout the project unless the PST approves changes. As the work is done you mark progress on the chart by filling in the bars to show the amount of work completed (see Figure 9.7).

If a key stage is late starting or takes longer than expected to complete, or the finish suffers a delay, this is shown clearly on the chart. The original position of the bar on the chart is unchanged; changing it would modify the baseline. Although doing so covers up the change that has taken place, you lose the opportunity later to ask why it happened and what everyone has learnt from the difficulties leading to the change.

Modifications to the plan are recorded as they occur to enable the experience to be logged for future projects. This may involve moving one or more tasks away from the original baseline position. This appears odd on the chart and tempts you to move the baseline with the comment, 'Well, we never actually expected it to happen like that!' When you move anything on the Gantt chart you are effectively modifying the project strategy for a reason. There must be a purpose in making a change, and leaving the baseline unchanged forces you to document fully the changes to the plan and schedule using the change management process. Later you evaluate the key learning points from the project and all these changes that occur. Of course, if any of these modifications applies to critical key stages or tasks then the project's completion is likely to be delayed. You then face the difficult task of recovery planning to try to recover the original project schedule or persuade the customer to accept the extended completion date.

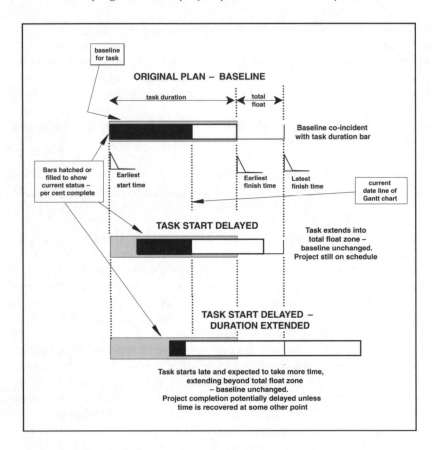

Figure 9.7 Showing current status on the Gantt chart

Deciding what completion means

Ask anyone engaged in project work how they are getting on and you can expect a reply like 'Fine, I'm about halfway through.' What does this really mean? Is it really true that the work is 50 per cent complete? It is probably a guess that, depending on the individual, may be accurate or well wide of the real situation and just gives information you expect to hear!

The bar on a Gantt chart is a linear graphical representation of effort. In real life, effort is never linear and depends on:

- the accuracy of the detailed planning of the tasks to be done;
- the complexity of the work;
- the amount of interruptions to the work;
- the availability of data and equipment;
- how the individual feels on the day.

The well-proven 80/20 rule applies: 80 per cent of the results come from 20 per cent of the effort and the remaining 20 per cent of the results take 80 per cent of the effort! Completing the last part of a piece of work can often take considerably longer than expected and extend into or beyond the total float zone on the Gantt chart. This brings you back to the metrics you agreed to use to measure progress.

Unfortunately, there are nearly always forgotten tasks that take a significant amount of time to complete:

- documentation;
- approval times;
- planning and developing test procedures;
- project reviews;
- project meetings;
- planning reviews;
- replanning meetings;
- customer meetings;
- user group meetings;
- negotiations with suppliers;
- expediting;
- searching for information;
- purchasing administration;
- training;
- travel and communication;
- updating project records.

Most of these and others will happen and occupy time assigned to project work. They will interfere with the effort given to planned tasks and are often ignored when assessing the percentage completion. You presume that all tasks will be completed on time using the durations entered into the schedule. Don't ask for percentage completion assessments when seeking progress data. These assessments are rarely accurate because of their historical basis. You need to know whether the task will finish on time, so ask for a forecast of when it will be completed. This focuses the individual responsible for the work to review other commitments due in the same period and give a more realistic assessment of the time to complete.

If the forecast completion date is then clearly unacceptable when compared to the schedule, you have the opportunity to take some prompt corrective action. You should persuade all your key stage owners to get into the habit of forecasting performance for their key stages. This proactive approach highlights potential problems before they have a serious impact on the project, allowing you to focus on corrective action.

In addition, forecasting has two other benefits. First, it improves everyone's ability to estimate time to do the work; forecasting is a 'real-time' activity, not looking into a crystal ball for the distant future. Second, it creates real targets for the individual doing the work; any delay beyond an agreed target cannot be tolerated.

The project status report (see Chapter 8) specifically requests that these forecasts be given when reporting, along with reasons for any changes to previous forecast completion dates. Encourage the team to use these reporting templates, and stress the importance of developing expertise in accurate forecasting. The analysis for variances at all stages must be a primary concern for the whole team, which must make sure that effective corrective action is taken when problems and hold-ups occur.

Good monitoring and tracking builds team confidence, anticipates problems and prepares future success.

CHECKLIST 21: MONITORING AND TRACKING

The main criteria for effective tracking are:

- Work content – is it to estimates (both time and cost)?
- Measurement – is everyone clear how to measure progress?
- Timescales – are work plans being completed on schedule?
- Quality – are standards being met in accordance with specifications?
- Teamwork – are responsibilities being adhered to?
- Changes – are problem-solving tools being used effectively?
- Stakeholders – are they being kept informed, consulted and involved?

Pay particular attention to:

- having regular contact with team members;
- having regular contact with the customer and project sponsor;
- encouraging rapid feedback of progress and problems;
- dealing with difficulties promptly;
- responding to requests for guidance and help;
- maintaining good communication with team and stakeholders;
- focusing everyone on watching out for risks;
- keeping the project records and file updated;
- issues arising:
  - resourcing problems;
  - technical problems;

- scheduling problems due to poor estimating;
- responsibility conflicts;
- checking that agreed action plans are implemented effectively;
- keeping everyone informed of project status.

At regular intervals, review the business case to ensure that your project is in compliance.

TAKING CORRECTIVE ACTION

The monitoring and tracking process identifies the problems that are interfering with the schedule and indicates the need for some action. The analysis for variance should help to expose the causes of the problem; then use problem-solving tools to derive an acceptable solution.

Taking corrective action has limited possibilities:

- Rearranging the workload(s) if a milestone is going to be missed – find others to take some of the tasks to relieve the loading, or even reallocate the tasks.
- Have the relevant team member put more effort into the job – not an easy option to demand in practice.
- Put additional resources into the job – resource constraints may negate this option.
- Move the milestone date, subject to the stakeholder's approval and the possibility of recovering time later in the project – difficult with activities on the critical path.
- Lower the scope and/or quality of the results demanded by the plan – only possible with agreement of the customer and sponsor. If doing so changes the business plan, you must consider whether PST approval is necessary before proceeding with this option.

Corrective action is normally approached using these options in this order. Record any assumptions you make when deciding action plans; they could have significance later! Any corrective action has a cost, and your obligation is to keep this to a minimum. You may have to seek the sponsor's approval to release contingency funds to cover this increased cost.

Before implementing any corrective actions carry out some simple checks that you have selected the best option based on the available information.

CHECKLIST 22: TAKING CORRECTIVE ACTION

Identify the possible options:

- Use cause and effect analysis to identify the problem's cause.
- Use brainstorming techniques to find the possible solutions.
- Use the expertise of the team and others.
- Identify the most flexible area out of scope, cost or schedule.
- Select the two or three most acceptable solutions.
- Record all assumptions.
- Derive a list of actions whereby you can implement the selected options.

Before deciding which option to use, check whether:

- the critical path will have changed;
- any individual workloads will be adversely affected;
- any milestones will be subject to slippage;
- any new HIGH risks will be exposed;
- any new issues (ie risks that actually occur) will be exposed.
- any cost over-runs will be introduced (do these need approval?);
- any localized schedule slippages are controllable (recoverable later?).

When selecting the option and setting the action plan, ask:

- What is the priority order of the tasks involved?
- Who is responsible for carrying out the actions?
- Who is monitoring implementation of the action plan?
- What is the target completion date?
- Who must be kept informed of progress?

PROBLEM SOLVING

Project work inevitably is faced with an astonishing range of problems. Some people regard problems as just a challenge to overcome! In the project a problem exists if you: 1) are faced with an unacceptable gap between what you currently have and what you desire as an outcome; 2) are unable to see an immediate way to close or remove the gap.

For example, problems in your project can be about:

- the schedule – work takes longer than planned;
- the effort planned – tasks are not carefully detailed to arrive at accurate estimates;

- resources are not available when promised;
- technical difficulties – technology doesn't work or is inadequate;
- inadequate training of team members – skills are not available;
- unforeseen absence of resources, equipment or materials;
- inadequate control – monitoring is not working effectively;
- failures in communication leading to misunderstandings and conflicts.

Much of your time goes into controlling the project schedule and taking prompt action when something unpredictable happens. If everyone focuses on risk management, you can hope to minimize the number of unpredictable events. When they do occur, you are faced with a problem that is treated as an issue to be resolved. Problem solving is dependent on a sequence of logical steps (Figure 9.8).

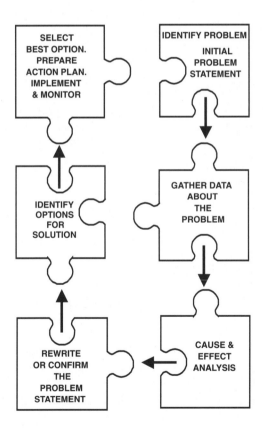

Figure 9.8 The steps of problem solving

Identifying the problem

It is important to frame the right problem. With the team, agree a statement that clearly describes the perceived problem. This may change later after data gathering is complete. Getting a consensus agreement of this statement is important as it must embrace everyone's perception of the problem. Avoid pre-judging the causes and reasons for the problem occurring now.

Gathering data

Collect information about the perceived problem. Collecting data helps to analyse the problem and confirm you are looking at the real problem and not a symptom of a deeper, hidden difficulty. You have limited time to resolve the problem and sometimes have to take decisions with information of doubtful accuracy. Usually a better solution is possible if some time is devoted to collecting data using sampling techniques to count or measure the data needed. Limit sampling to relevant data only and review any available historical data.

Identifying the real cause of the problem

Cause and effect analysis is a powerful tool for project work. It is easy to use and focuses everyone on a wide range of possible causes. Examining all the possible causes under the four headings allows you to develop the Ishikawa or 'fishbone' diagram, which is based on:

- people;
- process or method;
- materials;
- equipment.

An example is given in Figure 9.9. Start the diagram by drawing a large box on the right-hand side of a large piece of paper and writing the observed effect in the box. Then draw a horizontal line out to the left from the box across the paper. Now add four arrows, one for each of the headings from which causes are expected to come. Add possible causes under each heading to the relevant arrow to develop a wide range of possible causes of the effects observed. Some causes will appear on more than one arrow, but do not restrict them if you believe they are relevant.

When you feel you have enough causes to work with, eliminate any causes you are confident are obviously false. Then look for repeated causes on different arrows and link these together. These are possibly primary causes and you can then identify secondary causes.

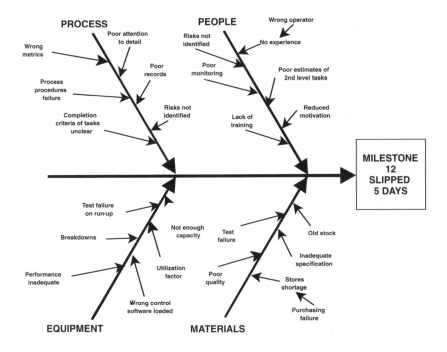

Figure 9.9 Example of a 'fishbone diagram'

Rewrite the problem statement

After analysis, review the problem statement and rewrite if appropriate, adding the causes identified:

'The problem is… which we believe to be caused by…'

This statement should now clearly identify the real problem with the probable causes, and is the basis for seeking a solution.

Seeking a solution

Solutions to problems do not just appear. They are based on a mixture of opinion, historical experience and facts available. Collect the team together and use brainstorming to derive possible ways to resolve the problem. Remember to observe the basic rules:

- Write down everything said, regardless of how apparently stupid.
- Suspend all judgement and criticism.
- Seek quantity, not quality.

When the list of ideas is significant, eliminate duplicates and obvious non-starters and then agree the list of possible solutions. Try to get three options as possible solutions to the problem and check the consequences of applying each. You must seek the 'best' option under the prevailing circumstances, based on cost, resource implications and effects on the schedule.

Implement the selected option

Develop an action plan to implement the agreed solution and confirm that responsibilities are clearly defined. Use the steps in Checklist 20 (p 206) for action planning. Then take the decision and monitor that the outcomes are the same as expected.

PROGRESS MEETINGS

Regular progress meetings are an essential part of the project control process. These meetings can take a considerable amount of time if you do not take specific actions to make them effective. Progress meetings give you an opportunity to:

- maintain team cohesion;
- inform the team of information and decisions you have received from the sponsor, customer and other stakeholders;
- review the risk and issue logs;
- reinforce the importance of the entire team sharing the responsibility of meeting the project's objectives.

Include both core team members and part-time team members in the meeting. Ask everyone to be prepared to give a short verbal *active task report* to the meeting to highlight any tasks that should have been completed but have not been, with reasons and forecast completion dates.

Project progress meetings are not an opportunity for ego boosting with a huge display of technical ability. All the good things that have happened before the meeting are good news, but ancient history. You want to know about the bad things that have happened which you do not yet know about:

- tasks that have slipped;
- resource conflict problems;
- equipment failures or absence;
- materials not available;
- milestones slipping;
- technical difficulties.

It is useful to ask key stage owners to prepare a *look ahead report* covering the next two reporting periods (the period between progress meetings) to indicate:

- what needs to be done according to the schedule;
- what will not be done according to the schedule, with reasons and actions to correct the potential slippage;
- the impact on the project schedule, if any.

Remember that time spent in a meeting is time lost to project work, so keep your meetings to the point, keep them strictly timed and avoid diversions. Effective meetings only come from good control by the leader. Try to develop a standard agenda and always have an updated version of the key stage Gantt chart available for reference. Identify the outstanding issues but do not try to solve them in the meeting; set up a separate discussion with the relevant people.

Always have a flip chart stand in the meeting room and record agreed actions on the sheet as they occur, with responsibility and target completion date. In this way there should be no doubt in the team as to who is responsible for which actions, and they do not have to wait for the minutes. The *action list* (Figure 9.10) is the most important document to

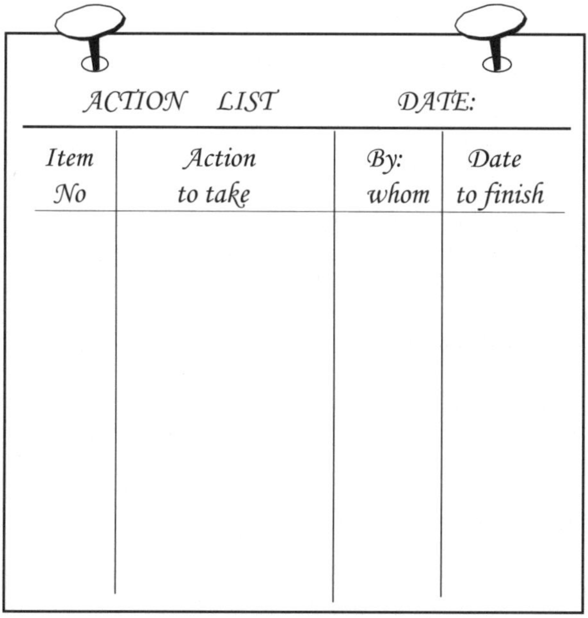

Item No	Action to take	By: whom	Date to finish

Figure 9.10 Prepare an action list on flip chart sheets

come out of the meeting and is the starting point of the next meeting – checking that all previous actions are completed.

Avoid letting the meeting get caught up with a long and detailed examination of a particular issue and its resolution. If a problem takes more than five minutes to solve, log it for a separate discussion. It is preferable to leave issue resolution to a separate meeting with the right people present and no time constraint.

Involvement of the whole team in progress meetings builds ownership and good team working. Peer pressure is a powerful enabler, and team members support each other. With the huge increase in electronic means of communication it is tempting to rely on these methods and hold virtual meetings. Don't fool yourself that these can replace the benefits of face-to-face communication. Body language sometimes conveys a mountain of meaning to an alert team and helps you recognize many relationship problems existing between individuals in the team. Run your progress meetings to make the best use of everyone's time.

> Yesterday is history – you can't turn back the clock. Focus the team on what must be done next.

CHECKLIST 23: PROJECT PROGRESS MEETINGS

Always have a timed agenda and keep the meetings short. Set the start and finish time – and stick to them. Ask questions to identify:

- What has been completed on time?
- Have there been any outstanding exceptions to the work done?
- What actions agreed earlier are incomplete?
- When will outstanding action plans be complete?
- Which milestones have been completed on time?
- Which milestones have slipped?
- Are action plans in place to correct slippages?
- Have any risks escalated to become issues?
- Are there issues still waiting to be resolved?
- Are any resource capacity changes forecast?
- What work is to be done in the next period?
- Which milestones are due in the next period?
- What problems are anticipated in the next period?
- Are there any risks that could affect the work in the next period?

- Are any problems anticipated with third party contracts in the next period?
- Are there any team performance problems and issues?

Encourage ideas and suggestions from the team but avoid:

- long verbal reports of what has been done;
- problem solving in the meeting – set up a separate meeting to resolve problems;
- long debates – they detract from the purpose and cause deviation;
- negotiations – they usually exclude most of those present;
- 'any other business' – the biggest time-waster.

PROGRESS REPORTING

At the launch of the project you decided the reporting and communication processes to use (see Chapter 8 to remind yourself). Throughout the execution phase of the project, check that these processes are working and providing the right information for effective control. If the methods are not working well then agree with the team how to improve them. Do not put this off until later or the next project. Continuous improvement is important, so grasp any opportunity to do the job better.

Check with your customer and the sponsor that they are getting all the essential information in the reporting process. You do not want to spend all your time preparing reports, so do make sure the process provides essential data only and avoids creating an enormous paper trail. It is very easy to generate large volumes of paper, particularly when using computers, and most of this information is never read. Keep reports short using templates, like the *status report* given in Chapter 8, but expect to make a more detailed presentation at a full project review.

Project control is dependent on good communication. It is your obligation to keep the process working always to avoid confusion and misunderstandings.

Project records

It is essential to maintain accurate project records and encourage everyone involved to accept this obligation from the outset. Write everything down so that you remember it! The *project file* is a source of all relevant information – current and historical – about the project and must be comprehensively maintained. This includes all latest issues of standardized records, including those held on computer systems. Do not rely on the integrity or availability of computer records alone. The information in the file includes at least:

- the stakeholder list;
- the project organization chart;
- the project brief;
- the scope of work statement;
- the project risk log;
- risk mitigation strategies;
- risk management forms;
- the plan schedules and all updates;
- estimating records;
- key stage responsibility charts;
- activity responsibility charts;
- the issue log;
- issue management forms;
- the project milestone schedule;
- status reports;
- meetings minutes/action lists;
- project change requests;
- project review reports;
- contracts;
- financial reports and documentation;
- customer and supplier information;
- closure checklist;
- handover checklist;
- completion certificate(s);
- evaluation report.

Remember, the project file is a living record of the project and becomes an invaluable source of data for future projects.

The project log book

If you opened a *project log book* at the start of the project, use it as a daily diary of events in the project. Always keep it with you and record events as they happen. The information you note here will help during the evaluation process after handover to the customer.

PROJECTS AND CONFLICT

Your project involves many individuals and groups of people. The hopes, desires and needs of these people are often incompatible with each other and these differences lead to conflict. When such differences surface they are often seen as difficult, troublesome, annoying or even embarrassing, and an intrusion into a calm and ordered life. Conflict and change are partners, never far apart, so accept the inevitable and be prepared to react when necessary.

A large part of your time can be occupied with fighting the fires and crises evolving from conflicts. Many conflicts occur from situations where roles and responsibilities are not clearly defined, leaving the team members confused.

Why does conflict occur?

Although many reasons for conflict are cited, some common causes are:

- diverse expertise in the project team;
- low level of authority given to the project leader;
- lack of understanding of the project's objectives by the project team;
- excessive role ambiguity in the team – unclear or shared responsibilities;
- unclear schedules and performance targets for team members;
- infringement of functional status and roles by project processes and procedures;
- remote functional groups operating almost independently on project work;
- local interference from high-level management involvement;
- the fact that people don't like each other or get on together in their work.

Most conflict arises from the way people behave with each other in a particular situation and, unfortunately, behaviour is not predictable. You need all your skills as a leader to resolve a conflict and identify whether it is good or bad for the project.

Conflict is good if it:

- brings problems and issues out into the open for discussion;
- brings the team together, increasing loyalty;
- promotes creativity, generating new ideas and work practices;
- focuses people on giving their work more detailed analysis.

Good conflict generates a win–win relationship between individuals, promoting sharing of information and improved motivation.

Bad conflict:

- creates stress, stirring up negative feelings;
- makes the working environment less pleasant;
- severely reduces the effectiveness of communication processes;

- interferes with the co-ordination of effort between groups and individuals;
- encourages an autocratic approach to working.

Bad conflict tends to cause a win–lose relationship to develop between individuals. In practice there is a spectrum of conflict between the two extremes of good and bad. You need to create a climate in the team where conflict is seen as healthy and valued for the results created. A team with no conflict could be perceived as complacent and lethargic with little creativity.

Types of conflict

The most common types involve one or more of the following:

- resources;
- equipment and facilities;
- budgets and costs;
- technical opinions and trade-offs;
- priorities;
- procedures;
- scheduling and estimating;
- responsibilities;
- personality clashes.

Personality conflicts are often the most difficult to resolve and may be resolved finally only by total separation of the parties.

Conflicts and risks

Many of the conflicts that occur can be predicted as potential events in a preliminary risk assessment. Resource allocation and prioritization between several active projects or other operational work is frequently a source of conflict, particularly as priorities are changed to satisfy external pressures. Examples of risks that can become a source of conflict include:

- unclear objectives and project definition;
- project priorities versus other work not being exposed;
- resources not being available when promised;
- delays in interfaces with other projects downstream;
- changes in the scope of work and project parameters;
- technical disagreements in innovation.

Conflict is a behaviour that hinders the project from achieving the expectations of the stakeholders. When it occurs, conflict must be regarded as an issue to be resolved as quickly as possible to avoid serious consequences.

Managing conflict

Any temporary management situation produces conflicts. These naturally result from the differences in the organizational behaviour of the individuals involved, who all come from different functional groups. You have a different view of the work and its priority to the functional manager (of your team members) who takes on the role of resource manager for all the project activity that has to be supported.

You operate in an environment of constant and rapid change. The functional manager works in a more standardized and predictable environment. You have to bridge the gap between these two environments to achieve success.

There is no single method of managing all conflicts in such temporary situations. The real skill is to:

- anticipate their occurrence;
- understand their composition;
- assess the consequences.

Project activity involves people, and it is their behaviour that directly contributes to conflict. Constantly look for possible areas of conflict, in the same way as you regularly review project risks.

Handling conflict

Everyone has a preferred behaviour in any particular situation that influences how they approach a conflict. Typically, the modes for handling conflict are the following:

- *withdrawal* – taking a retreat course: withdrawing from a potential collision course towards what appears to be a disagreement and hoping it will go away on its own;
- *smoothing* – seeking to establish and then emphasize the areas of agreement and avoiding the areas of disagreement initially, in the hope that the latter can be reduced to minor status as part of the whole and eventually be subject to *compromise*;
- *compromising* – starting from a rigid position on both sides but expressing a willingness to search for a solution: this allows both sides to the conflict to feel they are satisfied with the amount gained as well as the amount lost;
- *forcing* – exerting an opinion or view at the expense of the other: characterized by competitiveness, this leads to a win–lose result that ultimately becomes a lose–lose result, owing to the damaged relationship;

- *confrontation* – facing the conflict directly to cause face-to-face debate and discussion of the disagreements, deriving options for resolution: often defuses a violent situation and reduces the conflict to a level where *compromising* or even *smoothing* can resolve it.

In most conflict situations, you will work with *confrontation, compromise* and *smoothing* to resolve conflict in the team or between teams and functions. In dealing with management, *compromise* is the most likely mode, but behaviour will be influenced by your leadership style.

Resolving conflict is a real test of your ability to negotiate and influence others. You can achieve a successful outcome if you can focus the parties in conflict to identify and agree, first, the areas of full agreement, and second, the areas of disagreement. Then you can use the positive feelings about the areas of agreement to discuss the areas of disagreement one by one in a positive manner. Start with what appears to be the easiest to resolve and work through the list. Expect to fail with some, but if you can move the parties concerned to agree on a majority of points, it takes the heat out of the remainder.

> Effective conflict resolution is dependent on persuading everyone involved to listen in order to understand, not to evaluate and criticize.

ENCOURAGING GOOD TIME MANAGEMENT

Your primary objective in project work is to achieve a successful outcome that is generally interpreted as delivering the right results on time and to a pre-defined budget. Although this may require you to make changes to the technical elements of the scope and results required, the whole process is dependent on time. As time always moves inexorably on, it is common to assume things are happening according to the plans you spend much time developing. The reality is often far from expectations, and this is not just because the plans are wrong. Time management going out of control causes many of the difficulties you will encounter in managing a project. Some people are very skilled at organizing and managing how they use time effectively. Unfortunately, many are not so organized and their work output is extremely vulnerable to poor time management.

You are now thinking, 'What has this got to do with me?' A valid question to ask, but the answer is that it has everything to do with you. Remember, you are responsible for managing performance. Performance is directly related to effort that yields an output, and these results are dependent on how well an individual makes the best use of time. So, you have a direct interest in how everyone working on even the smallest part of your project is using the time allocated to the actual work. If you have an interest, you can influence how time is used, avoiding unnecessary work and duplication of effort, and ensure that attention is given to prioritizing the work. Time is your most valuable resource; if lost or misplaced, it is gone for ever. For you it is therefore a constraint, and you must demonstrate and encourage everyone involved to use effective time management principles to make best use of this resource.

A large number of projects are seriously understaffed, senior management believing (or hoping) that you will assume the additional workload created by the resource constraint. Unfortunately, this is usually easier said than done, since you are probably already burdened with other activities of an operational nature as well as, possibly, other projects! You do manage to cope with this burden of work, often working long hours, believing this is the only way to keep control of the project. The most significant problem with people and time management is actually recognizing and accepting that there is a problem. The problem can then be regarded as an opportunity to develop effectiveness, reduce the stress and improve the probability of success for your project.

Ask yourself some questions:

- Do you have trouble completing work to deadlines?
- How long can you work at your desk before being interrupted?
- How long can you work at your desk before interrupting yourself?
- How many interruptions (typically) occur each day?
- Have you a procedure for handling interruptions?
- Can you set aside a large block of time for something important?
- How much overtime do you work to get the job done?
- How is incoming mail handled?
- How much time do you spend attending meetings?
- How tough is it to say no?
- Do you carry out work you could allocate to team members?
- Do you make a fresh 'to-do list' every day?
- Is your list prioritized?
- How do you approach detailed work when it is necessary?
- Do you have flexibility in your diary for reactive time?
- Is your routine work made easier by having established procedures?
- Does the team understand your time management principles?

Converting time from a constraint to a manageable resource requires you to work towards dealing with the impact of these questions. As you are almost certainly doing some of the project work yourself, the barriers to effective time management affect you just as they do your team members.

Barriers to effective time management

If you spend too much time doing project work yourself then the consequence is a serious impact of all those things that rob you of valuable time to control the project. If you are unable to say no, you quickly become burdened with everyone's problems and the decisions needed to keep the project moving at every level. Many things can rob you of time, including:

- poor communication;
- unclear responsibility and authority;
- uncontrolled visitors and phone calls;
- lack of information;
- too many meetings;
- too many project reviews;
- casual conversations in the office;
- tracing data and information;
- record keeping;
- changing priorities;
- changes without explanation;
- unnecessary crisis interventions;
- procrastination;
- executive interference;
- too much attention to detail;
- over-commitment to non-project activities;
- unclear objectives and project scope;
- lack of support and commitment from others;
- lack of project tools;
- confirming resource commitments;
- bureaucracy;
- politics and power games;
- strong functional boundaries;
- fire-fighting – running from crisis to crisis;
- excessive paperwork;
- coaching inexperienced team members;
- inability to assess and take risks;
- desire for absolute perfection;
- lack of clear organization;
- unclear budget and financial controls;
- lack of business strategy.

You can probably think of many more, all influencing you to some degree and many having a serious impact on your effectiveness. The consequence of these robbers of time is a reduction in the working day for you and your team.

The productive output for most people is about 80 per cent of the available time, meaning that everyone really works only a four-day week. If you want proof, try completing a time log sheet for a week, recording what you are doing every 15 or 30 minutes of the day. Review the findings at the end of the week – you may learn something about yourself!

What can you do?

Start by addressing some fundamental issues. You cannot hope to encourage others in your team to improve their time management if you display all the symptoms of hopeless disorganization. Use your time effectively by the following means:

- Allocate work clearly to the team members.
- Delegate some of your authority where and when appropriate.
- Control your own assigned work to keep it to the project schedule.
- Don't take on more than you really know you can complete on time.
- Consult as required, but take decisions promptly and explain them.
- Prepare your own 'to-do list' and *update it every day.*
- Set your own priorities and generally stick to them.
- Focus on the areas of high risk in the currently active project work.
- Do the difficult tasks first, or when you can concentrate most effectively.
- Avoid unnecessary memos.
- Refuse to do the low-importance stuff.
- Control the time on the telephone – use a block of time for several calls together.
- Control the project work by exception, reviewing the plan charts each day.
- Set out a fixed agenda for project meetings.
- Don't hold meetings for the sake of getting together; have a clear purpose.
- Avoid wanderlust – monitor effectively when necessary.
- Focus everyone on the project's objectives.
- Show your concern for success.
- Turn problems into opportunities to progress and learn.

Regularly ask yourself some simple questions:

- What am I doing that really does not need doing?
- What am I doing that someone else could do just as well as or even better than me?
- What am I not doing that will not get done anyway if I avoid doing it?
- What have I done to establish clear priorities and targets for me and my team?
- Have I confirmed that everyone clearly understands what is expected of them?
- Have I communicated the current priorities to everyone who needs to know?
- Does everyone know and understand the consequences of ignoring the priorities?

- Is everyone aware of the high-risk areas and the triggers to identify potential issues?

The answers will lead you to improve the way you use time and encourage others to adopt the same process. Review your performance at the end of each day and give yourself a reward if you consider you are improving.

Working in a matrix

Or is it 'working in a maze'? – because that is how it feels sometimes. It is easy to be pulled in two or more directions at once, each promising the way out to a satisfactory conclusion. Most of the projects in an organization are carried out using people in different departments or divisions, or even on different sites or in different countries. How can you possibly hope to manage the team members' effective use of time and maintain your project schedule in such an environment?

The short answer is 'with great difficulty and a risk of increased stress levels', although there are some actions you can take to help make everyone's life more comfortable:

- Keep the stakeholder list up to date, particularly with the line managers of all the human resources you are using or plan to use in the future. These people control the time these resources can give your project and hold the keys to success. Your ability to influence them will be continually tested to ensure the project work is always started and completed on time. Keep them well informed of the project's progress and agree with them how the work is to be broken down into reasonable chunks for effectiveness. Remind them of the consequences for the business if the project suffers a slippage.
- One of the most significant time-wasters in project work is the effect of 'back-tracking'. When the project file is opened to start a piece of work, there is inevitably a need to review what was done the last time some work was carried out. If that was several days before, then there is a need to go back over what was done and achieved. The time for this 'back-track' is often significant, especially when you add up the number of times it happens in a project where people are only doing your work at intervals among other activities. Add up the total time used in this way in a project and it is almost frightening. The consequences of going back over previous work may cause a complete review and amendment of earlier work, which might be beneficial occasionally but is often unnecessary rework.
- Try to get agreement that project work is always given a sufficiently large chunk of time for some specific measurable output to be achieved

without any interruptions. Changes of priority are inevitable in departments you do not control, and putting out the fires in operational areas of the business is an essential activity. But fires are often encouraged or even lit for political reasons and you must try to get line managers to enter into firm commitments that your work will not suffer unnecessarily. Fire-fighting is often an excuse for lack of progress.

- Encourage your team members to work out their own time priorities, giving support and guidance when appropriate. Agree the time allocated to your project work and satisfy yourself that it is adequate for the work to be completed on time. Remember that everyone is different in the way they work and their pace. Encourage the team to expose and discuss their project work priorities with their line manager so that interruptions can be minimized and time used effectively. This helps the line manager to control and map his or her departmental resource utilization.

- With the agreement of the line manager concerned, set out personal targets for each member of the team. These are effectively the dates created in the project plan, but changes are often caused by changes to priorities, or minor slippages of earlier work. You must continually review these targets and take into account the slippages and the actions implemented to correct the time lost. The plan is dynamic and must be regularly updated for these changes, and the results distributed to everyone involved.

- Do not allow slippages to go unreported to you and the line manager, with missed targets pushing your project into fire-fighting mode. Try to keep proactive, continually monitoring future resource loadings and commitments so you can assess the impact on your project. This will minimize the incidence of unforeseen risks, and you can use 'what-if' analysis with the Gantt chart to decide on corrective actions to keep everything on track.

The most significant cause of failure in a matrix-type project is poor communication. This causes major chunks of time to be lost through misunderstandings. These are usually due to poor listening and unclear communications, with little or poor back-up documentation. Use the milestone schedule as a means of communicating to everyone the key dates which must not be missed and check that everyone understands his or her obligations to meet these dates. Keep the responsibility charts updated and reissued and insist that you need to know immediately if there is any doubt or lack of clarity by anyone about what is necessary or expected to meet those milestones on time.

The 'feudal kingdoms'

The hierarchical organizational structure, which is familiar to everyone, is a perfect arrangement for allowing the development of little empires within the organization. The consequent functional departmental empires become a collection of kingdoms each with their baron, who has total authority over the constituent manors or sections. This structural system from the 9th century still exists in some contemporary organizations, where departments have containing walls that can be breached only if you follow specific unwritten rules. The result is an organization with little integration, where the functional managers set their own rules and norms, making cross-functional co-ordinated working extremely difficult. Power games and political machinations occupy much management time and each manager is suspicious of the next, which leads to a high level of protectionism. Comments like 'we don't do things that way round here' are common, and consistent working practices such as those needed for project work are regarded with considerable mistrust. Such offices are almost like war zones, with missiles thrown at regular intervals to keep the 'enemy' at a distance and avoid being blamed when anything goes wrong.

This may sound like an extreme situation, but to various degrees it does exist too much today in many organizations. Projects identified as strategic and cross-functional have little real chance of success in such an environment. There are too many opportunities for individuals to attack and sabotage the efforts of a project team. Breaking down the walls or barriers to create an environment for successful co-operation with a common vision is clearly a task for the senior management of the organization. They must want to create an open environment where everyone is clearly focused on a strategic vision.

The consequences for your project are serious when a feudal kingdom is encountered. You find it virtually impossible to reach agreements, and even if you do, they are frequently ignored and broken. There is little sense of obligation demonstrated by the baron or lords of the manors and any attempt to create a real sense of good time management is hopeless. Your only course of action is to take the difficulties directly to your project sponsor with clearly illustrated evidence of the impact on the project. A strategic project has a 'must not fail' label that all functional managers must acknowledge, and your sponsor has the authority to cross the boundaries of these empires and force an atmosphere of willing co-operation.

Your project is always vulnerable, and all your efforts to encourage good time management and keep the project on track are wasted unless you respond promptly to such issues and escalate them for some very prompt action.

Have regular one-to-ones

Many of the time management problems can be reduced and their impact minimized with quick identification and realization that there is a problem. Performance management is an essential part of your job, and it requires regular contact with all your resources and the stakeholders, particularly if the latter have responsibility for some of the actual project work. The one-to-one meetings with each team member are essential to help you:

- demonstrate your concern and interest in their welfare;
- understand the team members as individuals;
- learn about their experience, skills, interests, beliefs and aspirations;
- discover how they feel about their work;
- find what concerns they have about their work;
- learn what problems they have with the work itself;
- discover what difficulties they have with managing their time effectively;
- agree personal targets aligned to the plan;
- monitor and discuss performance;
- identify areas for future training and development;
- agree any relevant recommendations to pass to their line manager.

The meetings are meant to be informal, but actions agreed are recorded and reviewed in the next discussion. Allow 30–45 minutes for each meeting and decide a frequency at the start of the project. Usually a monthly dialogue of this type is adequate, but it does depend on the length of the project. Diarized monthly discussions of this type never prevent *ad hoc* discussions and do not take the place of regular monitoring activities.

Your team members are giving a part of their available capacity to your work. In many situations their own line managers will not have much contact with them during this work, beyond some general concerns for their welfare. You have close and detailed information about each team member's performance and this needs to pass back to their line manager as part of the more formalized performance appraisal process. You can make an objective contribution to this process only through having a regular dialogue with each team member. A subsequent poor or indifferent appraisal review interview may be blamed on you, with quite serious impact on an individual's motivation!

Remember that you need a similar regular dialogue with your project sponsor to sustain your own motivation to achieve success.

CHECKLIST 24: ENCOURAGE GOOD TIME MANAGEMENT

Self:

- Identify your own time management problems.
- Regard time as a manageable resource, not a constraint.
- Focus on priorities, short and medium term.
- Create effective procedures and adopt them as a habit.
- Identify the barriers and time robbers that affect your work.
- Derive an action plan to eliminate the time robbers.
- Review your progress at regular intervals.

The team:

- Have regular one-to-ones to discuss performance.
- Encourage good time management practices.
- Support and give guidance where appropriate.
- Encourage self-evaluation and measurement of improvement.
- Create an open atmosphere where time problems are discussed.

Stakeholders:

- Keep up to date with progress and changes.
- Agree an acceptable breakdown of the work, avoiding too many small chunks.
- Eliminate the opportunities for excessive 'back-tracking'.
- Keep the focus on the project objectives and strategic priority.
- React promptly to structural barriers hindering the work.
- Escalate co-operation issues promptly to the project sponsor.
- Have regular one-to-ones with your sponsor.

CONTROLLING THE PROJECT COSTS

The control of expenditure is important to all organizations, yet many do not measure and monitor the costs of their business projects. The highest proportion of these costs is frequently associated with the resources used, and this is regarded as part of the operating costs of the business. Control of your project is not just about controlling the effort and work outputs, but should involve cost measurement. It is not just the domain of the finance department. You are keen to demonstrate success, and this is total only if you do not exceed the budget.

The data for setting up a budget and gathering expenditure information exist in every management information system. Often the projects have a low priority with finance people, who are mainly concerned to produce business operating statements rapidly each month. In many organizations the only way you can obtain accurate and up-to-date information on how much you have spent is to record it yourself. Once you make a commitment to spend some money in your project, it is out of your budget. The finance report may still not record this commitment until an invoice appears several weeks or months later. The budget report still shows you have more money left than is really true!

Of course, cost control is effective only if *all* costs are measured, including the costs of people working on the project. This means that everyone must record his or her time spent on project work so that this can be costed, with cost rates derived by the finance people. Cost rates often include all indirect costs such as rents, heating, lighting, etc for the organization. If the time data are not collected in a consistent and disciplined way then you cannot control the costs accurately. Your monitoring process must therefore include accurate measurement of:

- the time spent on each task;
- the resources used on all tasks;
- cost of materials (including wastage) used;
- the cost of equipment time used;
- capital expenditure committed (this may be treated separately);
- revenue expenditure committed (this may be included as an overhead in resource costs).

Normally you make these measurements over a specific period of two or four weeks or by calendar month.

For effective control you need information on:

- the project budget, a cumulative total divided into accounting periods;
- the costs incurred in the current accounting period;
- the costs incurred to date from the start;
- the work scheduled for completion according to the plan in the current period;
- the total work scheduled for completion to date;
- the work actually completed in the current period;
- the total work actually completed to date.

You can use the WBS and the key stage Gantt chart as the basis for collecting these data.

Cost performance

A graph showing cost planned and actual cost may seem to be a simple solution. An example is shown in Figure 9.11. However, although this chart can give you useful information, the information is incomplete. First, it does not tell you whether work planned is getting done. It shows only the rate of expenditure; expenditure above the planned level could be due to the work being ahead of schedule. Second, it does not tell you how up to date the cost data from the finance team are; accounting lag times can be four to eight weeks behind the current date.

It would seem from Figure 9.11 that the project will ultimately be over budget, but this chart cannot tell you what to forecast for the costs of the remaining months of the project. To get an accurate picture you need to

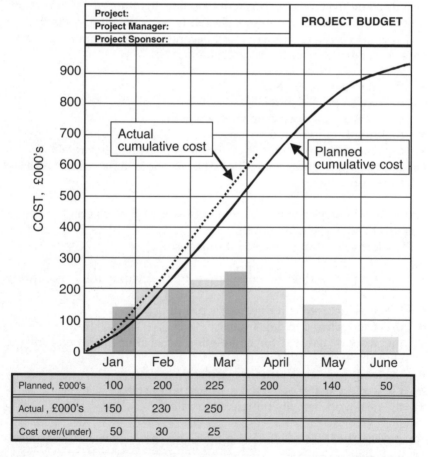

Project:				PROJECT BUDGET	
Project Manager:					
Project Sponsor:					

	Jan	Feb	Mar	April	May	June
Planned, £000's	100	200	225	200	140	50
Actual , £000's	150	230	250			
Cost over/(under)	50	30	25			

Figure 9.11 Planned versus actual project cost

measure the planned and actual costs of the work done. This is done with *earned value analysis*.

Cost control measures

To use earned value analysis, four essential measures are used for the control of project costs:

1. BAC – budget at completion

Budget at completion is based on the operating budget developed from the WBS for the whole project.

2. BCWS – budgeted cost of the work scheduled

At any specific time, the schedule shows that a certain amount of work should be completed. This is presented as a *percentage completion* of the total work of the project at that time. Then:

Scheduled completion $\times$ BAC = BCWS

3. BCWP – budgeted cost of the work performed

At any specified time the actual work measured as complete is compared with the scheduled amount and the *real percentage completion* calculated. Then:

Percentage actual completion $\times$ BAC = BCWP

The BCWP is known as the *earned value* of the work because it is the value of the work completed.

4. ACWP – actual cost of work performed

The actual cost of work performed at any specified time is the actual cost incurred for the work. The timing of the actual cost measurement coincides with the *percentage completion* progress measurement so that the actual cost can be compared with earned value (BCWP).

Other terms often used include:

5. FTC – forecast to completion

Forecast to completion is a forecast of the cost to be incurred to complete the remaining work. This may be an extrapolation using an analysis model or simply the costs to date added to your best estimates of all the costs to complete the project, eg:

FTC = BAC (ACWP/BCWP)

6. CV – cost variance

Cost variance is the difference between the value of the work performed and the actual cost for that work, ie:

$$CV = BCWP - ACWP$$

If the actual cost is above budget, the CV becomes negative!

7. CV% – cost variance per cent

Cost variance per cent is the cost variance divided by the planned cost, ie:

$$CV\% = CV/BCWP$$

If CV% is positive, it means that the work was performed under budget, whereas a negative figure shows that the project is running over budget at the point of measurement.

8. SV – schedule variance

Schedule variance is the difference between the value of the work performed and the value of the work that was scheduled to be performed, at the same measurement point in time, ie:

$$SV = BCWP - BCWS$$

If the work done is behind schedule, the SV becomes negative!

9. SV% – schedule variance per cent

The schedule variance per cent is the schedule variance divided by the budgeted cost of work scheduled to be complete at the date considered, ie:

$$SV\% = SV/BCWS$$

A positive SV% shows that more work has been completed than originally scheduled by the date considered. A negative SV% is bad news because it means less work than planned in the schedule has been done.

The variance measures are often used for trend analysis, because of their sensitivity to changes as the project progresses.

The cost control diagram

A convenient way to show the relationships between the cost measures in a graphic format is known as the *cost control diagram*. The ACWP and BCWP curves in Figure 9.12 are exaggerated to show the relationships clearly. In practice, both measures tend to cycle with time both above and below the budget curve (BCWS), and a mean curve is drawn through the scatter of points. The most accurate way is to tabulate all data using a spreadsheet program on a computer to calculate and update the data at regular intervals.

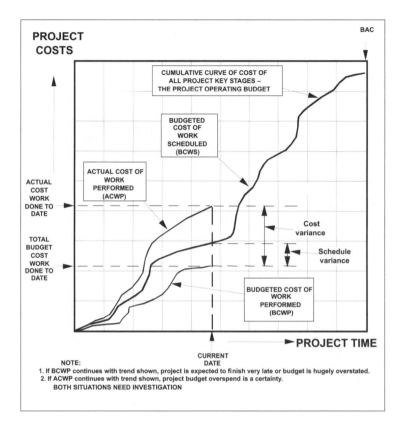

Figure 9.12 Cost control diagram

Using a spreadsheet on a computer makes it easier to incorporate any amendments to the budget resulting from major changes to the project. The data are then used to generate the diagram automatically for each reporting period.

The cost control diagram is a good tool for one project. For programmes and projects with several sub-projects a different charting approach can be used.

Cost and schedule performance chart

The *cost and schedule performance chart* shows at a glance the performance for several projects on one diagram. An example of a radar-type chart is shown in Figure 9.13.

Plot each project and sub-project as bullets using the values calculated for SV% and CV%; you can immediately see the relative performance of

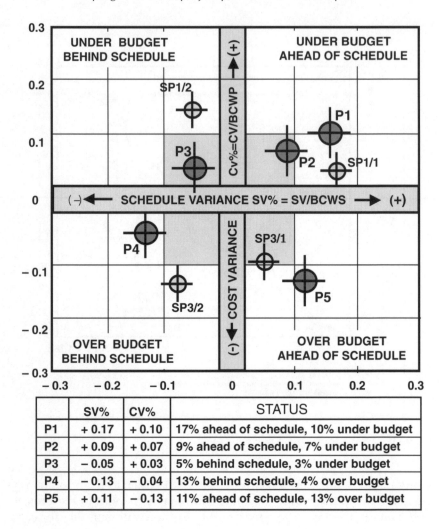

Figure 9.13 Cost and schedule performance chart

all the projects. Sponsors can use this type of performance chart for all the programmes and projects for which they are accountable. It is also useful for the PST, to help it effectively take an oversight view of the status of the organization portfolio of programmes and projects.

The PST can impose variance limits to show on the diagram, beyond which any project must be alerted for management decisions. On Figure 9.13 the inner grey area marked at the 10 per cent point indicates that any project moving beyond this area is alerted to the PST. Projects running well ahead of schedule may be using resources that could be transferred to others not doing so well. Projects running over budget and behind schedule may need to be carefully reviewed for possible scope reduction.

Accurate cost control is the most effective way to control a project, as variance to the project baseline schedule and budget is rapidly evident. If any project changes are approved that revise the balance between schedule and cost then the impact must be incorporated into the cost control. It is advisable to always retain the baseline unchanged for reference. The only valid time for a baseline to be changed is when the customer makes a radical change to the scope, causing a full replan of the project and a significant revision of the business case.

THE REGULAR 'GOTCHAS'

No, of course it is not simple. The processes you use in programme and project management are fundamentally not difficult to use; the difficulty is in getting people to use them effectively so they and you feel in control. All the techniques proposed here are proven, powerful tools and do work well, but they do not mean your project will be on time, on budget and have no issues or changes. The art of project management is applying the science to achieve the desired results. Many of the problems you encounter are seen over and over again, yet the solutions always seem a 'mission impossible'. When you hear comments like, 'Oh, that always happens!', it's time to react with avoiding actions. Some of the common problems are discussed below.

Lack of authority

Most projects cross functional boundaries within the organization. You are asking people to do the work and you have no authority over them because they work in other departments where the line manager does not feel involvement in the project. Ensure that:

- the business case includes a project charter that clearly lays out the responsibilities and your delegated authority limits;
- you convert the line managers, providing them with resources through which they can understand the stakeholder role and take steps to convert them to positive indirect influencers;
- keep stakeholders well informed with regular status reports;
- develop a strong working relationship with your sponsor.

Time management

Avoid floating start, phase and milestone dates. Fix dates with careful planning and watch out for people spending time on unnecessary activities. Don't try to do everything yourself – delegate, delegate, delegate. Help people prioritize their work and focus on activities that really matter, avoiding interesting tasks that don't count. Learn to say 'No', politely, when asked to add tasks that really bring nothing to the achieving of your objectives.

Too much reporting

Most people run away from bureaucracy, and written reports are no substitute for face-to-face contact with your team members and stakeholders. Avoid too much paperwork but use a standard format for progress reports as this conveys essential data only. Too often e-mails convey vague opinions that are of no added value to you when reviewing project status. Diarize regular one-to-ones with your team members and sponsor and let it be known how, when and at what intervals your progress reports will be issued. Keep your door open (if you have one!) unless you are in a meeting; don't leave a notice on your door asking people to make an appointment!

The 90 per cent problem

Watch out for the 90 per cent syndrome ('I'm almost done – about 90%'). This can even happen on two or more successive reports. The last 10 per cent may take longer than the first 90 per cent because of sub-surface problems that are not clear or not understood, or because there are just too many unknowns. Encourage honesty with estimates, particularly where a high level of creativity is needed. You may be getting a reported estimate that was originally fixed months ago in the schedule because the person giving you the estimate thinks it is what you expect to hear and wants to avoid exposing the reality. The truth will come out eventually and put you into a damage limitation exercise as other activities are impacted. If the schedule needs to be revised, you need to know as early as possible in order to allow replanning to take place.

Moving targets

Unfortunately, as project work proceeds, new ideas are appearing all the time. These can come from the customer, sponsor, stakeholders or your team. Creative ideas are great as they show that people are focusing on making the project successful. Changes are discussed earlier, so ensure they are clearly documented, not just tucked in here and there – a sure way to disaster. Always adjust the plan after changes are approved, not before, and revise the business case when appropriate.

Fighting fires and cost control

The techniques discussed earlier take time but they are designed to provide you and your team with a disciplined approach to achieving success. Remember that there are 'arsonists' about who will attempt to derail the project, and these people often consider such activities as clear definition and careful planning to be wasting valuable time. You are expected to dive in and correct as you go along in the interests of flexibility. Unfortunately, the price for this approach is often initially hidden and uncontrolled but surfaces eventually. Chaos will develop as costs spiral owing to uncontrolled use of resources in a situation where there are no clear responsibilities or commitment. Effective planning and good monitoring limit the fires to minor outbursts and keep costs under control. Do not rely on others to manage your budget; this is one task that is a priority for you.

Cost over-runs do not just happen. Poor communication and monitoring, lack of control of changes and irregular, inaccurate reporting all contribute to costs creeping ahead of the budget.

The right people

Projects are often seen by line managers as an opportunity to train a new recruit or pass on someone who has little to do right now. Are you just a little suspicious when you are enthusiastically offered a new team member by a manager? Building a team of enthusiastic people is a great motivator, but have you checked out their experience and skills? Enthusiasm is not a substitute for experience and skills. You do not have time in a project to train people with skills you need now. Unfortunately, telling people or their manager that the person offered is not acceptable is not easy to do and takes you into the political environment in the organization. Dead wood in the team will seriously slow down the project work, so do not ever delay acting to correct such situations. Remember, your main objective is the project's success, and that is not your ego in control but a business need delegated to you by the PST.

Mission impossible

It is not uncommon for project managers to incorporate more tasks in a project than are really necessary to achieve the objectives. Engaging on a project with unrealistic objectives, budget or schedule only leads to trying to achieve the impossible.

Try to avoid ever starting such a project even if there is pressure from higher management because it is someone's pet idea. Carry out a careful risk assessment to highlight the level of unacceptable and high risk involved. If you are still forced to start work, keep highlighting the risks and the issues as they occur and focus on the cost element. Maybe eventually they will see your arguments and either give you the scope to revise the requirements or scrap the project.

Sometimes a project runs into a brick wall! If the requirements start to clearly appear impossible tell your sponsor quickly. Avoid spending the organization's money on an impossible project. Either a major revision of the business case must be made or the project must be cancelled. Reluctance to take such decisions has cost many an organization huge sum of money and even bankruptcy.

You were not born with the ability to fly, so don't try to achieve the impossible and don't be afraid to admit a qualified and reasoned defeat!

APPROACHING THE CLOSURE PHASE

The day you never dared to expect will eventually arrive – when you realize that the work of your project is almost at an end. You can now look back over the many weeks and months of trials, tribulations, changes and successes and start to assimilate just what you have achieved. The team has worked well and can also recognize that the end is in sight – but it's not quite over yet. You cannot enter the final phase of the project until you have convinced the PST that you have satisfied the requirements set out in the current version of the business case. Provided you have kept the business case up to date with all changes approved during the project, the final step in this phase should be straightforward. To prepare for the presentation of your project to the PST, ask:

- Have all the requirements in the business case been met in full?
- Are any dependent projects/sub-projects/tasks incomplete?
- Are any unresolved issues outstanding that could affect closure?
- Are any action plans outstanding that could hold up closure?
- Are the cost records and variances to budget up to date?
- Has any revenue been generated to date?
- Have you lost any key resources needed for the next phase?
- Is the project documentation up to date?
- Are there any significant risks that could still hit your project?
- Is there anything you are aware of that could delay final closure and handover to your customer?

When you are satisfied you have everything under control and you have fulfilled the project's objectives, you can prepare a full presentation for the PST.

Prepare your PST presentation

The focus now will primarily be on the results achieved:

- objectives achieved;
- objectives not achieved, with reasons why;
- review of expected benefits;
- current state of the project budget;
- forecast project cost at completion;
- risks that could occur before closure;
- issues outstanding;
- summary of agreed revisions to the original business case.

The approval of the entry to the closure phase is an important and significant step. The PST must be satisfied that the project has generated the desired results and benefits, and that no rework or additional work is needed. Additional activities are better saved for a further, new project, even though there is a temptation to keep the team together and carry on. There is a risk of costs escalating, and careful control is essential. When you are ready to present your project to the PST, inform the PST administrator and fix the date.

PST approval

Before you make your presentation to the PST, ensure that your sponsor is fully appraised of the project's status; you do not want to find yourself without support in the meeting! Keep your presentation focused on facts. The PST is just as anxious as you to chalk up a successful outcome. Be prepared to recommend resolution actions for any outstanding issues and explain any potential risks remaining that you identified in your risk review.

The PST may give you a 'GO' decision, a conditional 'GO' decision or, more rarely, a 'NO GO' decision requiring more work to be done. Provided the decision is 'GO', you have approval to pass Phase Gate Four and enter the final phase of closure. The PST administrator will record the decision on the programme register and inform stakeholders.

SUMMARY

Figure 9.14 summarizes the key steps you repeatedly go through during project execution. Checklist 25 identifies some key leadership actions during this phase.

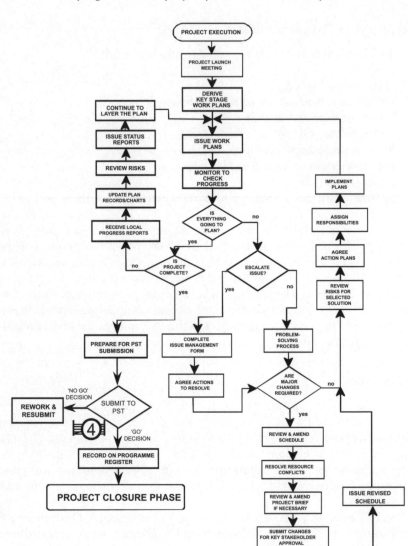

Figure 9.14 Process flow diagram: project execution

CHECKLIST 25: KEY LEADERSHIP ACTIONS DURING PROJECT EXECUTION

- The stakeholders:
  - Report regularly on progress.
  - Are involved in problem solving.
  - Maintain commitment with regular contact.
  - Encourage feedback of changing needs.
  - Regulate plan changes.
  - Seek approval of major changes.
- Project tasks:
  - Confirm resource commitments.
  - Continue to layer the plan detail.
  - Derive and sign off work plans as work progresses.
  - Modify the plan as appropriate.
  - Review progress against the project brief.
  - Track and record progress against the plan baseline.
  - Keep updated records of all cost information.
- Project team:
  - Co-ordinate team working.
  - Encourage participation of extended team members.
  - Involve everyone in replanning activities.
  - Resolve conflict and issues promptly.
  - Actively support team efforts with guidance and assistance.
- Team members:
  - Advise and coach when opportune.
  - Hold regular one-to-ones to discuss performance.
  - Stress priorities.
  - Recognize and praise effort.
  - Encourage participation in teamwork.
  - React positively to performance issues.

10

Closing your project

All good things must end – even your project! You have diligently nursed your project through the earlier phases and experienced the excitement of achieving the desired deliverables. You have overcome the trials and tribulations of the issues that seemed like 'mission impossible' at the time to emerge within sight of the finishing line. This final phase of your project still has all the potential for success or failure. Many issues can still occur and you must continue to monitor carefully to ensure a successful outcome. Closure of a project does not just happen; you must plan it with care.

As the project approaches the end it is easy for senior management to appear to lose interest. They are looking ahead to the next project, and this can be perceived as a lack of commitment. Your communication processes must keep them involved right up to the celebration of completion. The last thing you want is to become infected with a common virus: 'project drift'.

Project drift

Project drift occurs when you let the pressure off the control system as the end approaches. It is easy for the customer or any stakeholder to throw in a few add-ons: 'Just before you finish the project will you have a look at this modification?' This is the first sounding of the death knell! Control of late changes of mind adds significant extra work just as you are tidying up to prepare for handover to the customer. These extras are not budgeted, and can add considerable costs to the project and seriously affect the schedule. Any significant changes at this stage are best treated as a follow-on project after closing the current project.

Life after closure

There is also another consequence of add-ons: their effect on the motivation of your team. You are concerned about what happens next, and so are the members of your team. They are concerned about their next assignment, and this may show as a reduced motivation. The impact on remaining tasks is a possible slowing-down of effort and lack of commitment. You must keep the momentum going and avoid losing team members to other projects or operational activities. You and your team have worked closely together for some time now, so the next step is full of unknowns and will bring the severance of friendships and working relationships.

Similarly, your customer may suffer such effects and not bother to attend meetings so readily. The users will be anticipating the handover and may attempt to advance the completion by encouraging the taking of short cuts. If the changes the users have to accept at handover are still not popular or accepted, they may obstruct completion and create additional work to cause delays. All these difficulties can be anticipated if you have maintained effective communication and involve the stakeholders closely in the closure process.

WHY HAVE A CLOSURE PHASE?

A clean closedown of the project gives a sense of a job well done and satisfaction for everyone who has been involved. Success rubs off on people and affects how they feel about what they have achieved and how you led the team. This phase requires you to ensure that closure is carried out in a controlled and organized manner, just like all the work that was done before. The key steps involved include:

- meeting with all stakeholders to get their acceptance of the closure process;
- completing all contractual commitments to contractors and suppliers;
- establishing the closure criteria with the customer;
- preparing a plan for the staged transfer of responsibilities to marketing and manufacturing departments, including documentation;
- preparing a staged plan for the transfer of the team members to new projects or their original departments;
- releasing equipment and materials;
- completing and auditing the project accounts; the final project cost, paying all outstanding invoices and closing down the accounts;
- updating the project file and documentation;
- if required, preparing a final summary report of the project's performance.

Failure to formally close a project has been known to leave people still working on activities they think important with no control. The project manager left weeks ago and yet they are still hidden away working on an endless project! These valuable resources could be better used elsewhere but they are lost in the vast network of the organization, apparently busy but achieving little of value for the business.

The PST will expect a final presentation from you showing a clean and successful closedown, with a satisfied customer. You should demonstrate that you have:

- met the requirements of the business case;
- obtained the expected benefits;
- evaluated the project performance for lessons learnt;
- shut down all work other than those activities essential to handover to the customer;
- transferred responsibilities where necessary;
- prepared the ground for the transfer of the team to other activities;
- prepared a final report on the project.

ESTABLISHING COMPLETION CRITERIA

Agree with your customer and the customer's user group just what completion means to them. Identify the specific criteria they want to use to confirm completion.

Project completion is signified by the fact that:

- all tasks are finished;
- specific deliverables are finished;
- testing programmes are finished;
- training programmes are prepared and/or finished;
- equipment is installed and operating;
- documentation manuals are finished;
- process procedures are finished and tested;
- staff training is finished.

All criteria for completion must be measurable by agreed methods or conflict will be inevitable. Use the completion criteria to create a *closure checklist* to assist you and the team to ensure that all outstanding work is completed.

Checklist 26 gives some of the typical headings with some starter questions to create a closure checklist. Add more subject headings and questions as required, particularly with respect to the technical aspects of the project deliverables. Areas such as the handover to the sales and manufacturing functions can be added as separate headings and expanded to include specific details of the transfer of responsibilities.

CHECKLIST 26: QUESTIONS FOR A CLOSURE CHECKLIST

Deliverables:

- Have all deliverables been completed and handed over to the customer and new internal 'owners'?
- Has accountability for any outstanding deliverables been assigned?

Project tasks:

- Have all outstanding tasks been agreed, with firm completion dates?
- Have all outstanding tasks been assigned?
- Have the project file and documentation been completed up to date?

Issues:

- Have all issues been resolved?
- Have agreed completion dates been agreed for all outstanding issues?
- Has ownership for outstanding issues been agreed?

Project follow-on:

- Have all follow-on activities been agreed and assigned?
- Have all training needs been planned and activated?
- Have all documentation manuals been completed, signed off and issued?

Sales and manufacturing:

- Have necessary documentation and process details been transferred to these functions?
- Have responsibilities for transfer to these functions been agreed and assigned?

Business case:

- Has the business case been updated with the final outcome?
- Has the forecast of benefits been updated and communicated to others?
- Has accountability for monitoring and reviewing benefits been assigned?
- Have review points for measuring the benefits been agreed?

Team and stakeholders:

- Have all stakeholders been informed of the imminent closure of the project?
- Has a team member reassignment plan been agreed and issued?
- Have individual team appraisals been completed and passed to line managers?

Evaluation:

- Has the active evaluation of the project been completed?
- Has a date been fixed for conducting the post-project evaluation?

Project budget:

- Have all project costs been collected and finalized?
- Has the cost system been blocked to any further expenditure?
- Has the final cost been derived, with reasons for variance from budget?

Project amenities:

- Have all project amenities (office space, desks, computers, etc) been released?
- Have arrangements been agreed for the release of remaining amenities in use?

One of the key stages in your plan should be the acceptance process for handover to your customer. Your ultimate objective is to delight your customer, so validate the acceptance process now.

THE ACCEPTANCE PROCESS

For most projects it is easy for the team to identify the essential steps of handover. The acceptance process is based on the closure checklist, and you should get your customer and the user group to agree with this list of actions to reach a state of readiness for full acceptance. This checklist includes a list of activities that must be finished before acceptance is confirmed. The list includes questions on various topics, depending on the type of project:

- unfinished non-critical work;
- the project tasks – based on the WBS;
- the deliverables achieved – based on the project brief;
- quality standards attained – based on the scope of work statement;

- supply of equipment;
- installation of equipment;
- testing and validation of equipment;
- testing and validation of operating processes;
- documentation manuals;
- new standard operating procedures;
- design of training programmes;
- training of operating staff and management;
- training of maintenance staff;
- setting up of a help desk;
- establishing a maintenance function;
- outstanding issues awaiting resolution;
- identifying follow-on projects;
- limits of acceptability.

The acceptance process should also identify the customer representative who has the authority to sign the project completion certificate.

In addition, confirm:

- who is responsible for each step of the acceptance process and the work involved;
- what post-project support is required and who is responsible;
- what post-project support can be available;
- for how long such support must be given.

Once an agreed process is produced with the checklist, you are ready to implement the final stages of the project. You can then set up the *close-out meeting*.

THE CLOSE-OUT MEETING

Prepare the team well for this important meeting. It is the culmination of all your efforts over many weeks or months.

Hold a team meeting to review:

- the project WBS;
- the project brief;
- the key stage Gantt chart;
- the project risk log;
- the project issue log;
- the final key stage work plan charts;
- the project milestone schedule;
- the business case.

Check that all work is finishing on time and no forgotten tasks are expected. At this stage it is quite common to find a number of outstanding minor tasks from earlier key stages still unfinished. They are not critical and have not impeded progress, yet they must be completed. Set clear targets in this final sweep to complete all these tasks soon to avoid giving your customer an excuse to withhold acceptance.

Then go through the closure checklist with your customer and set targets for the team for any outstanding work to complete. Focus on outstanding issues and allocate responsibility for each, with clear target dates for resolution. When you are satisfied that everything is under control, confirm the date of the close-out meeting with your customer, the sponsor, key stakeholders and the core team. For programmes, ensure that the project managers of all dependent projects are also invited to attend the meeting. A typical agenda for the meeting is shown in Figure 10.1.

At this meeting your objective is to get agreement for the sponsor to formally close the project. To achieve this objective, you:

- review the project results achieved;
- receive feedback from everyone involved;
- go through the closure checklist and confirm completion of actions;
- confirm and explain action plans for any outstanding work to be tidied up;
- confirm and explain action plans for any outstanding issues;
- agree and confirm responsibilities for any ongoing work or support;
- confirm who is accountable for monitoring the project's benefits;
- present the completion certificate for approval and sign-off by the sponsor;
- thank the team for their efforts;
- thank the stakeholders for their support and commitment;
- thank the customer and your sponsor for their support and commitment.

Provided you have done everything the closure checklist demands, acceptance should be agreed and the completion certificate (see Figure 10.2) approved and signed by the sponsor.

You will probably leave this meeting with a feeling of considerable relief – if your project is signed off. But you have not quite finished yet! So, delay the final celebrations for a few days, because now you must carry out an evaluation of the project.

CLOSE-OUT MEETING AGENDA
DATE:
VENUE:

PROGRAMME/PROJECT NO:
PROGRAMME/PROJECT SPONSOR:
PROGRAMME/PROJECT MANAGER:

WELCOME BY THE SPONSOR

1. **DELIVERABLES**
   Confirm that the list of deliverables in the business case has been approved and accepted.
2. **OUTSTANDING ACTIVITIES**
   Review outstanding activities not complete, expected dates of completion and responsibilities.
3. **TRANSFER OF RESPONSIBILITIES**
   Confirm that the handover checklist is completed and actioned and all transfer of responsibilities is completed.
4. **OUTSTANDING ISSUES**
   Review outstanding issues and confirm that responsibilities to resolve are assigned and dates for completion of actions are accepted.
5. **BENEFITS AND BUSINESS CASE**
   Confirm that business case benefits are on target; report any revenue to date and whether forecast of future benefits is in accordance with expectations. Assign accountability for monitoring of business benefit development in the future and any future performance reviews.
6. **ACKNOWLEDGEMENTS**
   Thank the customer, sponsor, stakeholders and team for their efforts and contributions to achieving a successful outcome.
7. **LESSONS LEARNT**
   Highlight any key lessons learnt from what went well and what went badly. Indicate when the full evaluation report will be issued.
8. **FORMAL CLOSURE**
   Provided all present are in agreement, the completion report is signed off by the sponsor.

Figure 10.1 Agenda for the close-out meeting

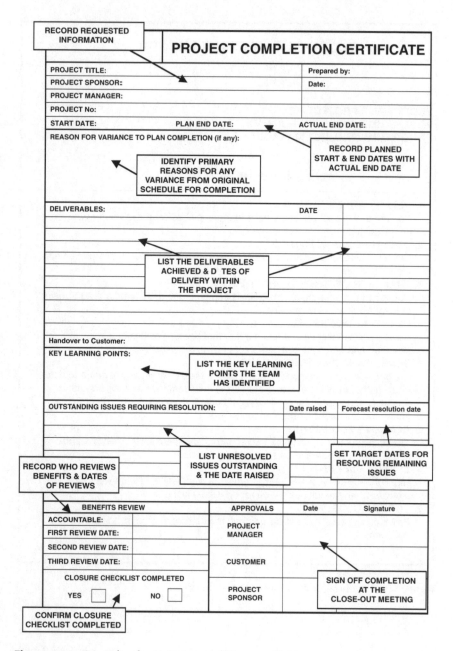

Figure 10.2 Example of a project completion certificate

EVALUATING YOUR PROJECT

Question: Why evaluate?
Answer: To learn.

Evaluation is the process used to review the project and identify what went well and what went badly, and then ask, 'Why?'

Question: What is evaluated?
Answer: The technical work, achievements, the project processes and the management of the project.

Evaluation of projects normally has two modes:

- active – a continuous process throughout the project's life, with occasional specific reviews or 'audits';
- post-project – after the project is handed over to your customer. The post-project evaluation provides data for future projects.

Evaluation is difficult to complete because everyone who has been involved in the project is looking to his or her next assignment. The work of the project has finished, with motivation and enthusiasm dropping to a low level. People do not want to be reminded of what went badly and start an inquest at this late stage, viewing the events as ancient history.

Active evaluation

Active evaluation often happens by default. Members of an effective project team are always keen to learn from what they are doing. Promote evaluation by encouraging the team to question the way it carries out the project work. This is particularly valid when issues are resolved by asking relevant questions. When you ask an open question about an event, there are always consequential questions that follow.

There are no rules for evaluation; just let the team focus on identifying opportunities for learning. This is continuous improvement in action, leading to better ways of doing things. What is more important is that anything learnt must be accepted and broadcast so that everyone can benefit from the experience. This is a more difficult activity for you to implement. Your primary concern is the project and you have little time to spend talking to other project managers about events that have occurred and how they were resolved. They may show only a passing casual interest since they are similarly focused on their projects.

Suggest to your sponsor that a forum of project managers meet occasionally to share learning from their project activities. Particularly important events and the resulting improvements in project process could be the subject of a special presentation. An alternative approach is to start a project newsletter for your project community. This has the additional benefit of giving publicity and recognition to particular projects, project teams and the results achieved. The newsletter takes some of the mystery and secrecy out of the organization's project activities. Checklist 27 gives some starter questions; ask others that are more appropriate to your project.

CHECKLIST 27: QUESTIONS FOR ACTIVE EVALUATION

For any event, ask:

- Why did this happen?
- What were the consequences?
- Was it good or bad for the project, stakeholders and team?
- Could the situation have been anticipated?
- Were there early signals that went unrecognized at the time?
- When was the situation first identified?
- Who should have reacted?
- Was it due to unclear responsibility or authority?
- Was it due to poor estimating?
- Was it due to poor planning?
- Has there been a failure by any stakeholders to fulfil their obligations?
- Has there been a communication failure?
- Where have our communication processes failed?
- Can we correct these failures now?
- Has the control system failed us?
- Is the event a direct result of current organizational policies?
- What have we learnt from the event(s)?
- What changes can we implement now to prevent a recurrence?
- Are policy changes necessary?
- Are the learning points valuable for other project teams?
- How can we check that the learning points are communicated now?

CLOSING DOWN THE PROJECT

So, you are ready to celebrate the fact that the many months of exhausting work are over and you are ready for a new assignment. Not quite yet, because you must conduct a clean closedown of your project. The completion certificate has been signed off; you have completed your initial evaluation of lessons learnt, and assigned responsibilities for outstanding tasks and issues. You should have updated the business case to align with the final project outcome. This should be a straightforward task if you have always maintained the document as the project progressed. Now you must prepare your final report for the PST, which will want you to demonstrate that you have satisfied the business case requirements and delighted your customer.

Inform the PST administrator that you are ready to submit your final report to the PST and arrange a date for the presentation. When you have a date for the presentation, ensure that the document has been issued before the meeting.

Prepare your PST presentation

The focus now will primarily be on the final results achieved:

- requirements achieved;
- benefits achieved;
- final cost of the project and variance from the budget;
- any issues outstanding, actions to resolve and dates for completion;
- summary of responsibilities transferred;
- summary of people reassignments;
- key lessons learnt;
- project documentation up to date and the file ready to be closed.

The approval of the final closedown is a significant step. The PST must be satisfied that no additional work is needed.

PST approval

At this final phase gate it is unlikely that the PST will give a 'NO GO' decision. Your presentation should be an occasion for celebration of a successful conclusion to your project. It is always possible that the PST may delay that final closedown until absolutely no outstanding tasks are completed, particularly as a decision may have been made to reassign you to a new project or other job. If such tasks exist, ensure that accountability for them is clearly agreed before the meeting. If you have completed the preparation carefully, you should not face this problem and it should not cause any difficulties with the PST.

Once the PST has agreed a 'GO' decision to close the project, the PST administrator will record the decision on the programme register and inform stakeholders that the project is completed.

After approval

After the PST meeting you must close down and archive the project file. The final task for you before you can close the file is to ensure that all reassignments of the team members are completed. Then you can call together everyone who has been involved in the project at any time for a celebration meeting. Include the stakeholders, without whom you would have not been so successful. Ask your sponsor to give a very short presentation to the group about how the senior management feel about the achievements, and acknowledge the contribution made by all present. If appropriate (or allowed), even provide a free lunch!

POST-PROJECT EVALUATION

Valuable experience and information are gained during a project. Much of this is lost in the archives and never recovered to help future teams. You and your team members will remember the highlights. As you all move on to other activities and projects, the learning points become dimmed with the passage of time. Lessons learnt should be documented and distributed to individuals engaged or likely to be engaged in project activities. Opportunities for improving processes and procedures are continually present. Some of the learning from projects should be incorporated into the organization's policy.

It is appropriate to carry out post-project evaluation asking in-depth and searching questions about each dimension of the project manager's role:

- managing the project stakeholders;
- managing the project's life cycle;
- managing performance of the stakeholders, yourself and the team.

In all areas when questions are asked, there are inevitably consequent questions of cause and effect to be answered by the project team as a means of checking that all possible learning points are identified. The results of this evaluation should be published in the post-project or post-mortem report. It is easy to avoid the events where things went wrong because of the potential risk of hurting someone's feelings. If these events involve senior management, evaluating them may be perceived as direct criticism, and therefore career limiting! Focus on facts, not perceptions, and avoid negative statements. Every negative has an equal and opposite positive, so seek the positives that will give the organization benefits in the future. For example, a statement about the poor performance of a sponsor can easily be perceived as highly critical. Turn this into a positive statement:

At week 6 a slippage of three weeks was incurred owing to delays in the approval of the primary plan (*fact*). This was caused by the sponsor being absent overseas resolving problems on project X (*fact*). The delay could have been avoided if another executive manager or the project manager had been given the necessary authority during this period of absence (*learning*).

Checklist 28 lists some typical questions to ask during the evaluation process. Such a list can never be exhaustive, because many specific questions are directly related to a particular project. Add further questions to ask for your project. Every question yields an answer that generates more questions to ask and you must decide where to stop. Remember that the purpose of this whole process is to learn.

> Evaluation is not an exercise in self-gratification. The process must be an objective one at all times, not one of placing blame or boosting individual egos.

CHECKLIST 28: QUESTIONS FOR POST-PROJECT EVALUATION

Ask question about the stakeholders:

- Were the needs correctly identified initially?
- Was the project purpose statement correct?
- Did the needs change during the project as a result of unforeseen events?
- Were the benefits correctly identified and satisfied by the project?
- Were the expected results obtained?
- Were unexpected results obtained?
- Is there a follow-up need to be examined in subsequent projects?
- Were all stakeholders identified at the outset?
- Did new stakeholders appear during the project?
- Were stakeholders managed effectively?
- Did stakeholders interfere unnecessarily with the detail?
- Did any external stakeholders fail in their obligations?

Ask questions about the project's life cycle:

- Was a feasibility study carried out?
- Who defined the project's purpose?

- Was the project manager appointed at the outset?
- Were responsibility, authority and accountability clearly defined for the project manager?
- Were realistic timescales established for the project?
- Were project objectives clear and understood?
- Were all tasks clearly established with accurate durations?
- Was the plan logic correct?
- Were project resources correctly estimated?
- Were work plans for each team member clearly established?
- Were all team members aware of their responsibilities and authority?
- Were all resource commitments honoured?
- Were milestones clearly established?
- Were project review meetings built into the plan?
- Were all resource constraints identified and resolved?
- Were risks identified and regularly monitored?
- Was there a documented control system understood by everyone?
- Were there clear lines of communication for monitoring and providing feedback?
- Did the reporting process work effectively?
- Did project meetings achieve their purpose?
- Were all issues resolved promptly?
- Were all changes to the project documented and handled promptly?
- How was individual performance measured and communicated?
- Was the budget communicated to everyone?
- Were cost and expenditure information monitored regularly and reported to the team?
- Were the end users satisfied with the results?
- Was the customer involved in the design of an acceptance process?
- Were the team and project manager satisfied with the results?
- Are there follow-up and maintenance activities?
- What actions are required to be able to close the project files?
- What have we all learnt from this project that will assist management in future?
- Was the business case maintained up to date throughout the project?

Ask questions about performance:

- Did the project's sponsor fulfil his or her obligations?
- Were there delays caused by any stakeholder?
- Did any stakeholders avoid their responsibility?
- Did the team meet regularly?
- Did the team work well together?
- Was individual performance appraised regularly?

- Were failures to meet personal targets subject to investigation?
- Were conflicts and grievances dealt with promptly?
- Did the team and project manager review their performance regularly?
- Have additional training needs been identified as a result of performance assessment?
- Is recognition appropriate?
- What recommendations can be made to improve future performance?

Technical evaluation

The technical evaluation is concerned to demonstrate that the best results were obtained with the skills, experience and technology available to you throughout the project. You need to focus the team to identify where successes were achieved and also where technical problems occurred. The technical work of the project is the principal area where you have endeavoured to encourage the greatest creativity from team members. Turning this creativity into innovative results is the underlying objective of the whole project. Much can be learnt from how this was done, a process that is fundamental to the growth of knowledge in the organization.

It is important to recognize that your technical achievements may have a value to others, often far more than you can realize at the current time. Do ensure that the technical part of your evaluation report is distributed to anyone who could benefit from your efforts. This is an essential activity in any organization with a commitment to grow. The information you gather through evaluation must be shared widely if the organization is to realize the maximum benefits from your efforts. You will similarly learn from the efforts of your colleagues with other projects.

CHECKLIST 29: QUESTIONS FOR TECHNICAL EVALUATION

Typical questions to ask include:

- Were the original objectives technically feasible and realistic?
- Were the customer's needs accurately specified?
- Was the customer accurately presenting the user's requirements?
- Did the technology exist?
- Did new technology have to be developed as part of the project?

- Were the right skills available to develop this new technology?
- Was specialized training necessary for the project?
- Were the products variations or derivatives of existing products?
- Was new equipment required?
- Did new equipment have to be developed?
- Were new test procedures required?
- How were these developed?
- Was specialized test equipment developed?
- How were technical difficulties resolved?
- Were consultants involved?
- Are any new designs and technology protected?
- Can we patent any of the developments?
- What is the confidence level of the technical performance?
- Have additional opportunities for improvements been identified?
- Can any technical developments be used on other projects?
- Have possibilities for other products been identified?
- Has all essential documentation been completed?
- Who else needs to know about the technical results obtained?

POST-PROJECT APPRAISALS

At some stage after the project handover, the project's benefits should be measured. When you carry out this evaluation, the project is complete and the customer has accepted the results. The benefits of the project are not all apparent. Some benefits could come from the project during the execution phase, depending on the type of project.

At the definition phase of the project you set out the project's benefits. These are likely to be concerned with:

- improvements in equipment and plant performance;
- new income from introducing a new product;
- improved efficiency from the re-engineering of processes and procedures;
- increased effectiveness from skills enhancement by training programmes.

All these benefits can be quantified and measured by metrics agreed with your customer. If a cost–benefit analysis exists from the project initiation then a forecast exists of the benefits against time. This is often presented as a cost saving through the improved efficiencies or increased income, contribution or profitability resulting from the new product's introduction.

At the closure of the project, agree who is responsible for the measurement of benefits and when they are to be reviewed. The customer may decide to take this responsibility and release you for the next project. However, if the project has had a successful outcome, you will almost certainly want an involvement, even if it only means getting regular reports over the next 12 months. Although you attempt to create a clean handover to the customer, you will probably have continuing contact for a short period as part of the post-project support process.

When the benefits accumulate later, give the team members some feedback; they will be interested.

WHAT NEXT?

You have finished the project, delighted your customer and reported your evaluation in a final report. When you prepared for the formal closure, you should have prepared a plan for the release of your team members to new roles in other active projects or back into a functional role. Before you celebrate your success, ensure that these plans are actioned and completed. It is very demotivating to finish work in a successful project team and then find that no job has been found for you. Then you can celebrate with your team – a job well done! Call a celebration team meeting and ask the customer and other stakeholders to come along. Ask your sponsor to address the group and put on record the success achieved. After the euphoria of this celebration, remember to make sure your project file is completely updated before you close it for the last time! Check that:

- you have agreed future responsibilities for the team members on post-project implementation;
- agreed reassignments for all other team members and actions are completed;
- you have identified any training needs for yourself and team members;
- you have informed line managers of team members that the project is complete;
- you have passed on training needs to relevant line managers and the training department;
- you have thanked the line managers for their support and commitment.

But what does come next? Perhaps another project, promotion or just back to operational activities? Ask yourself what you gained from the experience of managing the project and what actions you can take to improve your performance even more. Every project is unique, involving different people and different skills. Your continued development comes from this self-analysis, which will lead you on to greater success in the future. This success is directly related to your commitment. Develop the skills of project management further for the larger projects that are becoming part of working life in most organizations today.

Project work is enormously rewarding and creates a great sense of achievement.

SUMMARY

Figure 10.3 summarizes the key steps of project closure. Checklist 30 identifies the key leadership actions to which you should give particular attention during this final critical phase of the project.

CHECKLIST 30: KEY LEADERSHIP ACTIONS DURING PROJECT CLOSURE

- The stakeholders:
  - Maintain regular reporting.
  - Agree acceptance criteria.
  - Involve end users in handover checklist design.
  - Agree follow-on activities.
  - Evaluate performance.
  - Sign off all reports and completion documentation.
- Project tasks:
  - Seek sign-off of work breakdown structure.
  - Review outstanding issues.
  - Agree action plans for issues.
  - Confirm that all action plans implemented and complete.
  - Update the project records and file.
- Project team:
  - Maintain regular team meetings.
  - Maintain participation and consult regularly.
  - Anticipate risks and issues that hinder closure.
  - Review team performance.
  - Identify valuable learning points.
  - Reward team performance.
- Team members:
  - Confirm that all responsibilities are fulfilled satisfactorily.
  - Appraise performance.
  - Advise on additional training needs.
  - Recognize and reward performance.
  - Seek opportunities for further development.
  - Organize new assignments for everyone.

Celebrate your success!

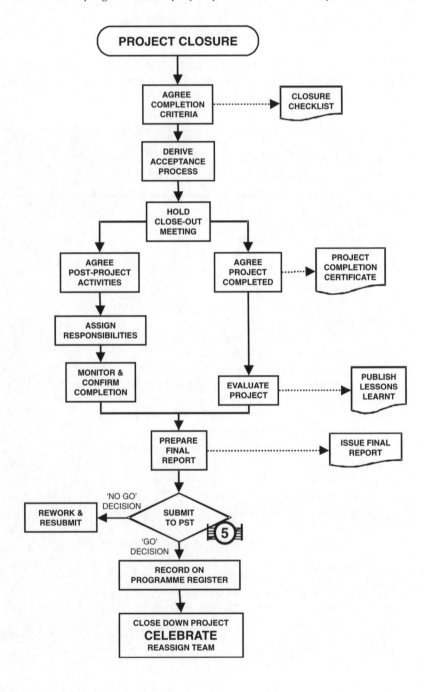

Figure 10.3 Process flow diagram: project closure

11

Using a computer

In common with many business processes today, the management of projects can benefit from using computer technology. A project is controlled and managed through the collection and use of information to take decisions, and software exists to help the project manager in this process. A wide range of project management software is available, from relatively inexpensive to very expensive. The explosion in graphic interface programs has made the use of computers more accessible to everyone, making the software easier to use and understand.

It is important to remember that computer software is a tool to help you manage the project from start to finish. It is not just a planning tool; that is a popular misunderstanding. The critical path techniques today are developed to enable you to plan, schedule and control your project, and computer software is based on these fundamental processes. The modern computer gives you access to some sophisticated techniques as a serious or casual user in programs that until recently were the domain of information systems gurus. However, there is one thing the computer cannot do for you. It cannot review your wealth of experience, select appropriate information, make a judgement and take the decision. The computer can only take decisions based on the information you input to the program; if these data are wrong then the resulting output is also at fault. Yet because it comes from the computer, people fall into the trap of believing the output – because the computer must be right! The critical problem is to make sure the correct data are given to the computer initially, which is easy to say but not so easy always to do.

One of the most valuable features of all project management software is the speed and ease of reporting a large amount of information in excellent formats. This makes a significant contribution to reducing the time you need to take decisions in support of the control process. Most software allows you to select the data you want to report and to design the formats to suit your particular needs.

WHAT CAN SOFTWARE DO?

Much of the processing of information in the derivation of a plan and schedule can be carried out effectively, with the advantage of rapid output of the results. It is quite common to find this software just being used to produce a Gantt chart at the start of a project. A presentable chart that looks good and is easy to understand helps to explain to management and others what is intended to happen in a project. This is only the beginning, but to go any further requires an understanding of the more complex features of the software. The computer allows you to turn data inputs to valuable information for reviews, issue management and decision making, as shown in Figure 11.1.

Project management software programs are really a combination of a graphics, spreadsheet and database program to make a complex operating system for managing all aspects of the project. The graphics part produces the Gantt chart, the logic diagram or PERT chart and the graphs used for reporting. The spreadsheet part is used for the forms, tables and reports produced using the available data. The database part stores and

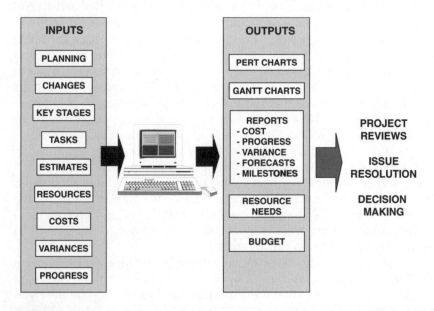

Figure 11.1 How the computer can help

manipulates the data provided for calculation, using the spreadsheet section to insert results into the tables, charts and diagrams viewed on screen. This combination gives the software a huge range of features with which to assist the project process. The difficulty is the learning curve to understand such complex software and remember how to use the many features without having to resort to the reference manual every time!

During the early part of the project it is relatively easy to input the essential planning data to generate a Gantt chart and insert the resources. You spend much of your time becoming familiar with the software. Then you move into the execution phase and have less time to use the program. You are probably going to update the schedule only once a week or even less frequently, and then the reference manual starts to become well thumbed! It is easy to forget how to use the many features provided for control unless you use them on a very regular basis. The time needed to update is often a major aspect of using software, and one that is ignored in the plan. You need more time than you expect to input the reported progress and update the information stored in the program. This is even more of a problem if the team members are not involved or do not have familiarity with the software. If the updating is completely your responsibility, it is quite possible you will rapidly fall behind with the inputting of information. The program is then so out of date that it has no added value for you and then acquires an unwarranted reputation. People start to complain that it is too complex, time-consuming and difficult to use.

So, treat the software as a tool in your toolkit. If the tool fits the job in hand, make good use of it, but make sure everyone in the team is given adequate training. Not everyone is comfortable with using computers or complex software. If you believe that it has value for your project, encourage and facilitate the learning process.

Most software programs are designed around some fundamental features that include:

- tabulating a list of tasks at different levels of the WBS;
- inputting duration data;
- inputting the dependency information;
- calculating the critical path and float data;
- deriving the Gantt chart;
- deriving the logic diagram or PERT chart;
- inputting a list of resources;
- assignment of resources by responsibility or capacity;
- inputting of cost data as resource cost rates and materials costs;
- deriving budget and cost curves, calculating earned value;
- scheduling the project on the basis of the input data;
- 'what-if' analysis of issues using the Gantt chart;

- reassignment of resources;
- identifying and correcting resource overloads;
- outputting a wide range of reports.

All programs handle the data in a slightly different way and include many other features to allow the optimization of the schedule in detail. More advanced software programs now include features for:

- recording project risks;
- recording and monitoring actions to mitigate risks;
- recording resource assignments across several projects;
- recording resource assignments across the whole organization;
- reviewing the whole project portfolio;
- managing the project pipeline to enable decision making by senior management.

Throughout this book, you are encouraged to record essential data about the project at each step of the project process. Most of the templates suggested for this purpose normally appear in software as default tables, although the layout and data formats may vary slightly. Some programs give you, the user, considerable freedom to design these tables to present the data in a format you desire – an important element when selecting software.

Some organizations have moved to using a custom-designed database program for recording project management data for a complete portfolio of projects. These programs are designed with direct links to specific project management software used in the organization. Alternatively, they are incorporated as a separate package integrated with a bundle of other packages including project management software, accounting and cost control software, contract management software, and resource management and levelling software. Typical features of these programmes include:

- tracking multiple projects;
- Internet publishing of data and reports;
- sub-project tracking;
- e-mail communications facilities;
- requirements for large projects – resources and tasks;
- corporate-wide resource assignments – operations and projects;
- corporate-wide resource levelling;
- budget and cost control systems, including earned value reporting;
- capital budget control;
- multiple reporting facilities, including custom reports;

- multiple calendars;
- advanced accounting systems, control and reporting;
- business case generation and tracking;
- variance reporting.

These programs are designed to operate at a corporate level to include both operational and project activities, as the example in Figure 11.2 shows. Such software systems are costly and complex, and usually require full-time administration technical personnel both to maintain and to operate the system. This type of software is difficult to learn to use, so many project managers prefer to use simpler systems to help them manage their projects.

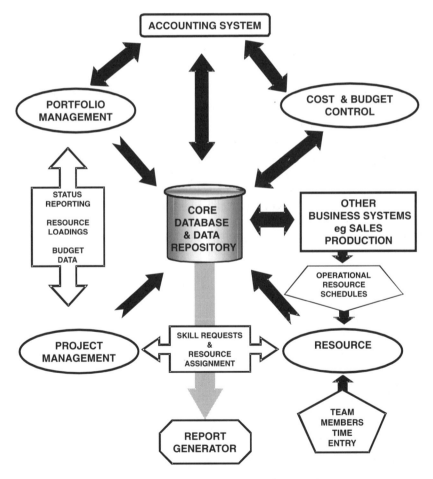

Figure 11.2 Example of the key elements of a corporate software system

USING A SOFTWARE PROGRAM

Most project management programs give you a number of different ways to input information and build the project plan. Each program gives you a recommended approach to use, but you are not restricted to that approach. Flexibility is important, and you are certain to be more comfortable with a program that works in the way that you think. The steps involved follow a sequence:

1. Open a new project file.
2. Insert project title, start date and project manager's name.
3. Set up the master calendar giving public and organizational holidays.
4. If possible, design the specific formats for the tables you require.
5. Input the project's organization – the core team – on a resource listing.
6. Set up resource calendars – one for yourself and each team member – to show their available capacity for the project, including holidays.
7. Input the list of key stages to a blank Gantt chart.
8. Assign responsibilities for the key stages. Select by responsibility; if capacity is used, the schedule is automatically adjusted when durations are added unless more than one person is assigned. Beware shared responsibility.
9. Input the durations for each key stage.
10. Input the dependencies between the key stages.
11. The program calculates the critical path, the key stage start and finish times, and floats.
12. A Gantt chart is produced, highlighting critical key stages.
13. A PERT diagram is produced.
14. A table generated is showing early and late start and finish times with total float.
15. Total project time is now available.
16. Input the cost data as resource cost rates and materials costs for key stages.
17. An operating budget cumulative curve is calculated.

You do not have to input cost data if cost control features are not used. This process gives you the base plan ready for optimization using the approach discussed earlier. Most programs use a default condition of FINISH to START for all dependencies. You have the option to:

- use an alternative condition – START to START or FINISH to FINISH;
- 'fix' a start or finish date – one that cannot move under any circumstances and is sometimes known as a 'must date';
- introduce 'lags' and 'leads' – with caution.

When you have optimized the schedule to arrive at an acceptable completion date, you can explore the detailed work inside each key stage. Use the template suggested in Chapter 7 to derive the data and responsibilities, then update the program as the work plan becomes a commitment by everyone concerned. To input this information you need to:

- add extended team members to a resource list;
- ideally, create resource calendars for each – otherwise the program assumes that each is 100 per cent available;
- add the task list at the lower levels in the relevant key stage on the Gantt chart;
- input the duration data;
- insert dependencies between the tasks;
- assign each task – by responsibility or capacity;
- update cost rate data for new resources assigned.

The program alerts you to any resource overloads created in assignment by capacity. If a person is assigned to work when that person is listed on his or her calendar as not being available, or is committed to an earlier assignment, two options are available: 1) assign someone else; or 2) extend the task duration on the schedule to a listed availability.

The consequence may be an extension of the project completion date, in which case further optimization is necessary by reiteration at key stage or lower levels of the plan. This is where the computer is powerful because of its speed at looking at the options available to take a decision. 'What-if' analysis allows you quickly to review the impact of moving or extending tasks, moving or adjusting resource assignments and changing the plan. Always check the consequences of these reiterations; the critical path may change.

When you have an acceptable schedule, freeze this as the baseline for control. Make sure everyone is issued with copies of the detail and keep copies of everything in the project file. Once you have frozen the baseline, it is prudent to keep a copy of the project file under a separate name as a back-up in case someone resets the baseline without your knowledge!

The next phase of the project, doing the work, provides you with feedback of what is happening. These data are inputted to the program using the 'update mode', whereby percentage completion is given to each active task up to the current date. Remember that the task is regarded as linear and it is better to calculate the percentage. Obtain the forecast of time required to complete and decide whether the task duration is extended into the float zone or further. The task bar can then show a true position, the percentage complete and the time to complete with a realistic completion date.

Updating the schedule, task by task, takes time to accomplish, and programs do vary in the features they offer and restrictions built in to make this process easy to complete. Any conflicts concerning resource assignments that arise from updating the progress are alerted, so you can take corrective action. Then you can explore the options available to view the impact on the rest of the outstanding work and take informed decisions.

WHAT SOFTWARE DOES NOT DO

The computer software works entirely on data you supply. Intuitive decision processing is beyond its capability, so there are some aspects of the work of a project that are entirely dependent on people:

- deciding the deliverables and benefits;
- identifying tasks and key stages;
- deciding the dependencies between key stages and the tasks inside;
- deciding the resources available to work on the project;
- doing the project work;
- identifying risks to the project;
- ranking of risks and allocating responsibilities for managing risks;
- reviewing the project risk log;
- deriving a milestone schedule;
- identifying issues – process and technical;
- problem solving;
- action planning to solve problems;
- resolving conflicts;
- monitoring and tracking the project activities;
- measuring the project's progress;
- reporting the project's progress.

These activities represent the major part of the project activity, so keep the project driving the software and do not allow the software to drive the project. The document templates suggested for status reports, risk and issue management are not included in most project software packages. However, you can easily construct these using existing word processors or spreadsheet programs. Experience with cost control suggests that setting up cost data and records using a spreadsheet is easy to accomplish, accurate and quickly updated.

Sending people on a two-day project management software training course does not mean all your projects will become successful the next week! A short course of this kind will only be a short exposure to the main features of a program, and expertise will only grow from extensive practical use. Software cannot ever replace the essential human inputs to project activity or the building and motivation of an effective team. The combined brainpower and experience of an effective team is far greater than the sum of the individual parts and surpasses the power of any computer software for project management.

SELECTING PROJECT SOFTWARE

The process of selecting software for project management is an emotive one in most organizations. Unless your organization is very focused on project activity, with a defined software policy, the selection process causes untold controversy and conflict. Everyone has their own favourite package for the work they do, and even the same software is configured to operate differently according to individual needs. Perhaps the information systems department will review available programs and make a selection that becomes policy. Experienced people with a record of success in managing projects are the best to review software and decide whether it is a valuable tool to make the job easier for the type of projects undertaken. Some packages are particularly suited to certain types of projects, so selection should not be based on price alone but should include a review of:

- track record of performance;
- ease of use and interface consistency;
- compatibility with other software in use;
- whether the software needs to be stand-alone or networked, and availability;
- what platforms are available;
- features for planning and scheduling;
- features for control and updating;
- quality and ease of reporting;
- networking features – passwords, access restrictions, etc;
- whether training is available;
- whether a helpline and back-up are available.

Project software is complex, so it is often the product of specialist suppliers, rather than just the major software suppliers that are household names in the industry. There is little evidence of compatibility problems with such specialist packages, but it is advisable to request detailed demonstrations of all the key features of a package before making a decision to purchase.

If you are selecting a software package then seek expert help and review what is available. Compile a list of things you want from the program, then review the feature lists to decide which program to put on test. Do not restrict this list too much. Involve people from all functions in the demonstrations. It is an important decision, to purchase project software, and as you gain in experience and confidence, you come to expect more from your software. However, changing later to accommodate additional features is costly.

Remember that no computer software can replace the essential management skills of communicating, decision making, negotiation, assessment and conflict resolution that are all important for you as the project manager.

THE PROGRAMME MANAGEMENT OFFICE

Variously termed the *programme or project management office* (PMO) or *programme support office*, this function is now increasingly recognized as an important element essential to achieving success with programmes and projects. It is not uncommon for new policies and procedures, such as the many offered to you in this book, to enjoy a limited life, and many people hope they will burn out and fade away just because they are perceived as a management fad.

There is no standard model for a PMO, but the concepts are all similar and the variance is only in the responsibilities and the roles involved. The primary purpose of a PMO is to establish a centre of excellence to maintain the procedures and processes used in the management and control of the active programmes and projects in the portfolio. The PMO promotes the use of these procedures throughout the organization and the permanent staff provide active support to programme and project managers as expert consultants.

Since the PMO is the centre of excellence, it is natural to give the PMO the authority to select and maintain the project management software used as a standard in the organization. Often the role of the PMO is extended to include provision of a scheduling service and provision of the data required for portfolio and pipeline management. Typical responsibilities of a PMO could include:

- maintaining and improving project standards;
- promoting best practices;
- spreading lessons learnt;
- organizing training at different levels;
- providing hands-on support;

- mentoring;
- providing consulting services;
- scheduling analysis;
- financial and budget analysis;
- enterprise-wide data and information collection, eg resource commitments;
- supervising and measuring programme and project managers' performance;
- selecting programme and project managers;
- having oversight of management on programme and project performance;
- career development.

The PMO can raise alarms when things seem to start going wrong in a programme, or project and influence managers and sponsors to take early corrective action.

The programme and project managers are not necessarily owned by the PMO. In some organizations they are: all programme and project managers work within the PMO, being assigned to new programmes and projects as the PST selects them.

Relationship between the PMO and the PST

With the increasing realization of the importance of the principles discussed in Chapters 2–4, many organizations have recognized that having a centre of excellence is essential to their success with programme management. To achieve this the PMO is managed by a senior executive, the Director of Program Management, who reports to the Chief Executive. This clearly establishes the PMO as a vital function in the organization in the drive to achieve strategic objectives. The PST can look to the PMO to provide both data and vital support in the effective management and decision making needed to administer the organization's portfolio of programmes and projects. The PST administrator is usually drawn from the PMO.

The PST should clearly define the responsibilities and authority of the PMO. Depending on this authority, the PMO will share some or all of the glory for success or blame for the failures!

Postscript

This book has been a project and you have come to the end. Has it been a success? You will only really know when you apply the techniques and processes suggested here. All are tried and proven, and there is nothing either astoundingly new or astoundingly reactionary in these techniques. This project has been focused on deriving a step-by-step process to help you achieve success with your programmes and projects in future, giving you tips to improve based on personal experience. If you do achieve success and feel more in control of your working life as a programme or project manager then the work of this project has been a success. If you have any interesting experiences to relate using the approaches given here, the author will be pleased to hear from you via the publisher.

Appendix 1

Glossary of terms

There is a considerable amount of jargon used by project managers today, enhanced by the rapid growth in the use of personal computers for planning and control of projects. This glossary gives some of the more common terms and their usual meaning.

Activity. A clearly defined task or tasks with known duration – usually a group of tasks that together complete a particular step or part of the work.

Activity on node diagram. A network diagram where all activities are represented by the node or event, usually shown as a box. Arrows are used to show the logical flow of the project from node to node.

ACWP. Actual cost of work performed – the actual recorded cost, including costs committed, of the work actually performed up to a particular point in the project schedule.

Backward pass. The procedure by which the latest event times or the finish and start times for the activities of a network are determined.

Bar chart. A graphical presentation of the activities of a project derived from the project logic diagram shown as a timed schedule.

Baseline plan. The final 'frozen' plan as signed off by the sponsor before implementation. This is also the *recorded plan*, against which all progress is measured and variances analysed and reported.

BCWP. Budgeted cost of the work performed – the budgeted cost, based on the operating budget, of the work that is actually completed up to a particular point in the project schedule.

BCWS. Budgeted cost of the work scheduled – the budgeted cost, based on the operating budget, of the work that is planned to be completed up to a particular point in the project schedule.

Benefit. A measurable gain from the project that is a primary underlying reason for the project's being initiated.

Change log. A sequential listing of all change requests raised during the life of a project with essential information about their handling.

Change request. A standard template on which to record and request approval from the key stakeholders for a change to the baseline plan.

Control system. The procedures established at the start of the project that provide the leader with the necessary data to compare planned status with the actual status at any instant in time, to identify variances and take corrective action.

Cost control diagram. A graphical representation of the actual and budgeted costs of the work actually performed against the scheduled and budgeted costs of the work planned.

Cost variance. The difference between the value of the work actually performed (BCWP) and the actual costs incurred and committed (ACWP).

Cost variance per cent. The cost variance divided by the value of the work actually performed (BCWP).

Critical activity. Any activity in the project that has been analysed to show it has zero float and must therefore be completed on time if the project is not to slip.

Critical path. The sequence of activities that determines the total time for the project. All activities on the critical path are known as *critical activities*.

Deliverable. A specific, defined, measurable and tangible output from the project. Most projects have several deliverables.

Dependency. The basic rule of logic governing logic diagram and network drawing: any activity that is dependent on another is normally shown to emerge from the HEAD event of the activity on which it depends.

Duration. The estimated or actual time to complete an activity.

EET. The earliest event time – the earliest completion time for an event that does not affect the total project time.

EFT. The earliest finish time of an activity without changing total time or the spare or float time.

Elapsed time. The duration of a piece of the work expressed in real, calendar working days – taking into account holidays, weekends, etc not worked.

EST. The earliest start time of an activity.

Event. A point in the progress of the project after total completion of all preceding activities.

Float. The difference between the time necessary and the time available for an activity.

Forward pass. The procedure for determining the earliest event times of a network.

Full-time equivalent. One single person-day divided between several persons working on a key stage or task.

Functional manager. The person accountable for a function or department in the organization and responsible for the employees allocated to the function.

Gantt chart. A graphical method of showing a project schedule that shows project time, dates, all activities, resources and their relationships. It is derived from the logic diagram when it has been analysed for float.

Issue. A risk to the project, or an unforeseen event that has become a reality and needs to be resolved if the project's integrity is not to be threatened.

Issue log. A sequential listing of all issues raised during the life of a project with essential information about their handling.

Key stage. A group of closely related activities that can be isolated together as a clear stage of the project that must be complete before passing to the next stage.

Lag. An intentional delay period introduced between two activities in a logic diagram.

Layering the plan. See **Multi-level planning**.

Lead. A specific amount of time a successor activity should start after the start of its predecessor even though the predecessor is not complete.

LET. The latest time by which an event can be achieved without affecting the total project time from start to finish.

LFT. The latest possible finish time without changing the total task or float times.

Logic diagram. A graphic representation of the activities in a project with clearly identified logical dependencies established.

LRC. The linear responsibility chart, which displays a complete listing of key stages and/or activities with the names of the resource(s) who have been allocated responsibility for each as part of the plan.

LST. The latest possible time an activity can start without affecting the total project time.

Milestone. Another name for an event, but usually reserved for a significant or major event in the project. Often used for identifying key progress reporting points.

Monitoring. The process of checking what is happening and collecting data on project progress.

Multi-level planning. Planning the project at several levels of detail, starting with the key stages and then exploding each key stage to show all the associated activities. Where necessary, any activity is further exploded to show further detail of associated tasks at the next level down, and so on.

Must date. A planned date when an activity or group of activities must be complete under all circumstances.

Opportunity. An idea for a potential programme or project that aligns with strategic needs.

PERT diagram. The logic diagram in the PERT (Programme Evaluation Review Technique) project control system.

Phase gate. A specific point in the life cycle when all work stops and progress to date is presented to the PST for approval. Approval at a gate allows work to proceed through to the next phase of the life cycle.

Portfolio. The total active programme and project activity in an organization.

Predecessor. The activity immediately prior to an event.

Programme register. A sequential listing of all programmes and projects approved as 'active' by the PST. May also include opportunities for programmes and projects under investigation.

Programme steering team (PST). A senior management committee, often made up of project sponsors who have the power to prioritize and steer projects in the direction necessary to meet corporate objectives.

Project-approved budget. The budget approved at the conception of the project, based on outline plans only, with contingency included.

Project file. A central file that must contain copies of all documentation, letters, faxes, etc relating to the project. It is the project archive and the basis for subsequent evaluation and continuous improvement activities.

Project life cycle. A systems approach to a project in which the project is described as passing through four phases, from conception to termination.

Project log book. A bound A4 book with numbered pages where the project leader records all events, action plans and project activities. It comprises a complete event record cross-referenced to the project file. On larger projects each team member should also maintain a project log book.

Project operating budget. The budget derived at operating level after detailed planning to first or preferably the second level is completed.

PST administrator. The person appointed by the PST to organize the PST meetings and programme portfolio documentation.

Resource. Anything other than time that is needed for carrying out an activity but most commonly used to refer to people involved in the project.

Resource levelling. Utilization of available float within a network to ensure that resources required are appreciably constant.

Resource smoothing. The scheduling of activities within the limits of their total floats to minimize fluctuations in resource requirements.

Risk. An event that has been identified as potentially threatening the project's integrity if it actually happens.

Risk log. A sequential listing of all risks identified throughout the project's life and information about their ranking, probability and management.

Risk management form. A standard template recording risk data and the proposed actions to take when the risk occurs so as to minimize the damage to the project.

Risk mitigation plan. A standard template recording risk data and the actions required to avoid a risk occurring – usually used for 'unacceptable' or 'high' risks.

Risk score. The product of probability and impact; used for ranking risks.

Schedule. The project plan converted to 'real time' against a calendar by inserting realistic agreed time estimates and resource capacity factors into all the project activities.

Schedule variance. The difference between the value of the work completed (BCWP) and the budgeted cost, from the operating budget, of the work planned to be completed at a particular point in the schedule.

Schedule variance per cent. The schedule variance divided by the budgeted cost of the work scheduled to be complete (BCWS) at the date considered.

Scope creep. Adding additional features and extras during the project work that are not recorded and approved using the change process. Many incur extra time and cost consequences.

Single person-day. A method of estimating activity durations using 100 per cent of one individual's capacity to carry out the work. It represents a full working day, but in estimating ignores holidays, etc.

Soft project. A project where the objectives are only broadly stated and the resources needed are unknown and flexible, the scope left open intentionally and deadlines not defined clearly.

Sponsor. The senior manager who takes ownership of the project on behalf of the organization.

Stakeholder. Any individual who has an interest or stake in the project at any time during the project's life cycle.

Stand-alone project. A project that is independent of a programme.

Sub-project. A significant part of a project that is treated as separate for management and control purposes, usually because of its size or location. A sub-project is always linked to a parent project.

Successor. The activity immediately following an event.

Task. A specific defined piece of work, usually carried out by one person in a finite measurable time. A sub-unit of a project activity.

Time-limited scheduling. The scheduling of activities such that the specified project time is not exceeded using resources to a predetermined pattern.

Total float. The total spare time possessed by an activity beyond the estimated duration.

Tracking. The process of taking progress information gathered in a control system and inserting this into the original plan to show the actual status, ie the compliance or deviation from the planned status of the project at that point in time.

Work breakdown structure. The diagrammatic presentation of all the key stages and their associated activities arranged in a hierarchical format, showing each level of planning.

Work plan. A standard format form or chart for recording an agreed listing of the tasks to be carried out by an individual or department, complete with agreed start and finish times for each within the overall project schedule.

Appendix 2

Further reading

Baker, Sunny and Baker, Tim (1998) *The Complete Idiot's Guide to Project Management*, Alpha Books, New York

Barker, Alan (1993) *Making Meetings Work*, The Industrial Society; London

Burke, Rory (1993) *Project Management Planning and Control*, 2nd edition, John Wiley, Chichester

Carter, Bruce, Hancock, Tony, Morin, Jean-Marc and Robins, M J (1994) *Introducing Riskman Methodology*, The Stationery Office, London

Cleland, David I and King, William R (1988) *Project Management Handbook*, Van Nostrand Reinhold, New York

Crawley, John (1992) *Constructive Conflict Management*, Nicholas Brealey, London

Davenport, Jenny and Lipton, Gordon (1993) *Communications for Managers*, The Industrial Society, London

Eales-White, Rupert (1992) *The Power of Persuasion*, Kogan Page, London

Frame, Davidson J (1994) *The New Project Management*, Jossey-Bass, San Francisco

Hall, Elaine M (1997) *Managing Risk*, Addison Wesley Longman, Boston, Massachusetts

Hardingham, Alison and Royal, Jenny (1994) *Pulling Together: Teamwork in practice*, Institute of Personnel and Development, London

Hurst, Bernice (1996) *The Handbook of Communication Skills*, 2nd edition, Kogan Page, London

Kindler, Herbert S (1990) *Risk Taking*, Kogan Page, London

Lockyer, Keith (1984) *Critical Path Analysis and Other Project Network Techniques*, Pitman, London

PMI Standards Committee (1996) *A Guide to the Project Management Body of Knowledge*, Project Management Institute, Philadelphia

Pokras, S (1989) *Successful Problem Solving and Decision Making*, Kogan Page, London

Pritchard, Carl L (ed) (1997) *Risk Management Concepts and Guidance*, ESI International, Arlington, Virginia

Rosenau, M D (1991) *Successful Project Management*, Van Nostrand Reinhold, New York

Senge, P (1990) *The Fifth Discipline*, Doubleday, New York

Stewart, Dorothy M (ed) (1990) *Handbook of Management Skills*, Gower, London

Vincent, Geoff (1988) *Taming Technology: How to Manage a Development Project*, British Institute of Management, London

Young, Trevor L (1993) *Leading Projects*, The Industrial Society, London

Young, Trevor L (2000) *Successful Project Management*, Kogan Page, London

SOME USEFUL WEB SITES

All these sites give many links to other useful Web sites.

Project Management Institute (USA)	www.pmi.org
Project Management Forum	www.pmforum.org
Association for Project Management (UK)	www.apm.org.uk
Australian Institute for Project Management	www.aipm.com.au
PMI Bookstore	www.pmibookstore.org
IT project management	www.gantthead.com
Project management training	www.esi-europe.com
Risk management software	www.risk-management.org
Programme management	www.e-programme.com

Index

acceptance process 254
accountability 59, 123
  for change decisions 184, 187
activity, concurrent 132
activity, critical 148
activity, series 132
ACWP 239
administrator, PST 44, 55, 83, 168, 247, 261,
  286
appraisals, post project 266
approval, project definition 124
  project execution 247
  project planning 164
  project closure 261
assumptions 89, 144
authority 58
  lack of 243
avoidance risks 116

BAC 239
baseline plan, checklist for 164
BCWP 239
BCWS 239
benefits 15, 17, 19, 24, 107, 255, 266
budget 88, 237
  approved 162
  operating 162, 180
  reviewing 162
business case 38, 40, 49, 50, 83, 84, 89, 124,
  246, 252, 255
  reviewing 159
business plan 13
business planning 22
business strategy 13

change 3, 7
  approval of 187
  log 182, 185
  management process 144, 182, 183
  management process flow diagram 183
  managing 180
  request form 184, 186
  sources of 181
close out meeting 255
  agenda for 257
closure 250, 251
  phase, approaching 246
  process flow diagram 270
  questions, checklist for 253
communication 70, 175, 179
completion certificate 256, 258
completion criteria 252
computer, using a 271
conflict 224
  and risks 226
  handling 227
  managing 227
  types of 226
constraint(s) 29, 81, 117
contingencies 144
continuous improvement 38
control 30, 193
  system 193
  system designing the, checklist for 196
  system essential elements 195
core team 70, 89, 91, 104, 131
corrective action, taking 215
  checklist for 216

cost   108, 236
  and schedule performance chart   241, 242
  control and fighting fires   245
  control diagram   240, 241
  control measures
  earned value analysis   239
  performance   238
critical path   146, 148, 273
critical success factors   173
customer   45, 60, 62, 64, 80, 85, 104, 223, 244,
    252, 255, 266
  contract   87
  identifying customer needs, checklist for
    86
  needs and expectations   84
  satisfaction   64
CV   240
CV%   240

definition   102
  checklist for developing   126
  leadership actions, checklist for   127
  process flow diagram   128
documentation, project   94, 251
  change log   182, 185
  change request form   184, 186
  completion certificate   256, 258
  issue management form   204, 206, 207
  issue status log   202, 210, 220, 255
  key stage responsibility chart   140, 196
  key stage work plan chart   169, 170, 196,
    255
  milestone schedule   171, 174, 177, 187,
    196, 255
  organization chart   94, 95, 124
  project brief   38, 98, 102, 103, 106, 109, 126
  risk log   108, 119, 126, 177, 196, 199, 220
  risk management form   108, 120, 122, 126
  risk mitigation plan   111, 120, 121, 126
  stakeholder list   62, 103, 105, 126, 196, 232
  status report   176, 178, 214, 223
duration   141
  estimating the   141
dynamic action cycle   25
  life cycle   24, 68
  life cycle, managing   68

earned value analysis   239
environment, programme and project   1, 4
estimating   139, 145, 148
  duration   141
evaluation   259
  active   259

post project   262
  questions for active, checklist for   260
  questions for post project, checklist for
    263
  questions for technical, checklist for   265
  technical   265
executing   192
  process flow diagram   248

feudal kingdoms   234
financial case   88
fishbone diagram   219
float time   157, 273
  total   148, 194, 213
FTC   239
functional manager   57
further reading   289

Gantt chart   150, 154, 171, 211, 212, 255, 272
  key stage   156, 160, 171, 196, 211, 237
  showing current status   212
glossary of terms   283
growth, incremental   22
  step change   23

issue management   17
  process flow diagram   210
issues(s)   111, 123, 124, 162, 177, 255
  definition   201
  escalation   203
  escalation process   205
  management form   204, 206, 207
  managing   201
  ownership   204, 206
  questions for owners, checklist for   206
  rating   203
  resolution strategy   206
  resolution strategy, tracking   207
  reviewing project   208
  status log   202, 210, 220

key stage owner   137, 168, 177
  responsibility chart   140, 196
  work plan chart   169, 170, 196, 255
  work plans   168, 187
key stages   132, 133, 145, 146, 211
  splitting to improve project logic   134
kick-off meeting   90
kick-off meeting project, checklist for   92

lag   149, 157
launching a project   168
  seeking approval for   164
  process flow diagram   191

lead   149, 157
leadership   65
  actions during definition, checklist for   129
  actions during planning, checklist for   167
  actions during project closure, checklist
    for   269
  actions during project execution, checklist
    for   249
  actions during project launch, checklist
    for   190
  actions during project selection, checklist
    for   100
  actions for effective, checklist for   76
  dimensions of   67, 262
  managing performance   68
  role relationships   67
log book   97, 224
logic diagram   133, 134, 146, 147, 272
  analysing   150, 151, 152, 153
  deriving the, checklist for   135

matrix structure   33
  working in   232
meeting close out   257
  close out, agenda for   257
meetings   179
  action list   221
  agenda for the PST   44
  launch   187
  launch, checklist for   188
  of the PST   43
  schedule   179, 187
  team   198
milestones   155, 171, 177, 194
  schedule   171, 174, 177, 187, 196
monitoring and tracking, checklist for   214
monitoring process   199
  progress   197
  taking corrective action   215
  taking corrective action, checklist for
    216

opportunity   24, 45
ownership   12, 34
  of issues   204
  of risks   123

performance, managing   68
  managing, checklist for   69
PERT   147, 273
phase four   25, 247, 250
  approaching   246
phase gate one   50, 89

phase gate three   164, 181
phase gate zero   84
phase gates   27, 28
phase gates decisions   29, 30
  intermediate   162
phase one   25, 89, 102
phase three   25, 192, 211
phase two   25, 130
phase zero   25, 89
phases   24
planning   130
  activity, concurrent   132
  activity, critical   148
  activity, series   132
  baseline plan   187
  baseline plan, checklist for   164
  key stage owner   137
  key stages   132, 133, 145, 146
  leadership actions, checklist for   167
  logic diagram   133, 134, 135, 146
  process flow diagram   166
  task   132
portfolio management   18, 46, 47
post project appraisal   266
priority   29, 89
problem solving   38, 216
  fishbone diagram   219
  identifying the cause   218
  identifying the problem   218
  steps of   217
programme management   4, 5, 15, 17, 19
  characteristics   19, 20
  definition   18
  organizing for   32
programme manager   5, 8, 10, 15, 23, 38, 45,
    56
  as a leader   65
  qualities   65
programme portfolio   5, 18, 37
  primary screening   49
  secondary screening   50
  pipeline   51
programme register   37, 38, 39, 44
  operating   40
programme steering team   27, 34, 35, 82, 89,
    163, 242, 246, 247, 252, 281
  meetings   43
programme(s)   4, 5, 7, 13, 38, 40, 42, 70, 77
  definition   13
  example   14, 41
  how derived   22
  processes   77
  selection   46

selection, effective, checklist for   48
selection, inputs to effective   48
programme management office (PMO)
    280, 281
progress meetings   220
    checklist for   222
progress records   223
progress reporting   223
    frequency   198
    monitoring   197
project drift   250
project management   4, 5, 18, 19, 20
project management characteristics   19, 20
    definition   18
project management software   272
    corporate system   274, 275
    software selecting   279
    using   276
project manager   5, 8, 10, 23, 57
    qualities   65
project(s)   4, 5, 7, 9, 14, 70, 77
    approval to launch   164
    benefits   107
    brief   38, 98, 102, 103, 106, 109, 126
    change log   182, 185
    change management process   182, 183
    change request form   184, 186
    changes, managing   180
    changes, sources of   181
    characteristics   11, 12
    charter   99
    closure   250, 251
    completion certificate   256, 258
    control system   193
    cost and schedule performance chart
        241, 242
    cost   108, 236
    cost control and fighting fires   245
    cost control diagram   240, 241
    cost control measures
    cost performance   238
    cost, earned value analysis   239
    definition   10, 102
    definition leadership actions, checklist of
        129
    definition, approval of   124
    definition, checklist for   126
    definition, process flow diagram   128
    deliverables   106
    documentation   94
    executing   192
    file   96, 196, 223
    how derived   22

key stages   132, 133, 145, 146, 211
launch   168
launch baseline plan, checklist for   164
launch leadership actions, checklist for
    190
launch meeting   187
launch meeting, checklist for   188
launch, seeking approval to   164
log book   97, 224
manager   35, 38, 45, 50, 262
manager, as a leader   65
meetings schedule   179, 187
objective   67, 106
organization chart   94, 95, 124
planning   130
planning process flow diagram   166
processes   77
risk   110
risk assessment   103, 113
risk assessment questions, checklist for
    114
risk benefits   112
risk category   119
risk category matrix   119
risk log   108, 118, 119, 126, 177, 196, 199,
    220, 255
risk management   108, 110
risk management flow diagram   125
risk management form   108, 120, 122, 126
risk management, benefits of   112
risk management, when necessary   112
risk management, why necessary   111
risk mitigation plan   111, 120, 121, 126
risk monitoring   113
risk ownership   123
risk quantifying   117
risk response strategy   116
risk score   120
risk, definition of   110
risk, questions for assessment   114
risk, reviewing   199
risk, reviewing, checklist for   200
risk, types of   116
scope of work (SOW)   99, 113, 108, 126, 254
selection   46
selection, effective, checklist for   48
selection, inputs to effective   48
specification   98
stakeholders   58, 59, 67, 103, 144, 179,
    236, 255, 262
stand-alone   18, 40, 54, 77
starting up   79
status reports   176, 178, 214, 223
strategy   107

projects(s) evaluation 259
PST 27, 34, 35, 82, 89, 163, 242, 246, 247, 252,
  281
  administrator 44, 55, 83, 168, 261, 247
  hierarchies 37
  meetings 43
  responsibilities 42

reporting, too much 244
residual risks 116
resource(s) allocating responsibility 136
  analysing requirements 155
  needs 87
responsibilities, functional manager 57
  programme manager 56
  project manager 57
  PST administrator
  sponsor 56
responsibility 58, 123, 158
  allocating 136
  guidelines for allocating, checklist for 138
  of issue ownership 204
  recording allocated 139
risk assessment 103, 113
  questions, checklist of 114, 161
  category 119
  category matrix 119
  log 108, 119, 126, 177, 196, 199, 220
  management 17, 108
  management form 108, 120, 122, 126
  management process flow diagram 125
  management, benefits of 112
  management, when necessary 112
  management, why necessary 111
  mitigation plan 111, 120, 121, 126
  monitoring 123
  ownership 123
  quantification 117
  response strategy 116
  reviewing 199
  reviewing, checklist for 200
  score 120
  types of 116
roles and responsibilities 54
roles relationships 55

schedule crash impact 160
  crashing 159
  fast tracking
  impact of risks and 112
  optimizing 157
  preliminary 87
scope creep 13, 181
scope of work statement (SOW) 99, 108,
  113, 126, 254

selection leadership actions, checklist for 99
  effective, checklist for 48
  inputs to 48
  inputs to effective 48
SMART test 173
sponsor(s) 34, 35, 44, 45, 56, 61, 80, 104, 113,
  181, 182, 177, 223, 244, 255, 259
stakeholders 58, 59, 67, 103, 144, 179, 236,
  255, 262
  identifying 60
  identifying and managing, checklist for 60
  influence matrix 63
  key 45, 59, 81, 103, 182, 203, 244
  list 62, 103, 105, 126, 196, 232
  managing 61
start-up 79
statement of needs 85
statement of requirements 86, 98, 103
status reports 176, 178, 214
strategic needs 27, 79
  objectives 24, 40, 48
strategy 24, 107
sub projects 10, 15, 77
  characteristics of 12
  definition 11
  ownership 12
SV 240
SV% 240

task 132
  responsibilities 158
taskboarding 133
team members, selecting 71
teamwork 70
  building 72
  test 74
time limited scheduling 145
time management 228, 224
  actions 231
  barriers to effective 230
  encourage good, checklist for 236
  feudal kingdoms 234
  regular one-to-ones 235
  working in a matrix 232
tracking 209
  issue resolution strategy 207
  monitoring and, checklist for 214
transfer risks 116

WBS 136, 211, 237, 254, 255, 278
Web sites, useful 290
work breakdown structure 136, 160
working in a matrix 232

CD ROM

The CD ROM that accompanies this book gives you a collection of process tools, guide notes, instruments and presentation information that is useful in the introduction and practice of programme management. The contents are aligned to support the processes and procedures given in the book and expand many of the processes with the essential detail necessary to enable their use on an everyday basis. All have been tried and tested extensively.

The content is divided into a number of folders containing the appropriate material:

- programme templates;
- project templates;
- programme steering teams;
- portfolio management;
- stakeholder management tools;
- programme and project process guides;
- assessment tools;
- presentation materials.

INSTRUCTIONS FOR USING THE CD ROM

To use the CD ROM insert the CD in your CD/DVD drive on your computer. From here you can either:

1. Open Internet Explorer or other Web browser. Then from the menu system click on File_Open. In the dialog box that appears click on 'Browse' and locate the CD/DVD drive. Click on the 'index.html' file and click on 'Open'. This returns you to the browser 'Open' dialog Box. Click on 'OK' and the browser will open the file that explains the contents of each folder and how to view or access the information.

Or

2. From the Start menu, select 'Run' and enter: D:\Index.htm and then click on OK.

System requirements:

Personal Computer running Windows® 98, or later.

CD ROM/DVD drive.

Internet Explorer® 4 or higher.